PRETTY DEADLY

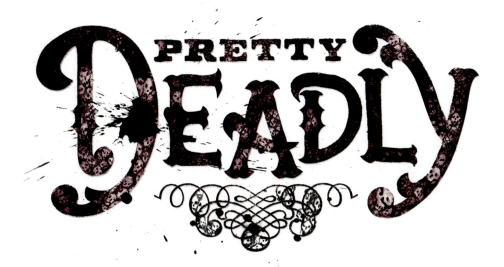

VOLUME TWO
THE BEAR

ROBERT KIRKMAN - chief operating officer ERIK LARSEN - chief financial officer TODD MCFARLANE - president MARC SILVESTRI - chief executive officer
JIM VALENTINO - vice-president ERIC STEPHENSON - publisher COREY MURPHY - director of sales JEFF BOISON - director of publishing planning & book trade sales
JEREMY SULLIVAN - director of digital sales KAT SALAZAR - director of pr & marketing BRANWYN BIGGLESTONE - senior accounts manager SARAH MELLO - accounts manager
DREW GILL - art director JONATHAN CHAN - production manager MEREDITH WALLACE - print manager BRIAH SKELLY - publicist
SASHA HEAD - sales & marketing production designer RANDY OKAMURA - digital production designer DAVID BROTHERS - branding manager OLIVIA NGAI - content manager
ADDISON DUKE - production artist VINCENT KUKUA - production artist TRICIA RAMOS - production artist JEFF STANG - direct market sales representative
EMILIO BAUTISTA - digital sales associate CHLOE RAMOS-PETERSON - library market sales representative

KELLY SUE DECONNICK
Script

EMMA RÍOS
Art & Covers

JORDIE BELLAIRE
Colors

CLAYTON COWLES
Letters

LAURENN MCCUBBIN
Design

SIGRID ELLIS
Edits

TRICIA RAMOS
Production

LAUREN SANKOVITCH
Managing Editor

PRETTY DEADLY logo designed by Maiko Kuzunishi.

ON TWITTER: @kellysue @emmartian @whoajordie @claytoncowles @laurennmcc @sigridellis @pancakelady

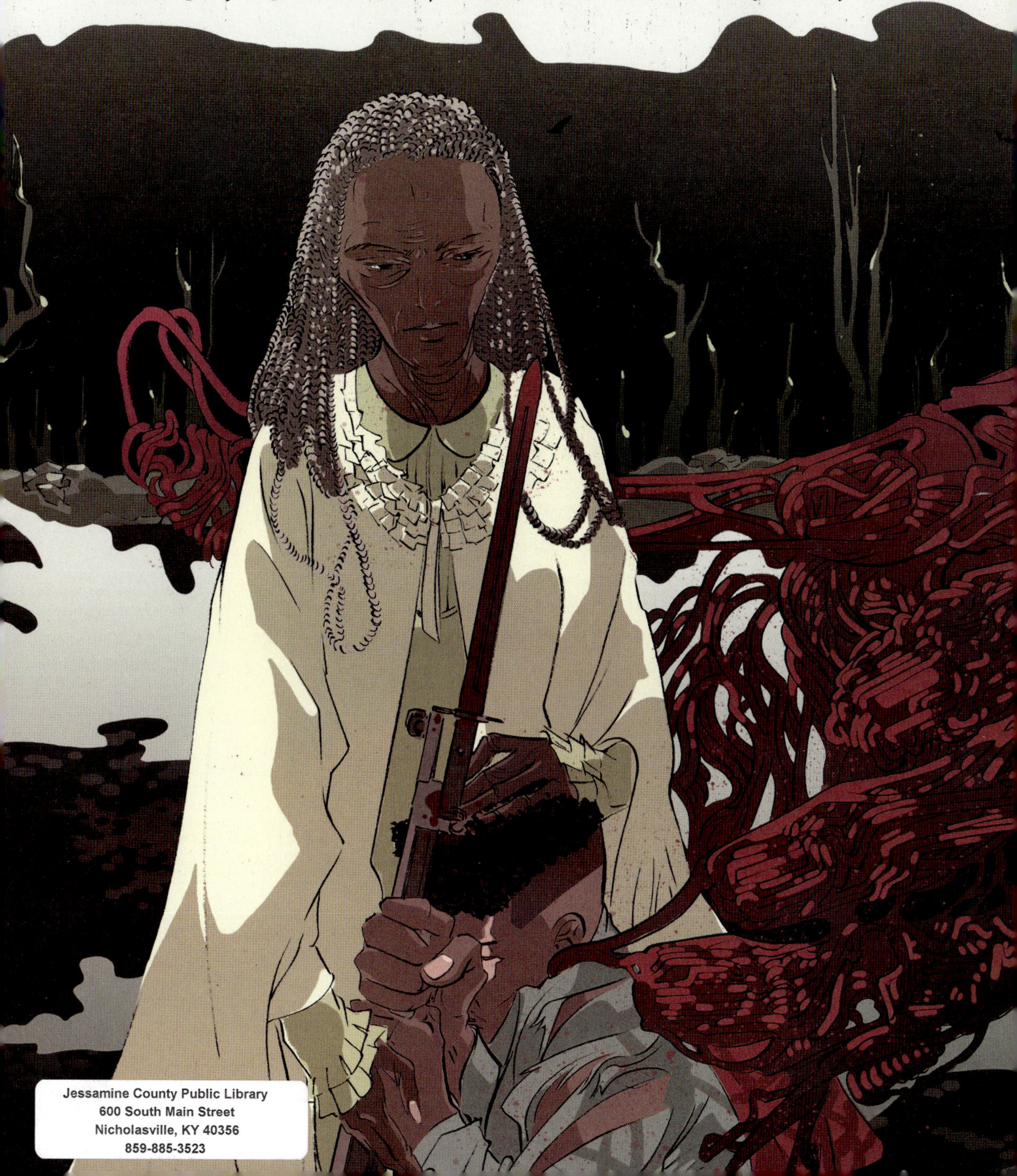

To my mom, María.
— Emma

To Henry Leo, my beautiful hummingbird,
your dream made the Bones Bunny real to me
and your heart made it all matter. Please whisper
my gratitude to Ginny when you see her next.

To Tallulah Louise, you got your anger from
me, baby girl. I'm sorry. You got your courage
from your daddy, though, so you're gonna be
all right.
— Kelly Sue

To Madison, the best and brightest.
— Jordie

To Rebecca Rafferty, who is still the pretty
deadliest person I know.
— Clayton

For the cosplayers and all other avatars of
modern gods.
— Sigrid

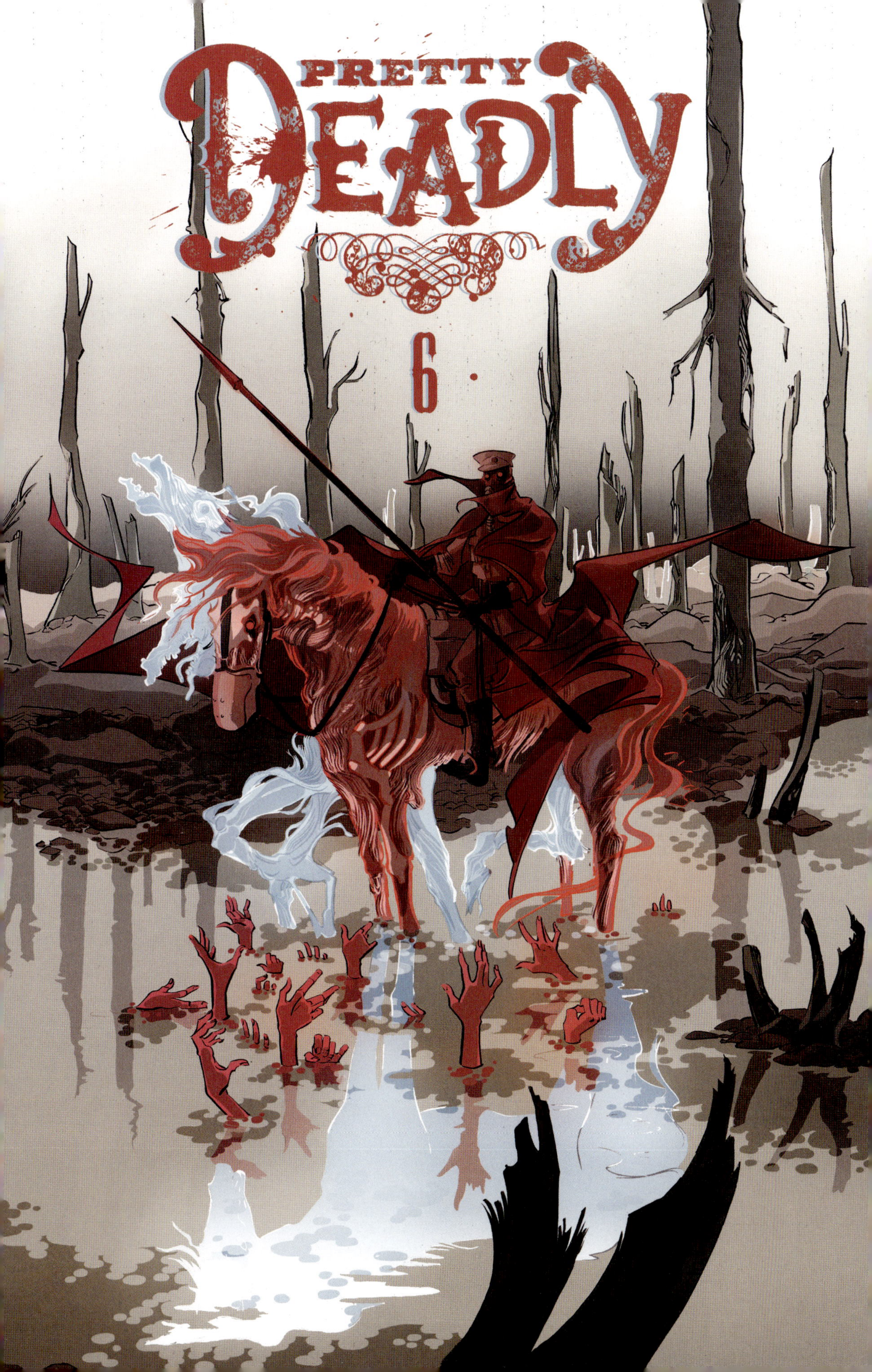
PRETTY
DEADLY
6

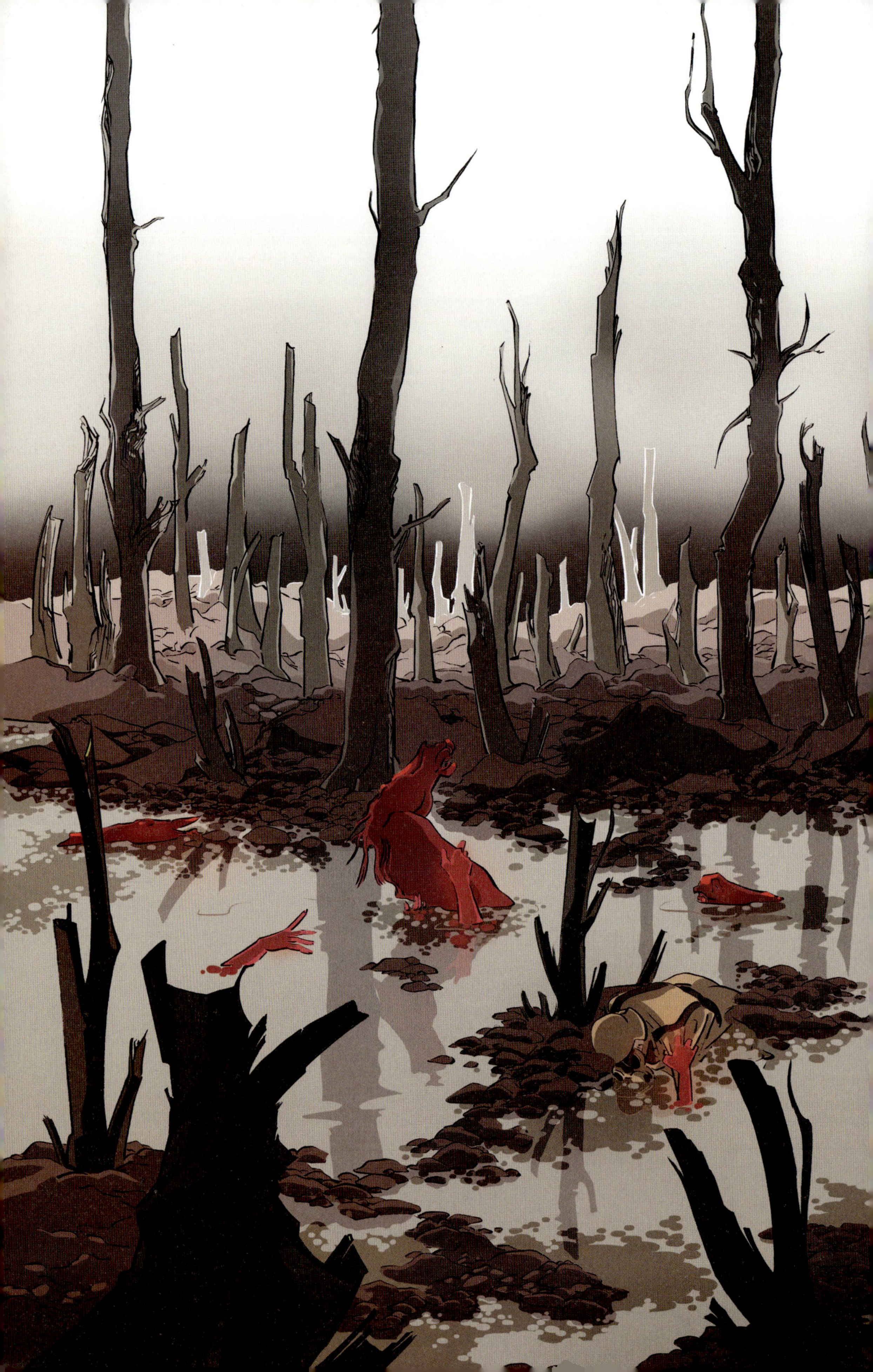

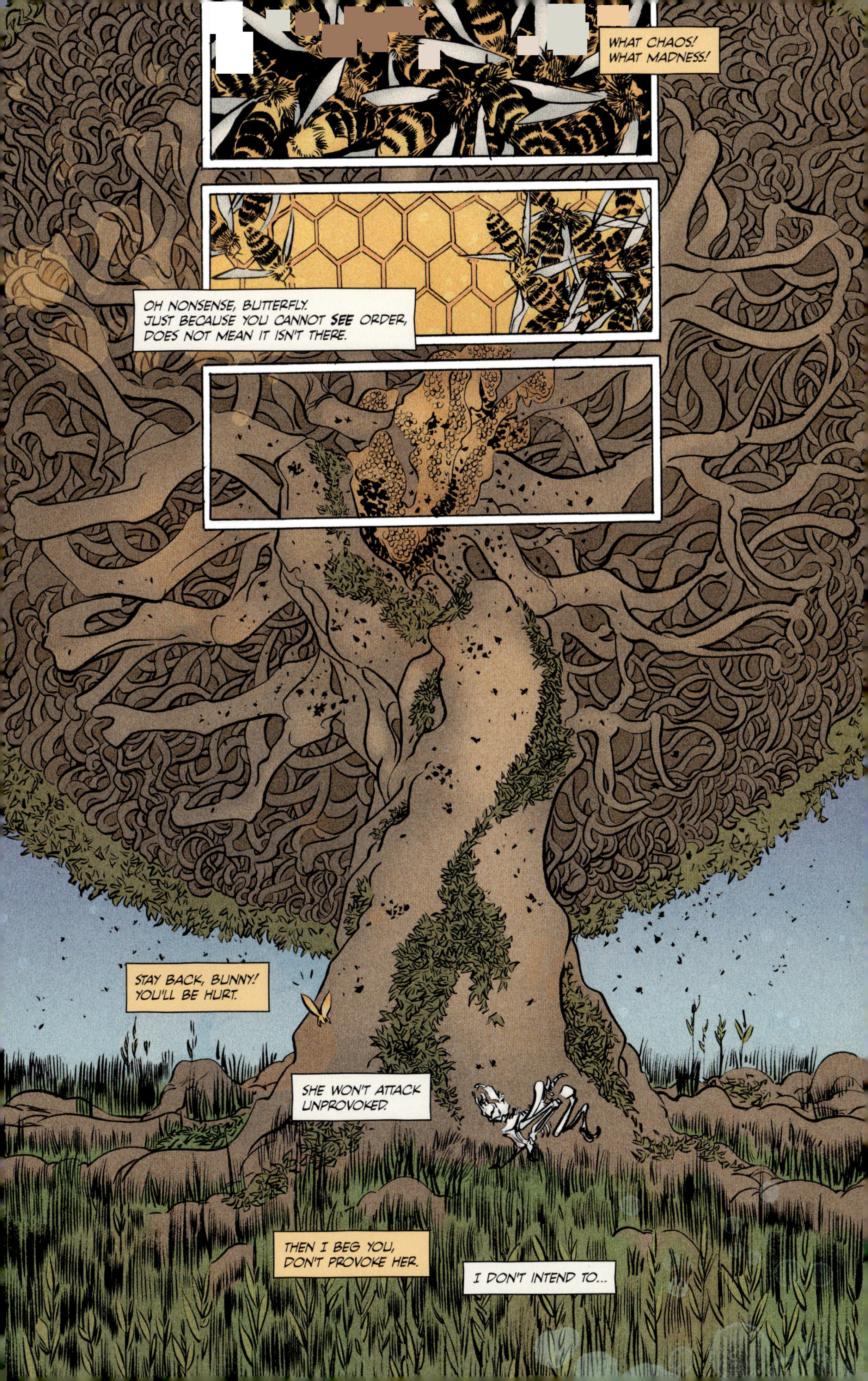
WHAT CHAOS!
WHAT MADNESS!
OH NONSENSE, BUTTERFLY.
JUST BECAUSE YOU CANNOT SEE ORDER,
DOES NOT MEAN IT ISN'T THERE.
STAY BACK, BUNNY!
YOU'LL BE HURT.
SHE WON'T ATTACK
UNPROVOKED.
THEN I BEG YOU,
DON'T PROVOKE HER.
I DON'T INTEND TO...

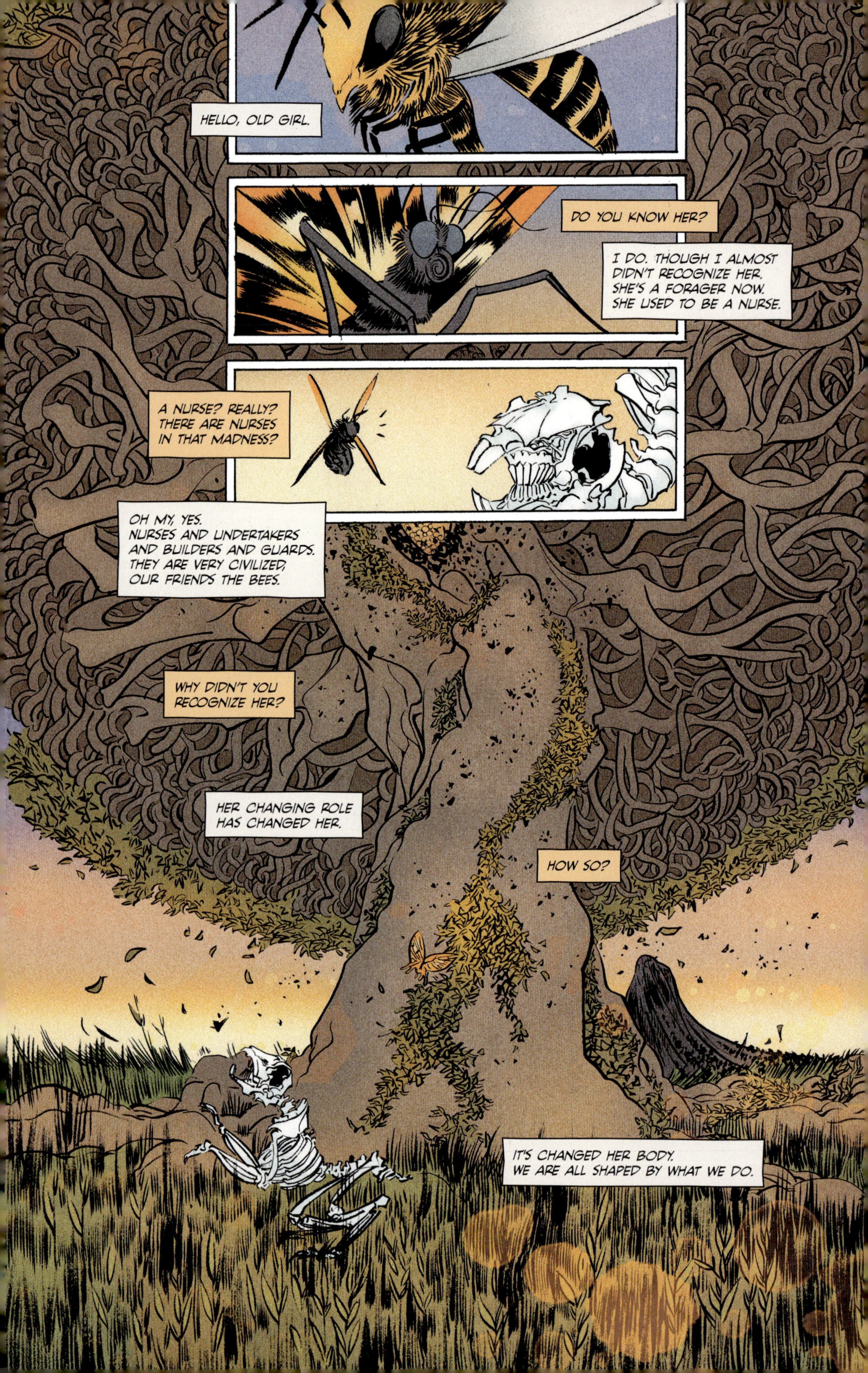
HELLO, OLD GIRL.
DO YOU KNOW HER?
I DO. THOUGH I ALMOST DIDN'T RECOGNIZE HER. SHE'S A FORAGER NOW. SHE USED TO BE A NURSE.
A NURSE? REALLY? THERE ARE NURSES IN THAT MADNESS?
OH MY, YES. NURSES AND UNDERTAKERS AND BUILDERS AND GUARDS. THEY ARE VERY CIVILIZED, OUR FRIENDS THE BEES.
WHY DIDN'T YOU RECOGNIZE HER?
HER CHANGING ROLE HAS CHANGED HER.
HOW SO?
IT'S CHANGED HER BODY. WE ARE ALL SHAPED BY WHAT WE DO.

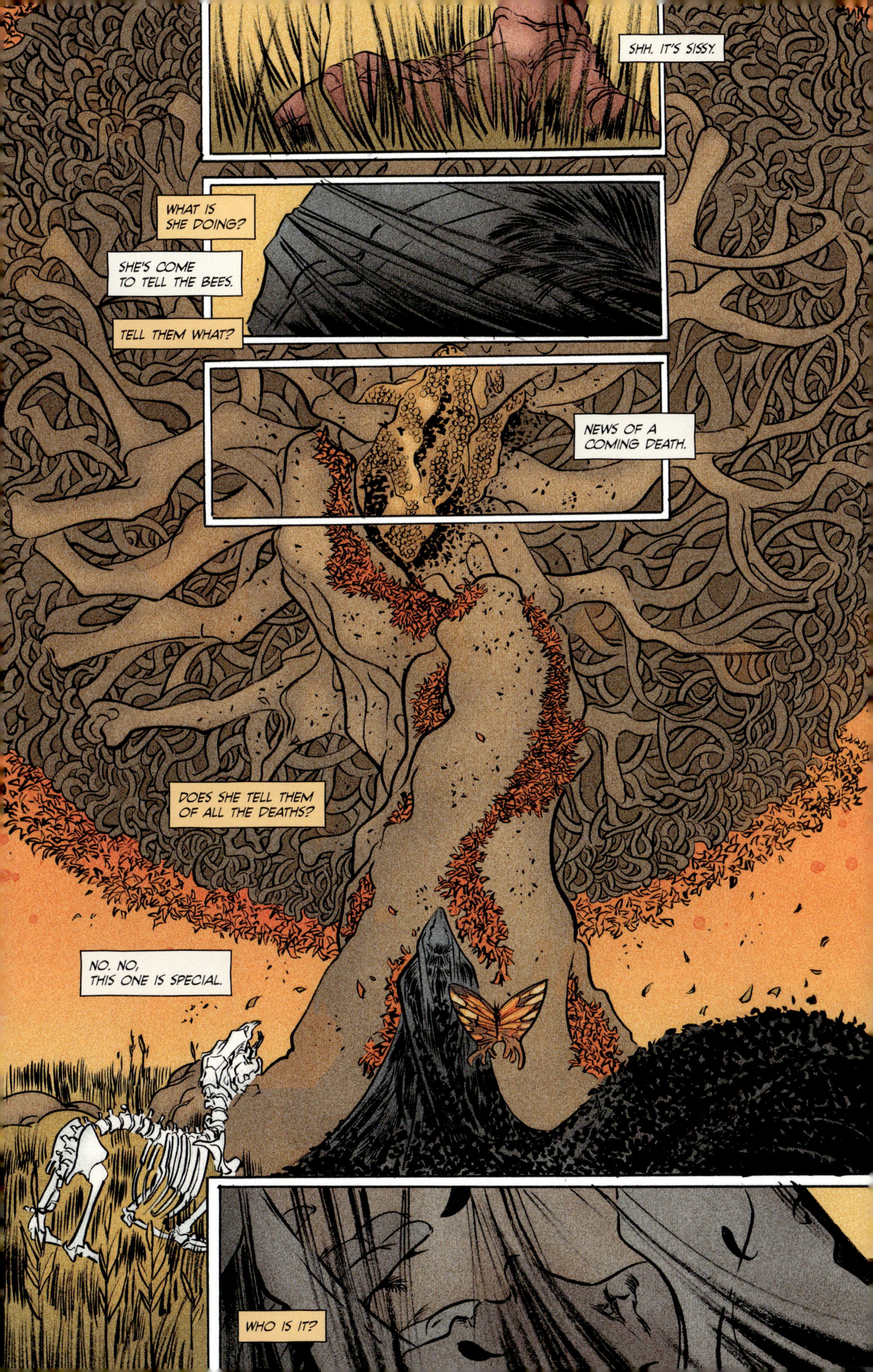
SHH. IT'S SISSY.
WHAT IS SHE DOING?
SHE'S COME TO TELL THE BEES.
TELL THEM WHAT?
NEWS OF A COMING DEATH.
DOES SHE TELL THEM OF ALL THE DEATHS?
NO. NO, THIS ONE IS SPECIAL.
WHO IS IT?

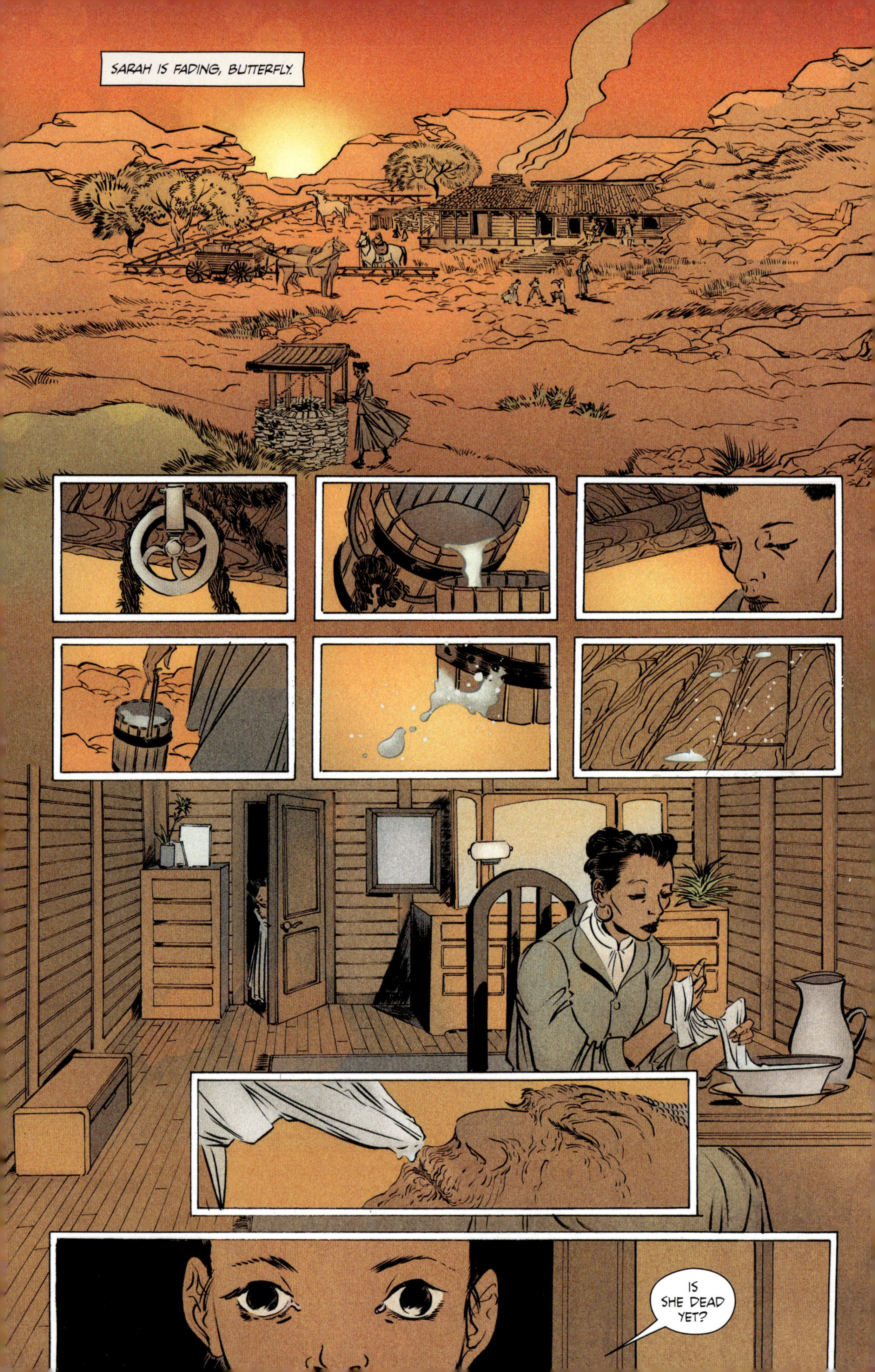
SARAH IS FADING, BUTTERFLY.
IS SHE DEAD YET?

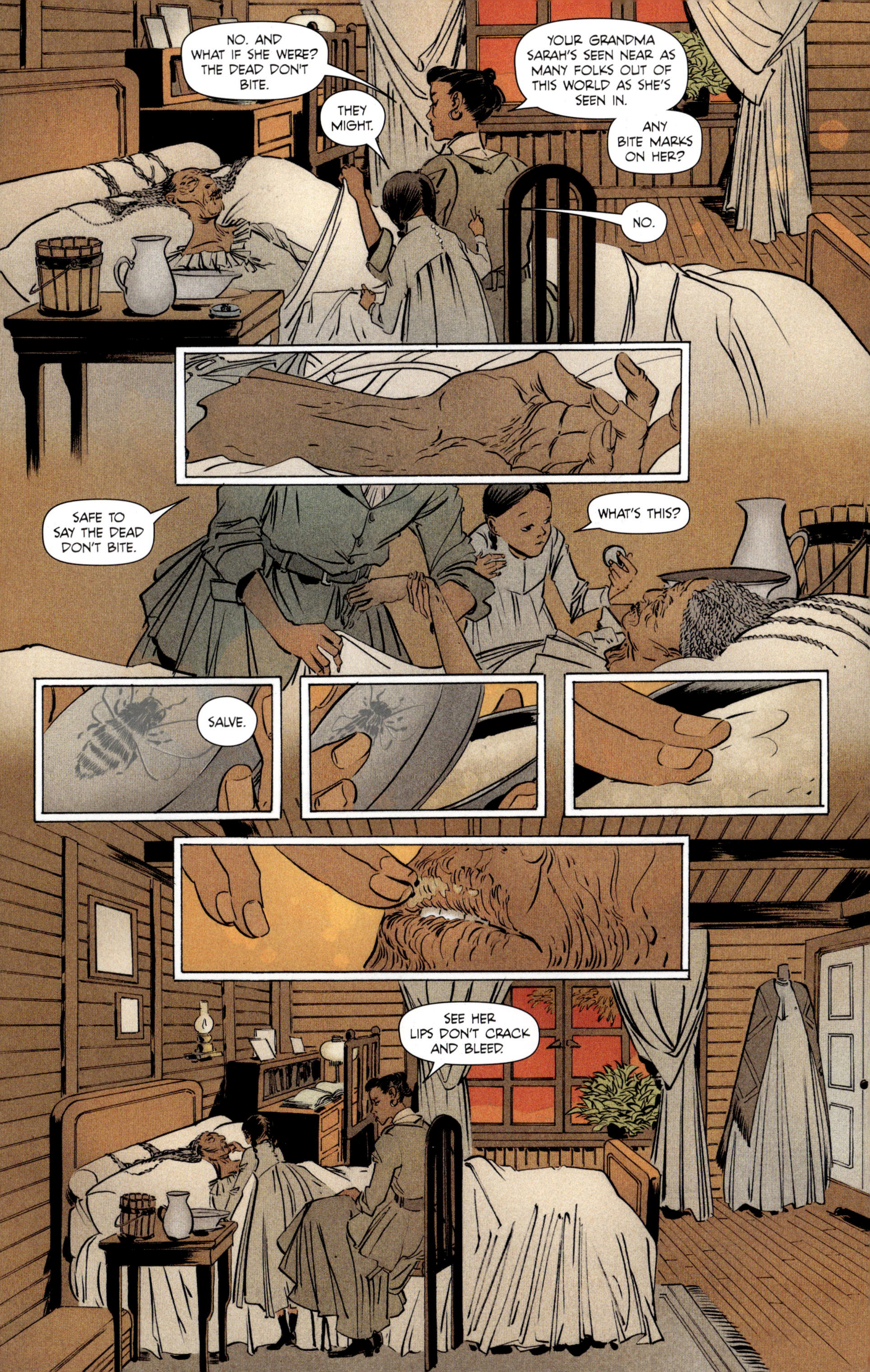
NO. AND WHAT IF SHE WERE? THE DEAD DON'T BITE.
THEY MIGHT.
YOUR GRANDMA SARAH'S SEEN NEAR AS MANY FOLKS OUT OF THIS WORLD AS SHE'S SEEN IN.
ANY BITE MARKS ON HER?
NO.
SAFE TO SAY THE DEAD DON'T BITE.
WHAT'S THIS?
SALVE.
SEE HER LIPS DON'T CRACK AND BLEED.

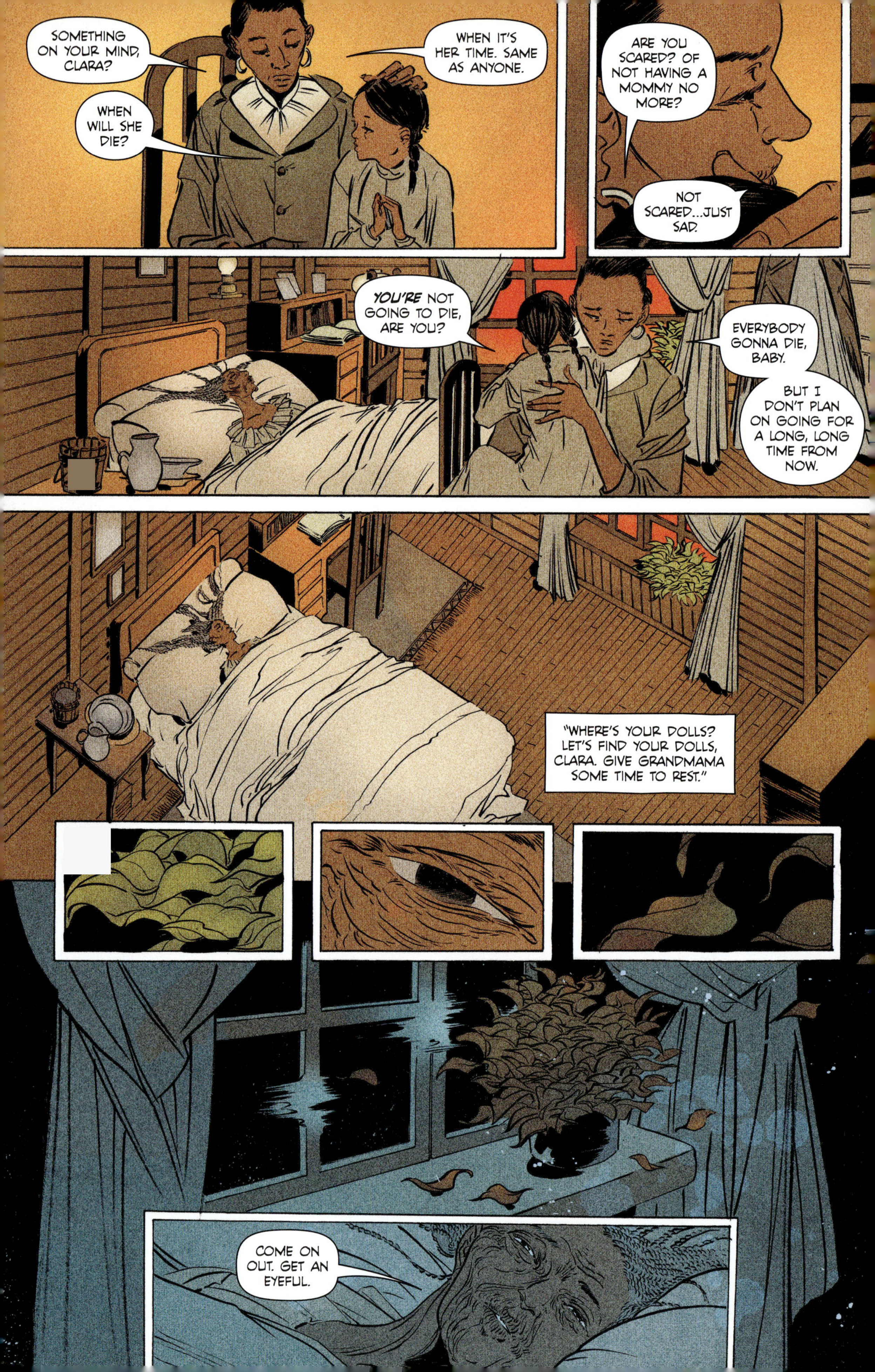
SOMETHING ON YOUR MIND, CLARA?
WHEN WILL SHE DIE?
WHEN IT'S HER TIME. SAME AS ANYONE.
ARE YOU SCARED? OF NOT HAVING A MOMMY NO MORE?
NOT SCARED...JUST SAD.
YOU'RE NOT GOING TO DIE, ARE YOU?
EVERYBODY GONNA DIE, BABY.
BUT I DON'T PLAN ON GOING FOR A LONG, LONG TIME FROM NOW.
"WHERE'S YOUR DOLLS? LET'S FIND YOUR DOLLS, CLARA. GIVE GRANDMAMA SOME TIME TO REST."
COME ON OUT. GET AN EYEFUL.

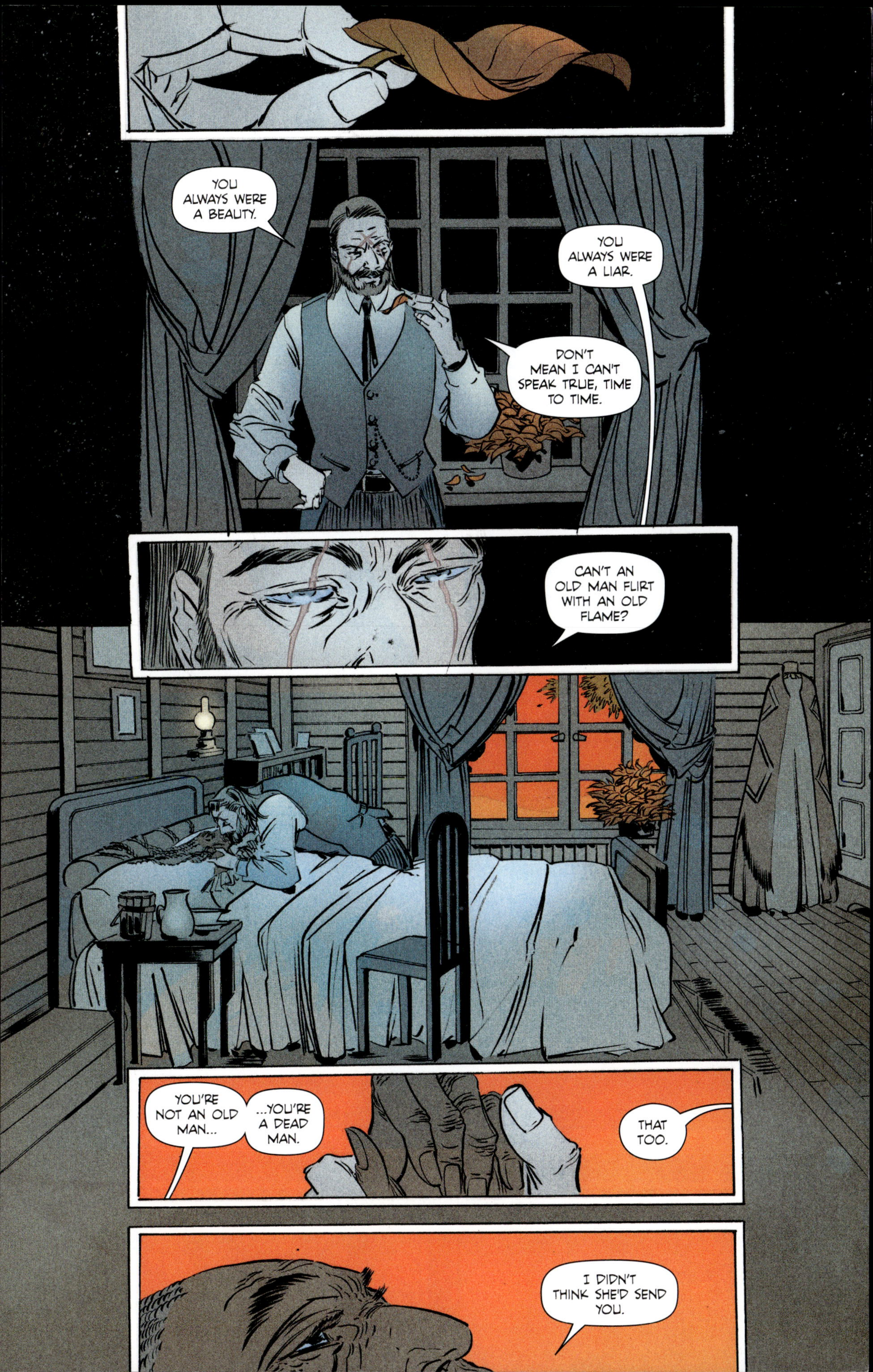
YOU ALWAYS WERE A BEAUTY.
YOU ALWAYS WERE A LIAR.
DON'T MEAN I CAN'T SPEAK TRUE, TIME TO TIME.
CAN'T AN OLD MAN FLIRT WITH AN OLD FLAME?
YOU'RE NOT AN OLD MAN...
...YOU'RE A DEAD MAN.
THAT TOO.
I DIDN'T THINK SHE'D SEND YOU.

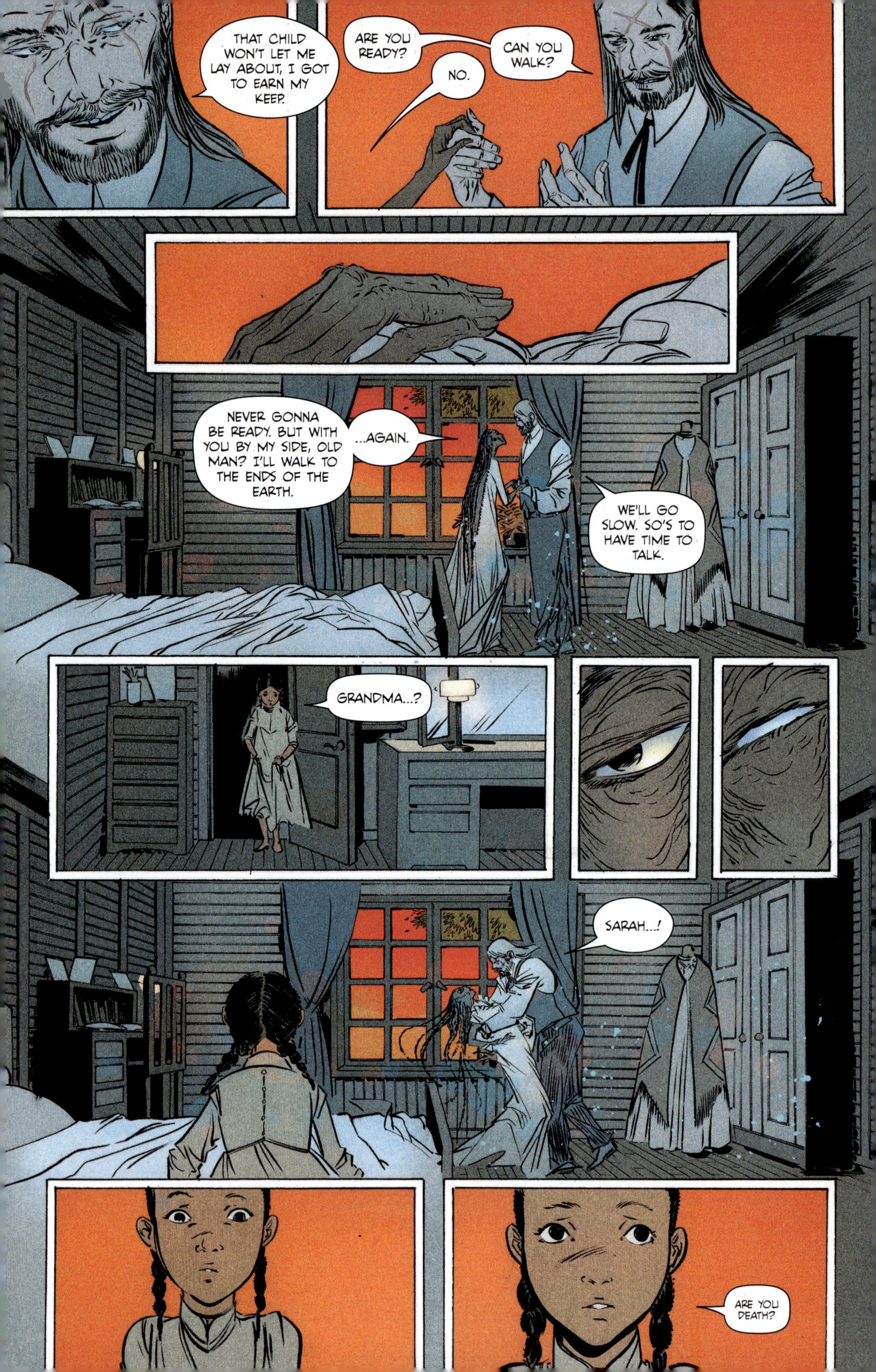
THAT CHILD WON'T LET ME LAY ABOUT, I GOT TO EARN MY KEEP.
ARE YOU READY?
CAN YOU WALK?
NO.
NEVER GONNA BE READY. BUT WITH YOU BY MY SIDE, OLD MAN? I'LL WALK TO THE ENDS OF THE EARTH.
...AGAIN.
WE'LL GO SLOW. SO'S TO HAVE TIME TO TALK.
GRANDMA...?
SARAH...!
ARE YOU DEATH?

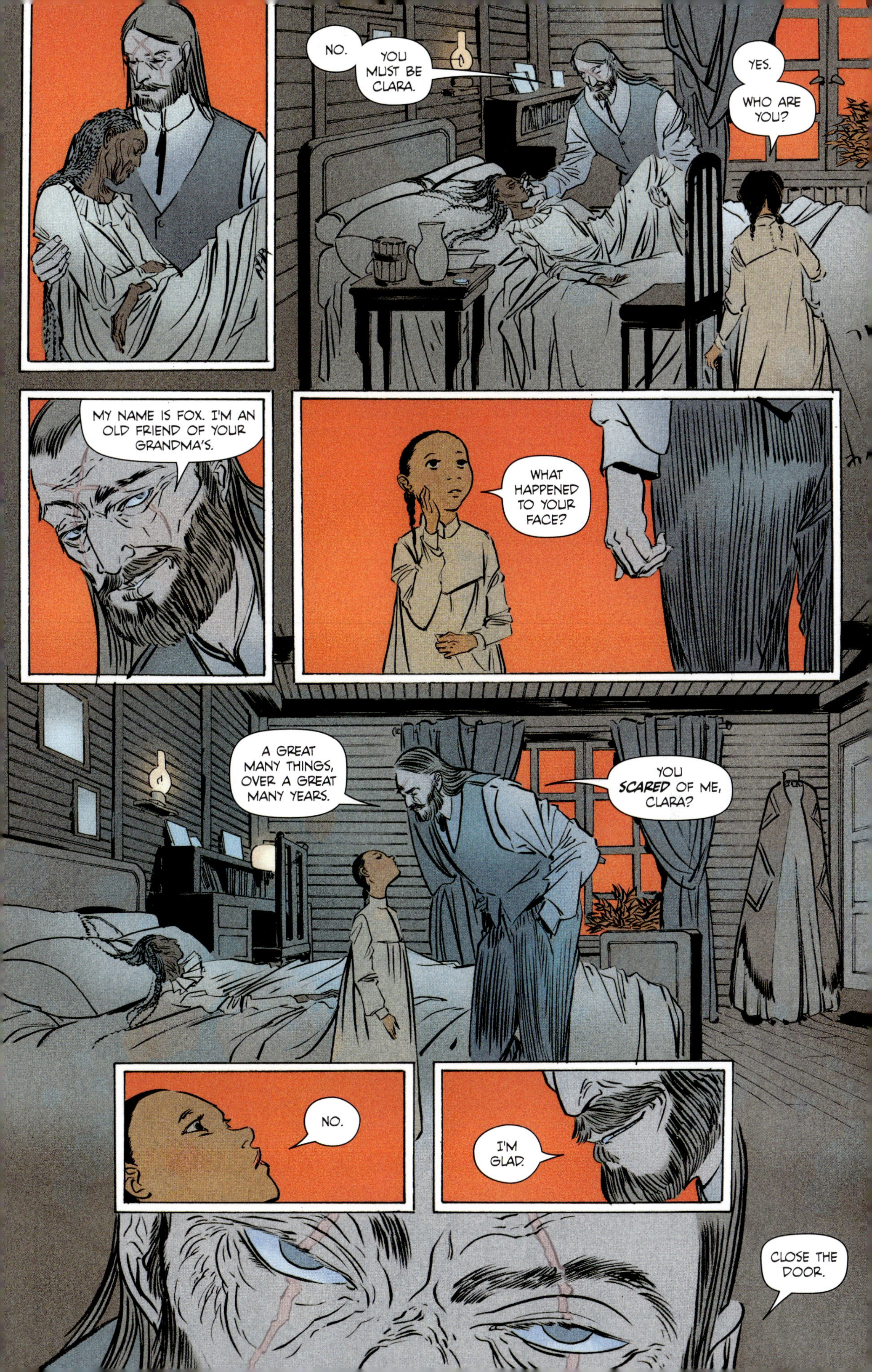
NO.
YOU MUST BE CLARA.
YES.
WHO ARE YOU?
MY NAME IS FOX. I'M AN OLD FRIEND OF YOUR GRANDMA'S.
WHAT HAPPENED TO YOUR FACE?
A GREAT MANY THINGS, OVER A GREAT MANY YEARS.
YOU *SCARED* OF ME, CLARA?
NO.
I'M GLAD.
CLOSE THE DOOR.

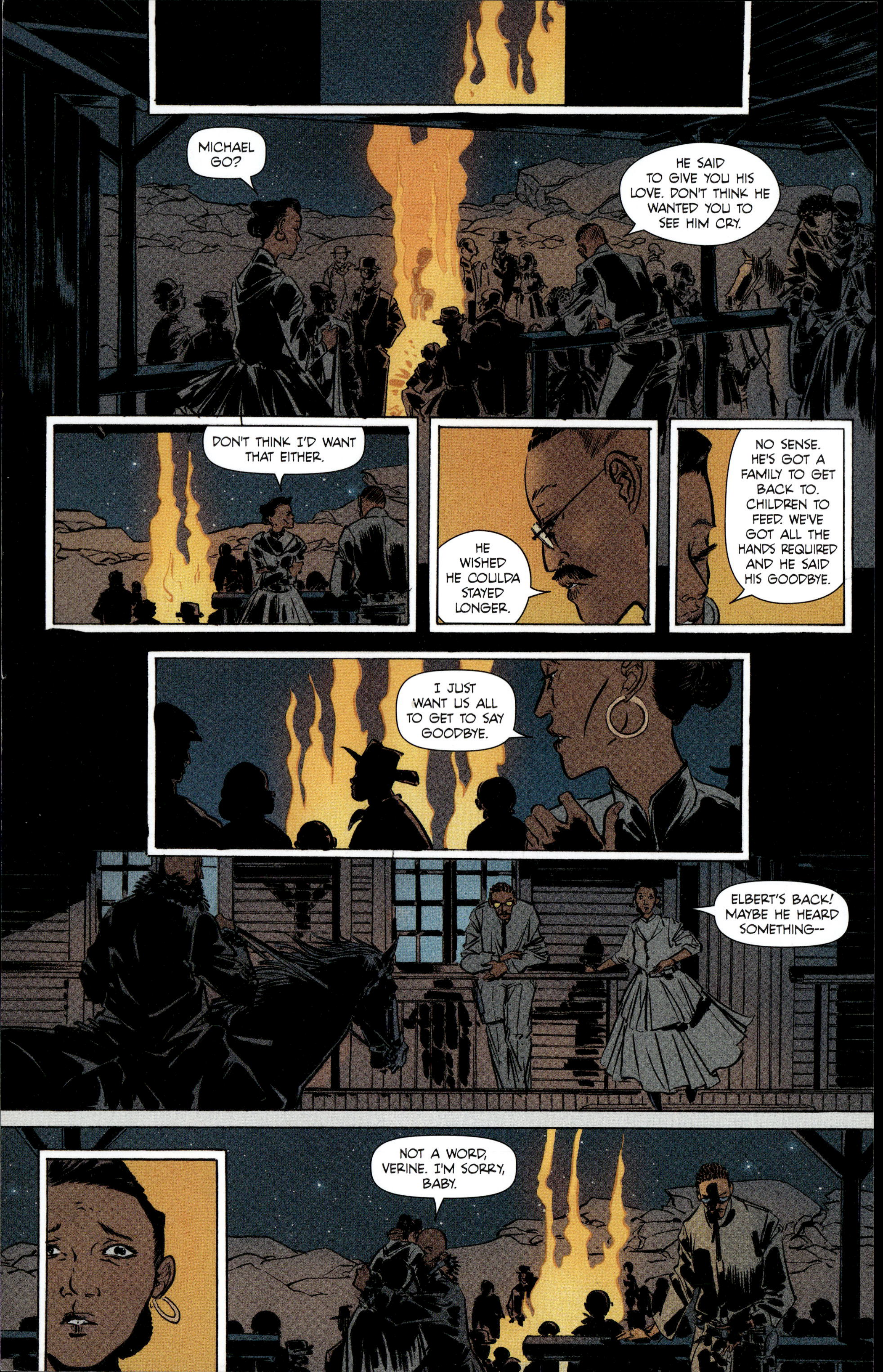
MICHAEL GO?
HE SAID TO GIVE YOU HIS LOVE. DON'T THINK HE WANTED YOU TO SEE HIM CRY.
DON'T THINK I'D WANT THAT EITHER.
HE WISHED HE COULDA STAYED LONGER.
NO SENSE. HE'S GOT A FAMILY TO GET BACK TO. CHILDREN TO FEED. WE'VE GOT ALL THE HANDS REQUIRED AND HE SAID HIS GOODBYE.
I JUST WANT US ALL TO GET TO SAY GOODBYE.
ELBERT'S BACK! MAYBE HE HEARD SOMETHING--
NOT A WORD, VERINE. I'M SORRY, BABY.

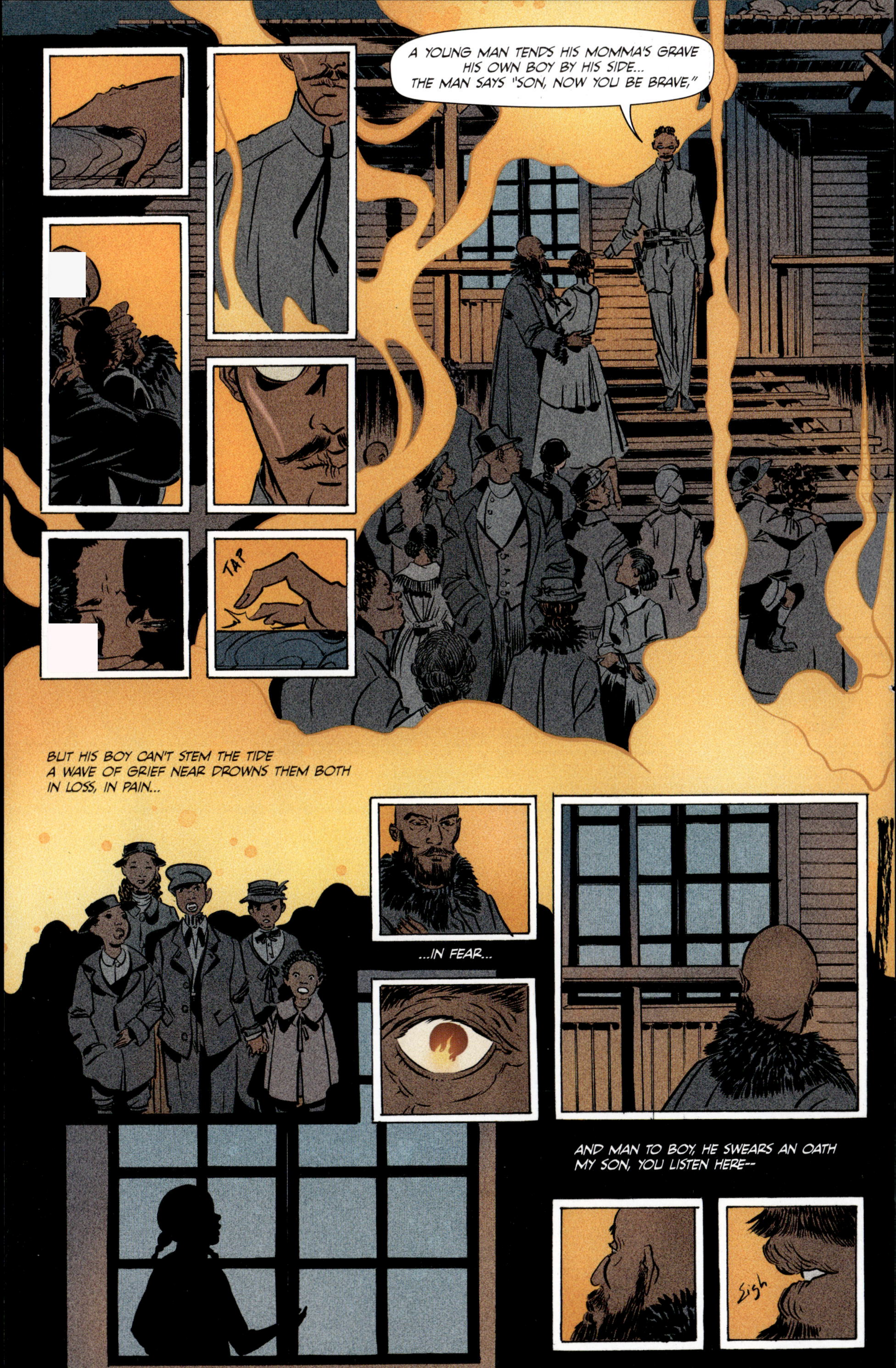
TAP
A YOUNG MAN TENDS HIS MOMMA'S GRAVE
HIS OWN BOY BY HIS SIDE...
THE MAN SAYS "SON, NOW YOU BE BRAVE,"
BUT HIS BOY CAN'T STEM THE TIDE
A WAVE OF GRIEF NEAR DROWNS THEM BOTH
IN LOSS, IN PAIN...
...IN FEAR...
AND MAN TO BOY, HE SWEARS AN OATH
MY SON, YOU LISTEN HERE--
SIGH

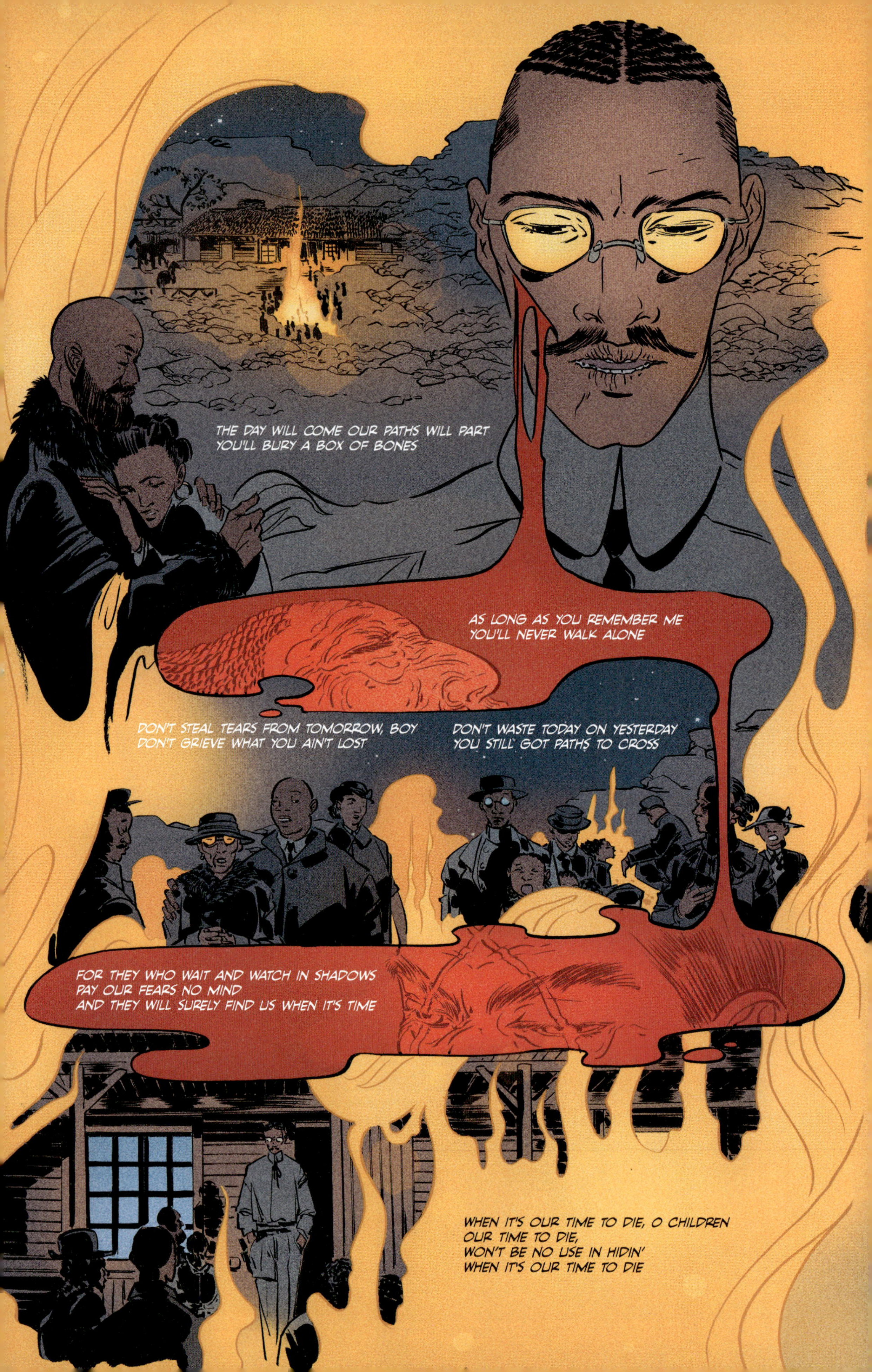
THE DAY WILL COME OUR PATHS WILL PART
YOU'LL BURY A BOX OF BONES
AS LONG AS YOU REMEMBER ME
YOU'LL NEVER WALK ALONE
DON'T STEAL TEARS FROM TOMORROW, BOY
DON'T GRIEVE WHAT YOU AIN'T LOST
DON'T WASTE TODAY ON YESTERDAY
YOU STILL GOT PATHS TO CROSS
FOR THEY WHO WAIT AND WATCH IN SHADOWS
PAY OUR FEARS NO MIND
AND THEY WILL SURELY FIND US WHEN IT'S TIME
WHEN IT'S OUR TIME TO DIE, O CHILDREN
OUR TIME TO DIE,
WON'T BE NO USE IN HIDIN'
WHEN IT'S OUR TIME TO DIE

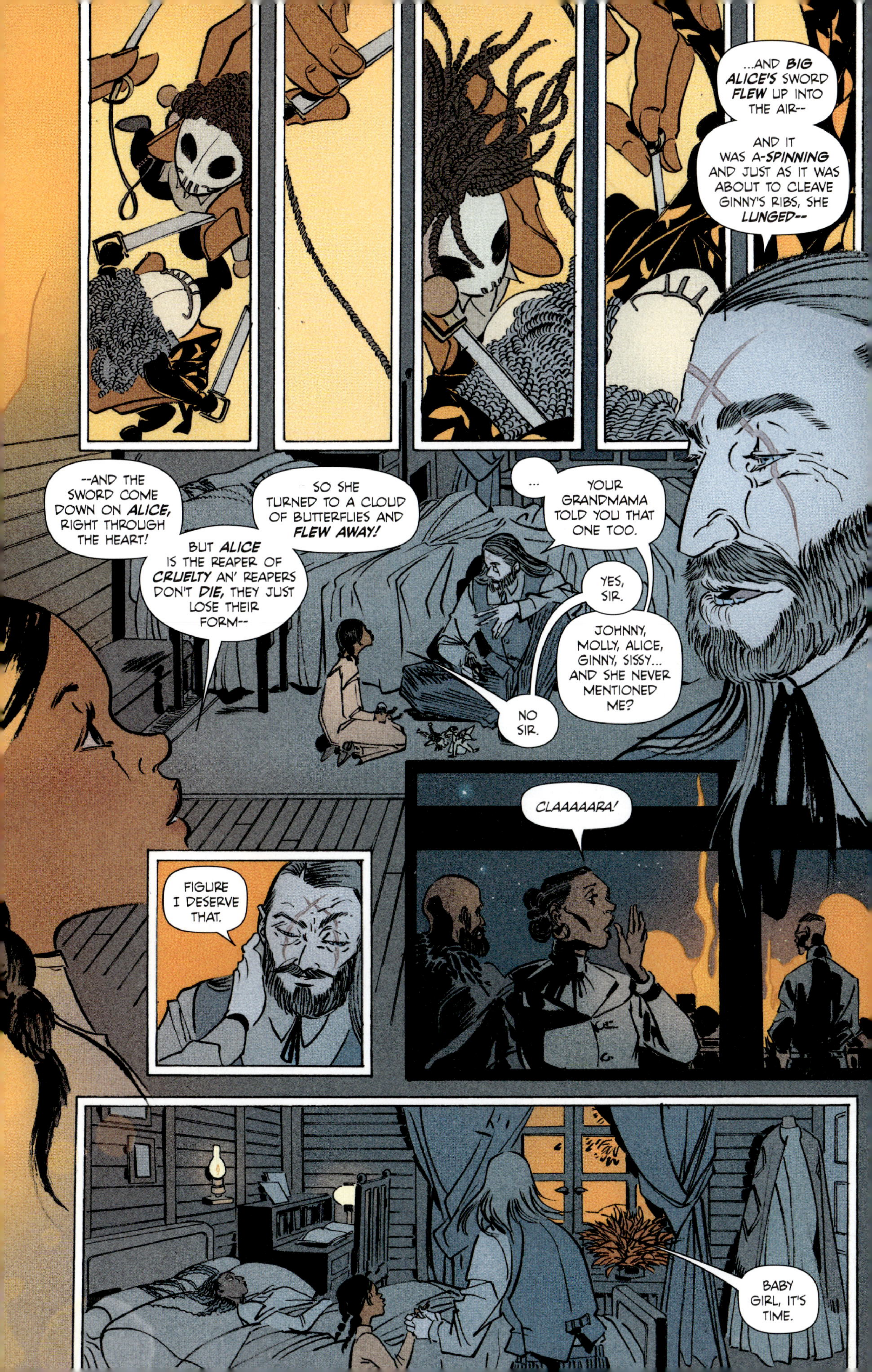

...AND BIG ALICE'S SWORD FLEW UP INTO THE AIR--
AND IT WAS A-SPINNING AND JUST AS IT WAS ABOUT TO CLEAVE GINNY'S RIBS, SHE LUNGED--
--AND THE SWORD COME DOWN ON ALICE, RIGHT THROUGH THE HEART!
BUT ALICE IS THE REAPER OF CRUELTY AN' REAPERS DON'T DIE, THEY JUST LOSE THEIR FORM--
SO SHE TURNED TO A CLOUD OF BUTTERFLIES AND FLEW AWAY!
...
YOUR GRANDMAMA TOLD YOU THAT ONE TOO.
YES, SIR.
JOHNNY, MOLLY, ALICE, GINNY, SISSY... AND SHE NEVER MENTIONED ME?
NO SIR.
FIGURE I DESERVE THAT.
CLAAAAARA!
BABY GIRL, IT'S TIME.

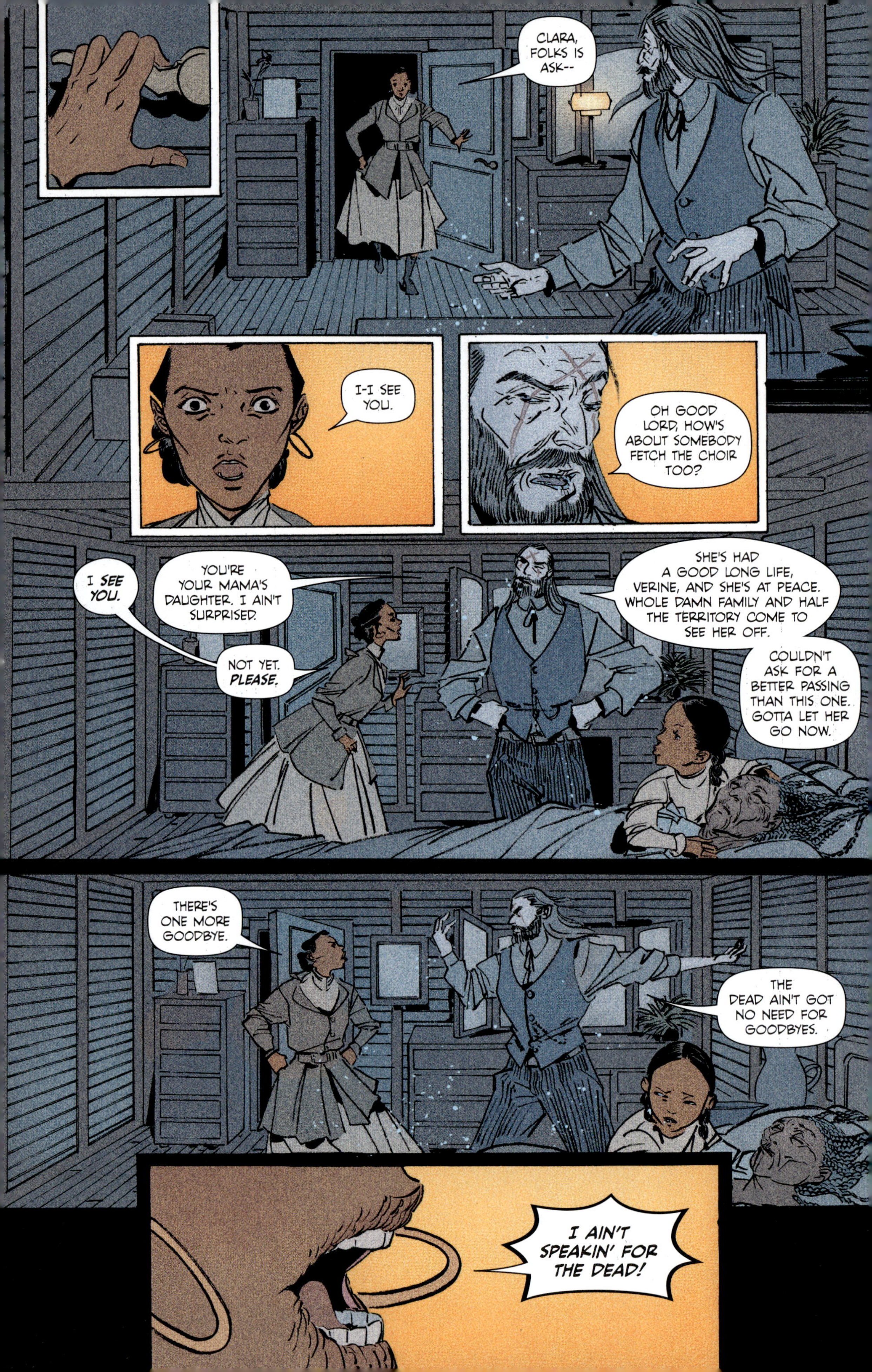

CLARA, FOLKS IS ASK--
I-I SEE YOU.
OH GOOD LORD, HOW'S ABOUT SOMEBODY FETCH THE CHOIR TOO?
I *SEE YOU.*
YOU'RE YOUR MAMA'S DAUGHTER. I AIN'T SURPRISED.
NOT YET. *PLEASE.*
SHE'S HAD A GOOD LONG LIFE, VERINE, AND SHE'S AT PEACE. WHOLE DAMN FAMILY AND HALF THE TERRITORY COME TO SEE HER OFF.
COULDN'T ASK FOR A BETTER PASSING THAN THIS ONE. GOTTA LET HER GO NOW.
THERE'S ONE MORE GOODBYE.
THE DEAD AIN'T GOT NO NEED FOR GOODBYES.
I AIN'T SPEAKIN' FOR THE DEAD!

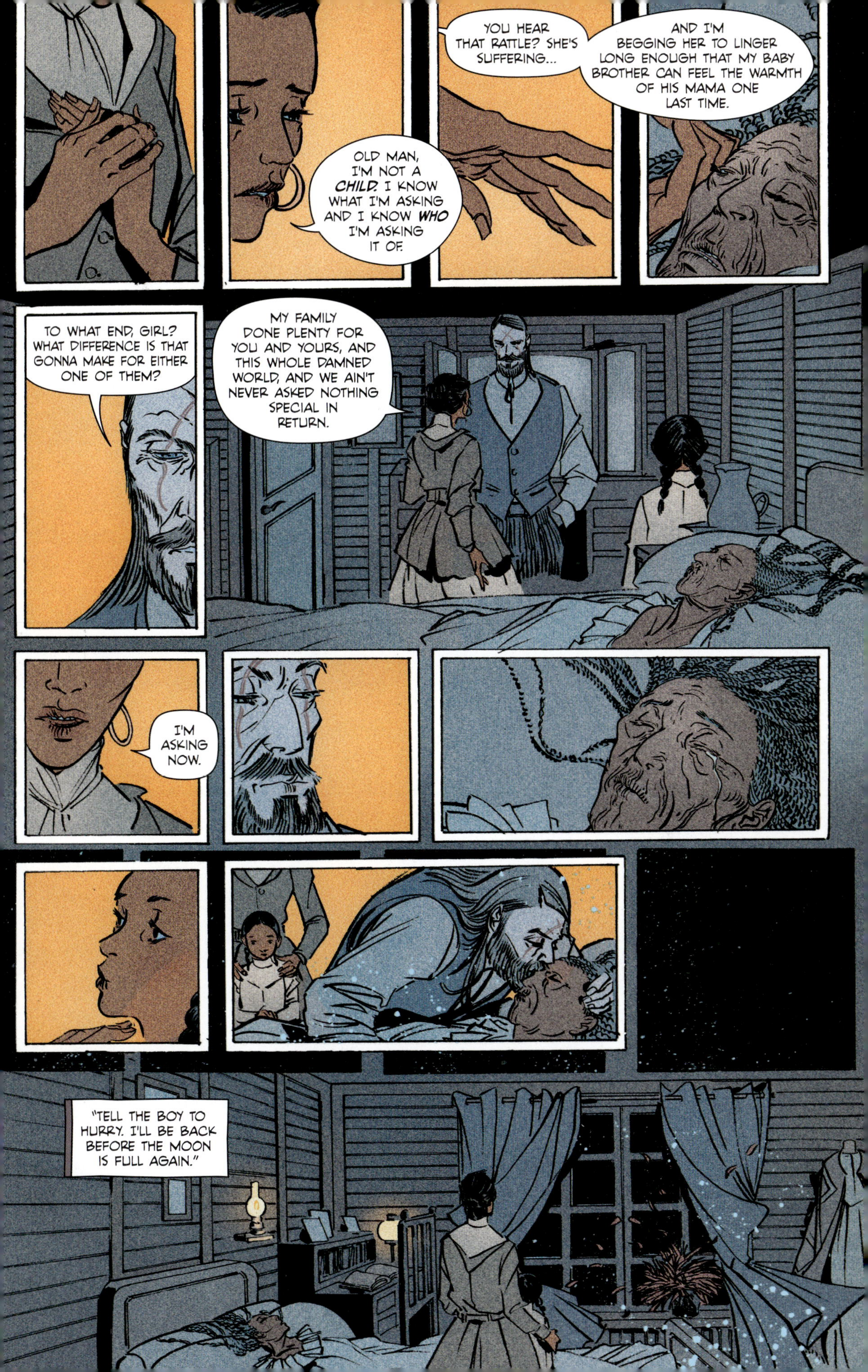
OLD MAN, I'M NOT A *CHILD.* I KNOW WHAT I'M ASKING AND I KNOW *WHO* I'M ASKING IT OF.
YOU HEAR THAT RATTLE? SHE'S SUFFERING...
AND I'M BEGGING HER TO LINGER LONG ENOUGH THAT MY BABY BROTHER CAN FEEL THE WARMTH OF HIS MAMA ONE LAST TIME.
TO WHAT END, GIRL? WHAT DIFFERENCE IS THAT GONNA MAKE FOR EITHER ONE OF THEM?
MY FAMILY DONE PLENTY FOR YOU AND YOURS, AND THIS WHOLE DAMNED WORLD, AND WE AIN'T NEVER ASKED NOTHING SPECIAL IN RETURN.
I'M ASKING NOW.
"TELL THE BOY TO HURRY. I'LL BE BACK BEFORE THE MOON IS FULL AGAIN."

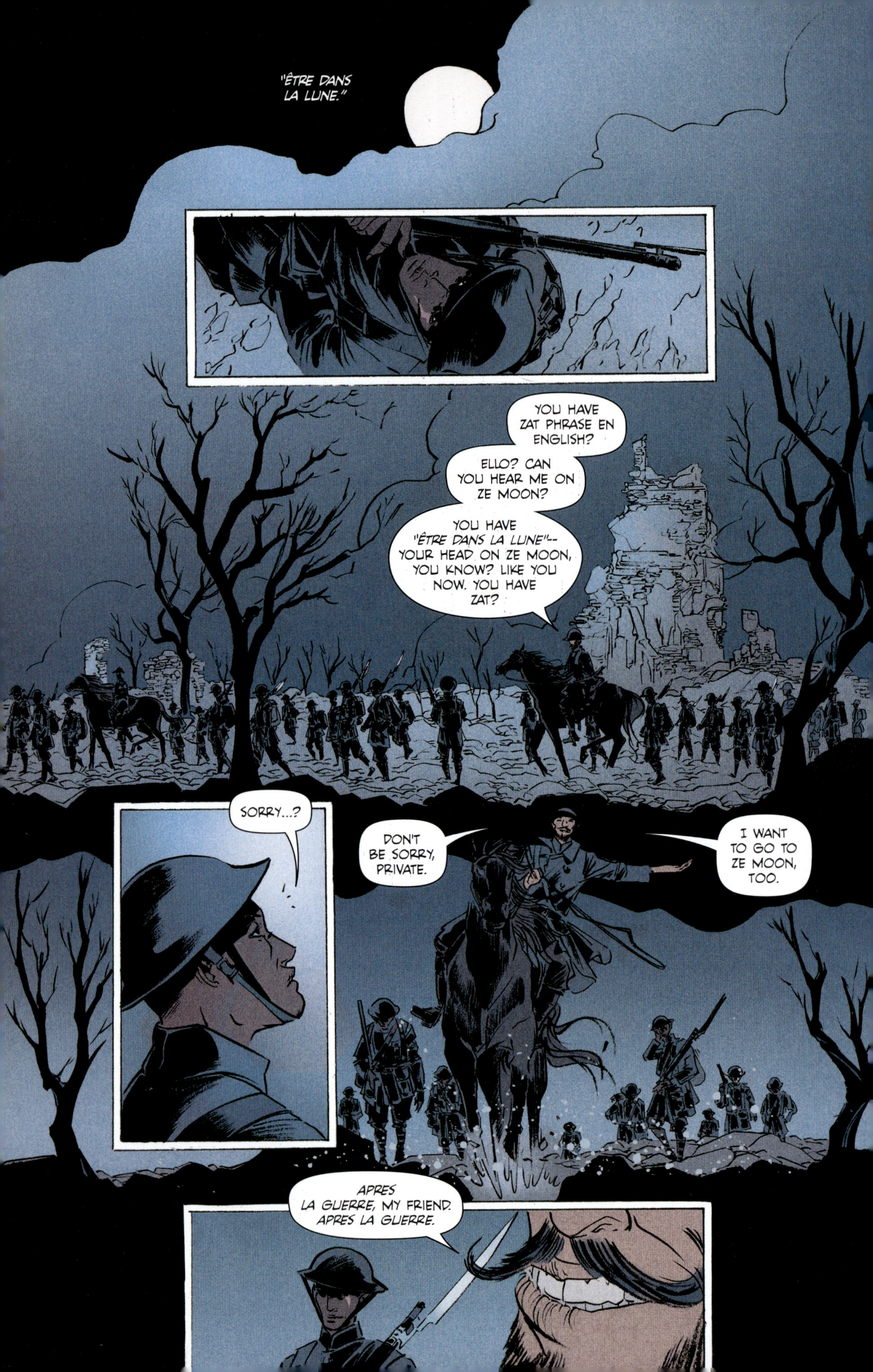
"ÊTRE DANS LA LUNE."
YOU HAVE ZAT PHRASE EN ENGLISH?
ELLO? CAN YOU HEAR ME ON ZE MOON?
YOU HAVE "ÊTRE DANS LA LUNE"-- YOUR HEAD ON ZE MOON, YOU KNOW? LIKE YOU NOW. YOU HAVE ZAT?
SORRY...?
DON'T BE SORRY, PRIVATE.
I WANT TO GO TO ZE MOON, TOO.
APRES LA GUERRE, MY FRIEND. APRES LA GUERRE.

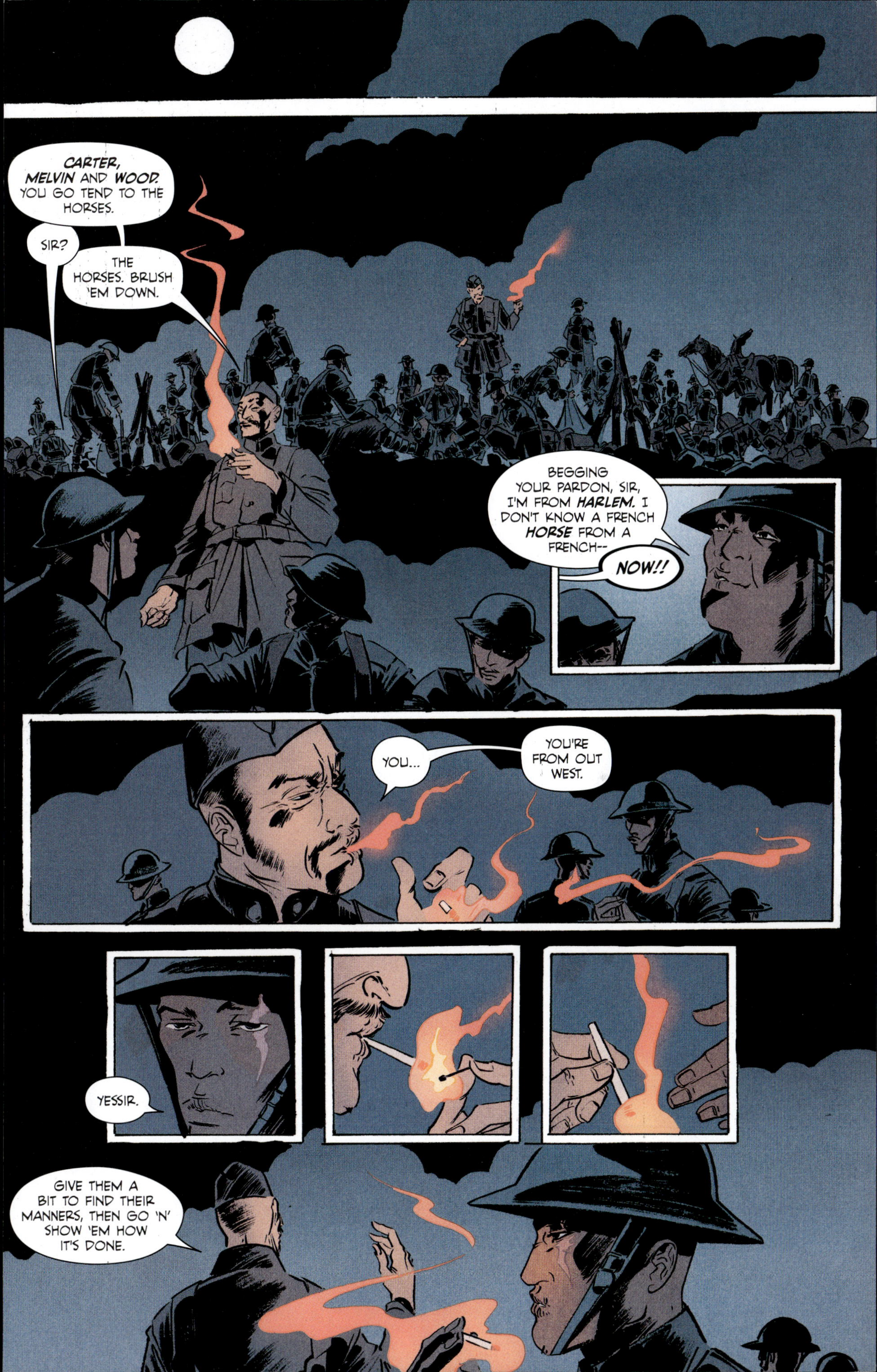
CARTER, MELVIN AND WOOD. YOU GO TEND TO THE HORSES.
SIR?
THE HORSES. BRUSH 'EM DOWN.
BEGGING YOUR PARDON, SIR, I'M FROM HARLEM. I DON'T KNOW A FRENCH HORSE FROM A FRENCH--
NOW!!
YOU...
YOU'RE FROM OUT WEST.
YESSIR.
GIVE THEM A BIT TO FIND THEIR MANNERS, THEN GO 'N' SHOW 'EM HOW IT'S DONE.

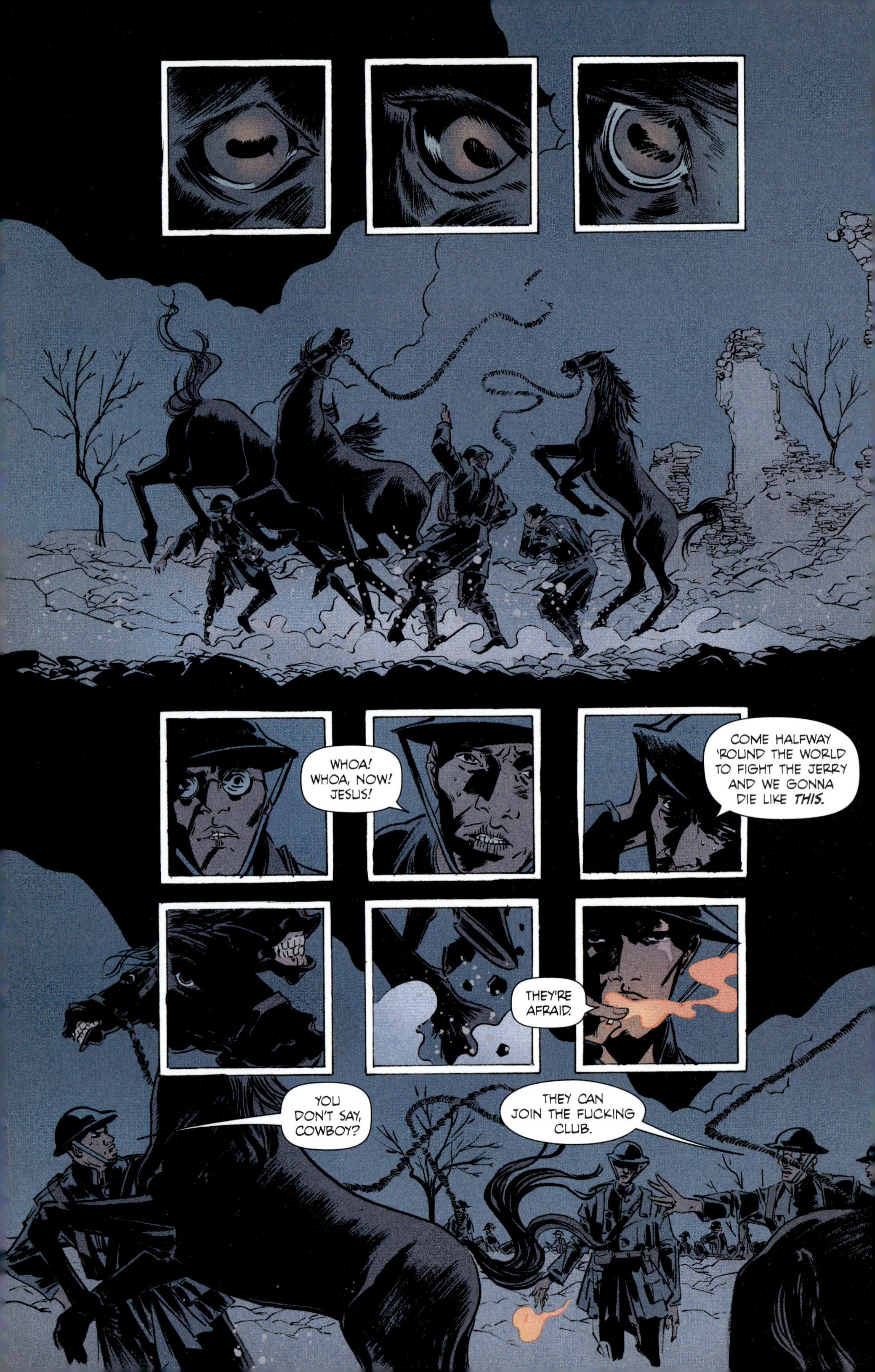
WHOA! WHOA, NOW! JESUS!
COME HALFWAY 'ROUND THE WORLD TO FIGHT THE JERRY AND WE GONNA DIE LIKE *THIS.*
THEY'RE AFRAID.
YOU DON'T SAY, COWBOY?
THEY CAN JOIN THE FUCKING CLUB.

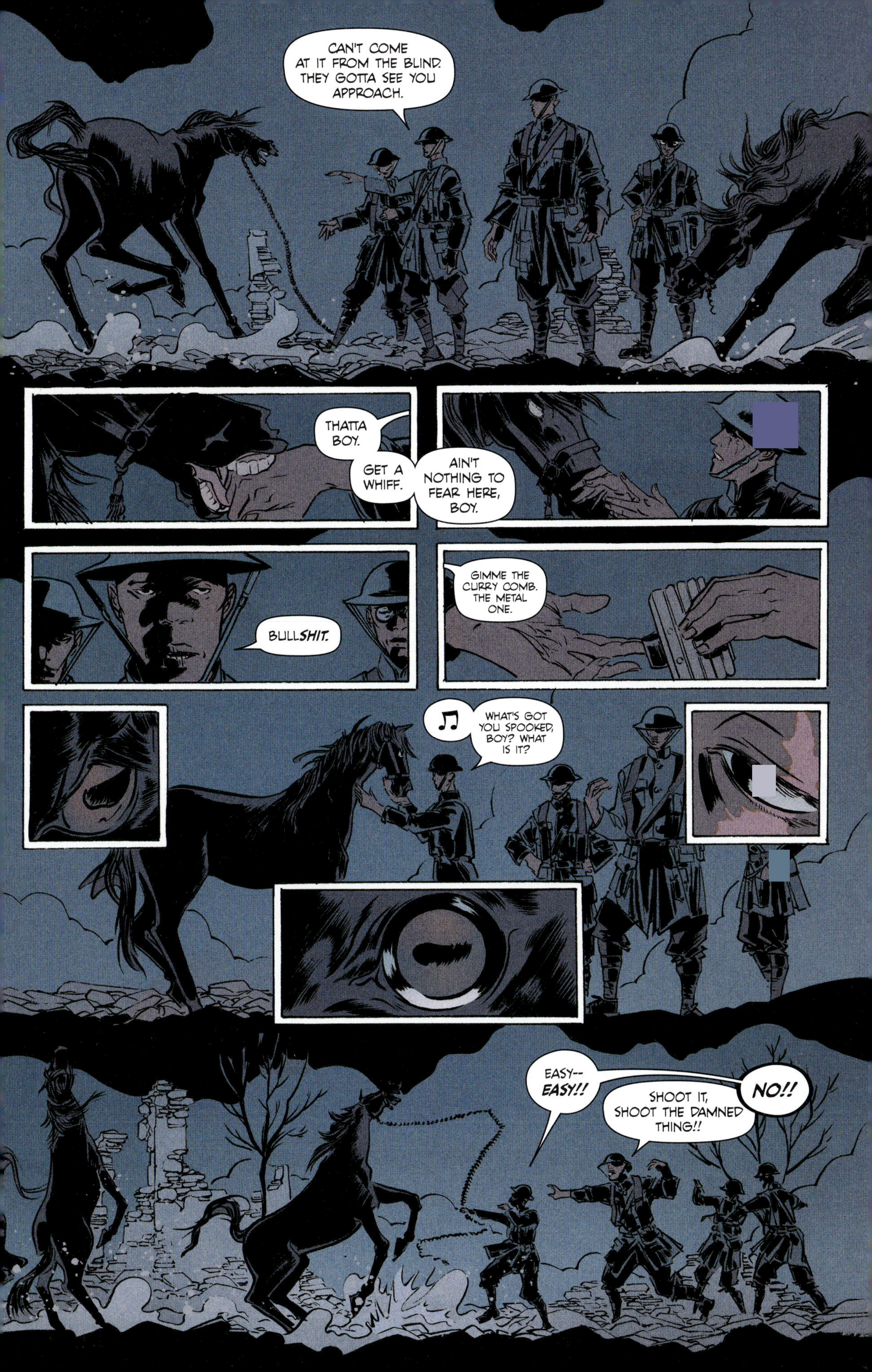
CAN'T COME AT IT FROM THE BLIND. THEY GOTTA SEE YOU APPROACH.
THATTA BOY.
GET A WHIFF.
AIN'T NOTHING TO FEAR HERE, BOY.
BULLSHIT.
GIMME THE CURRY COMB. THE METAL ONE.
♫
WHAT'S GOT YOU SPOOKED, BOY? WHAT IS IT?
EASY-- EASY!!
SHOOT IT, SHOOT THE DAMNED THING!!
NO!!

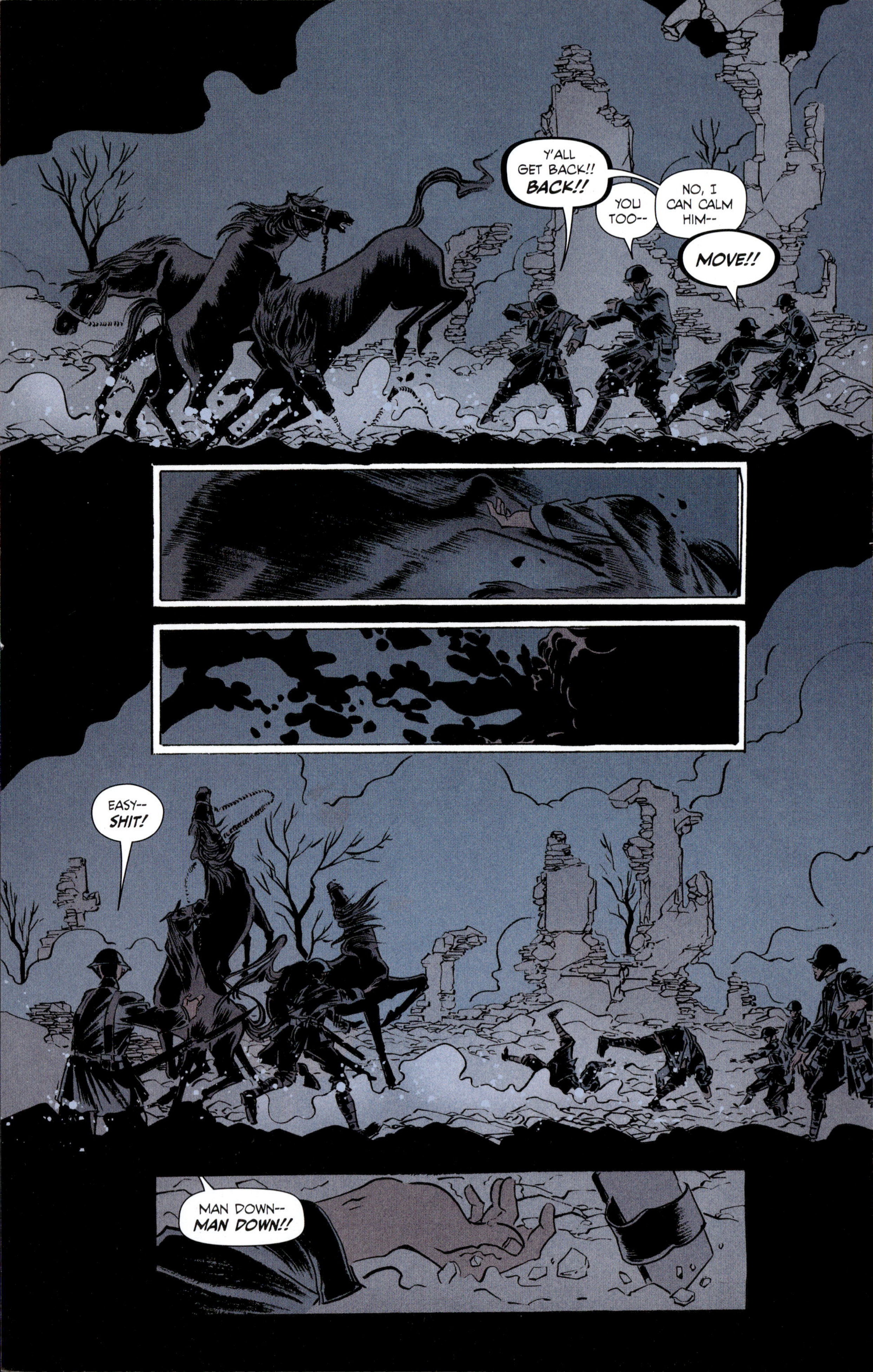
Y'ALL GET BACK!! BACK!!
YOU TOO--
NO, I CAN CALM HIM--
MOVE!!
EASY-- SHIT!
MAN DOWN-- MAN DOWN!!

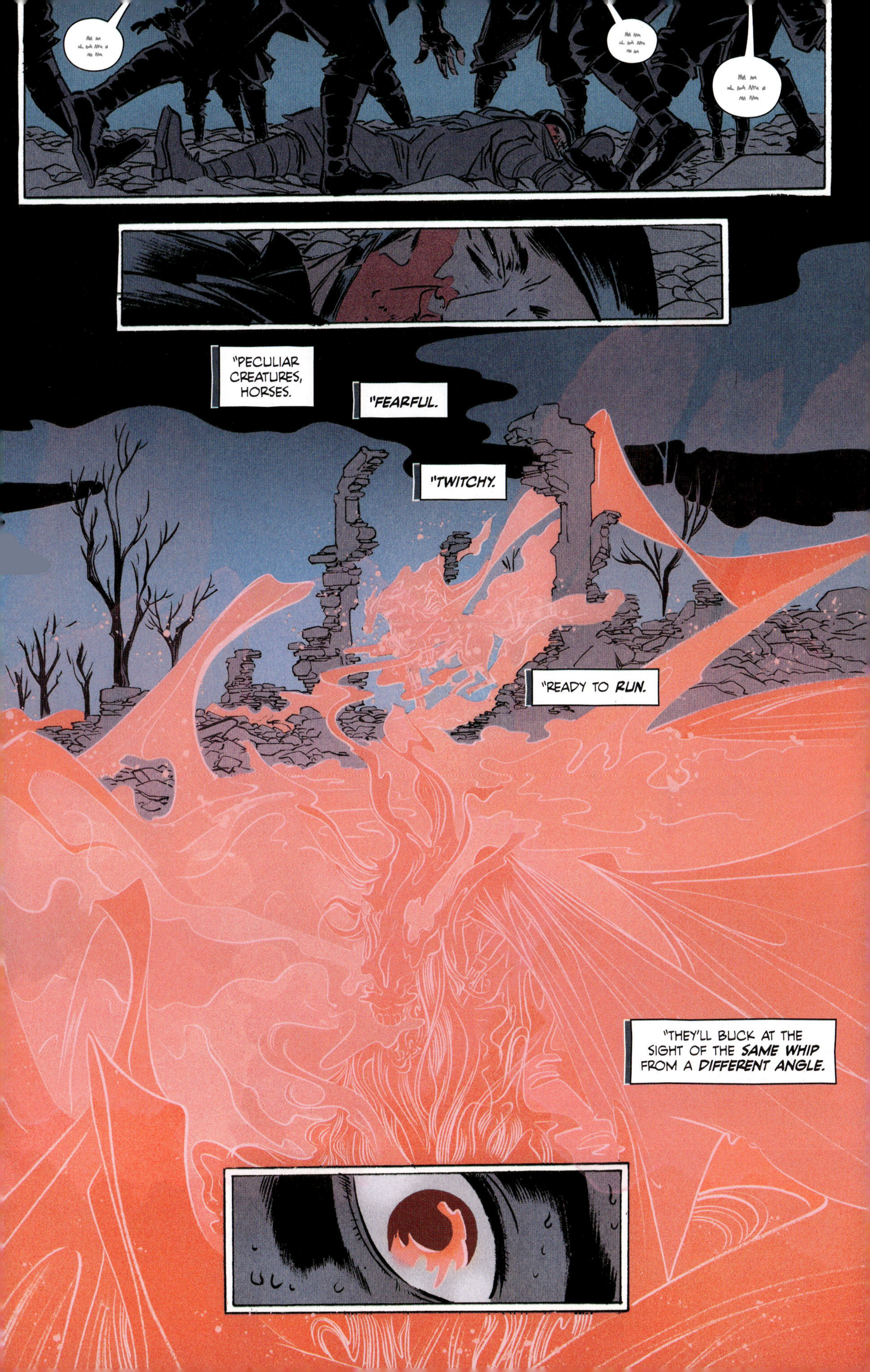
"PECULIAR CREATURES, HORSES.
"*FEARFUL.*
"*TWITCHY.*
"READY TO ***RUN.***
"THEY'LL BUCK AT THE SIGHT OF THE ***SAME WHIP*** FROM A ***DIFFERENT ANGLE.***

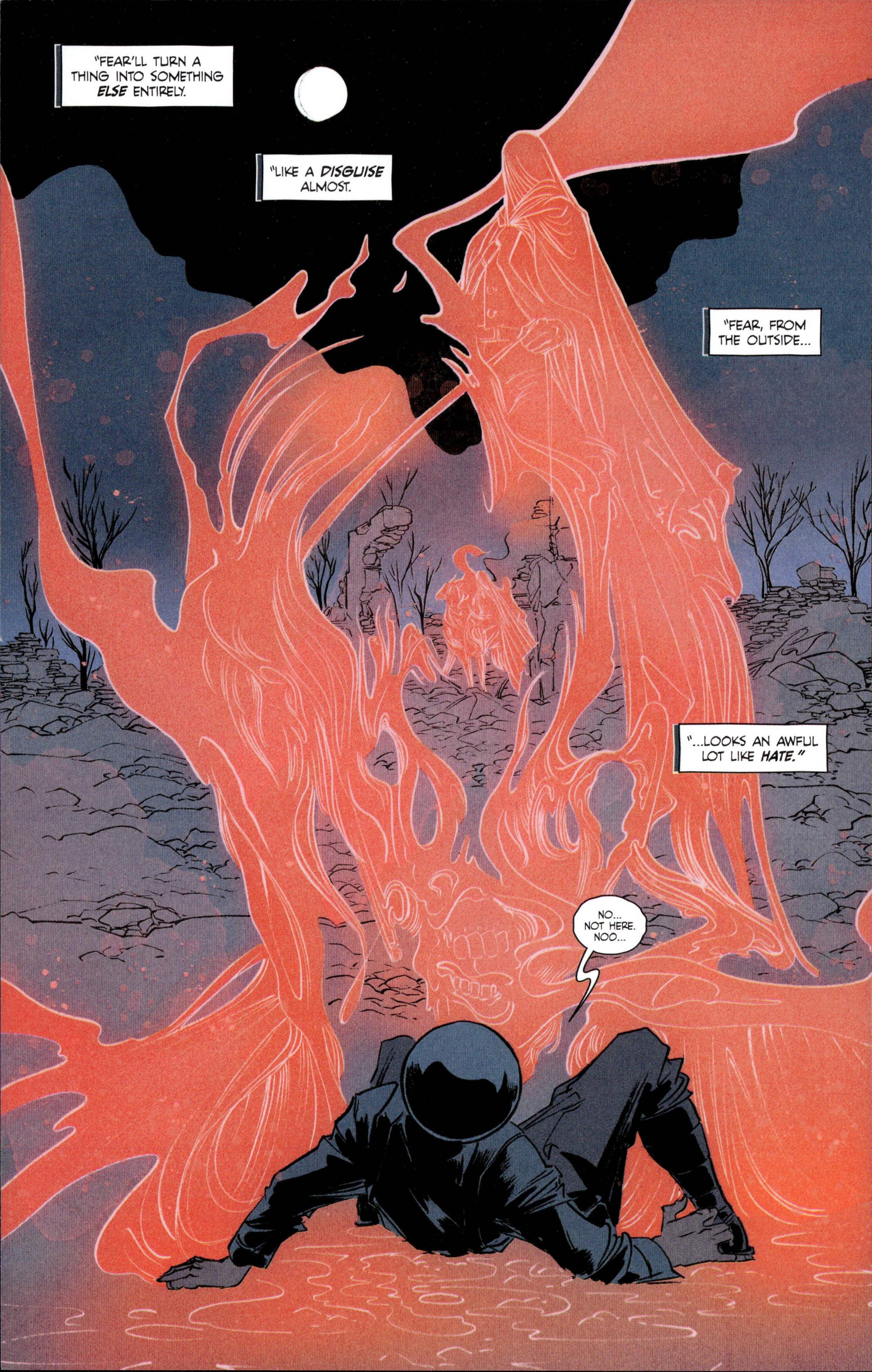
"FEAR'LL TURN A THING INTO SOMETHING *ELSE* ENTIRELY.
"LIKE A *DISGUISE* ALMOST.
"FEAR, FROM THE OUTSIDE...
"...LOOKS AN AWFUL LOT LIKE *HATE."*
NO... NOT HERE. NOO...

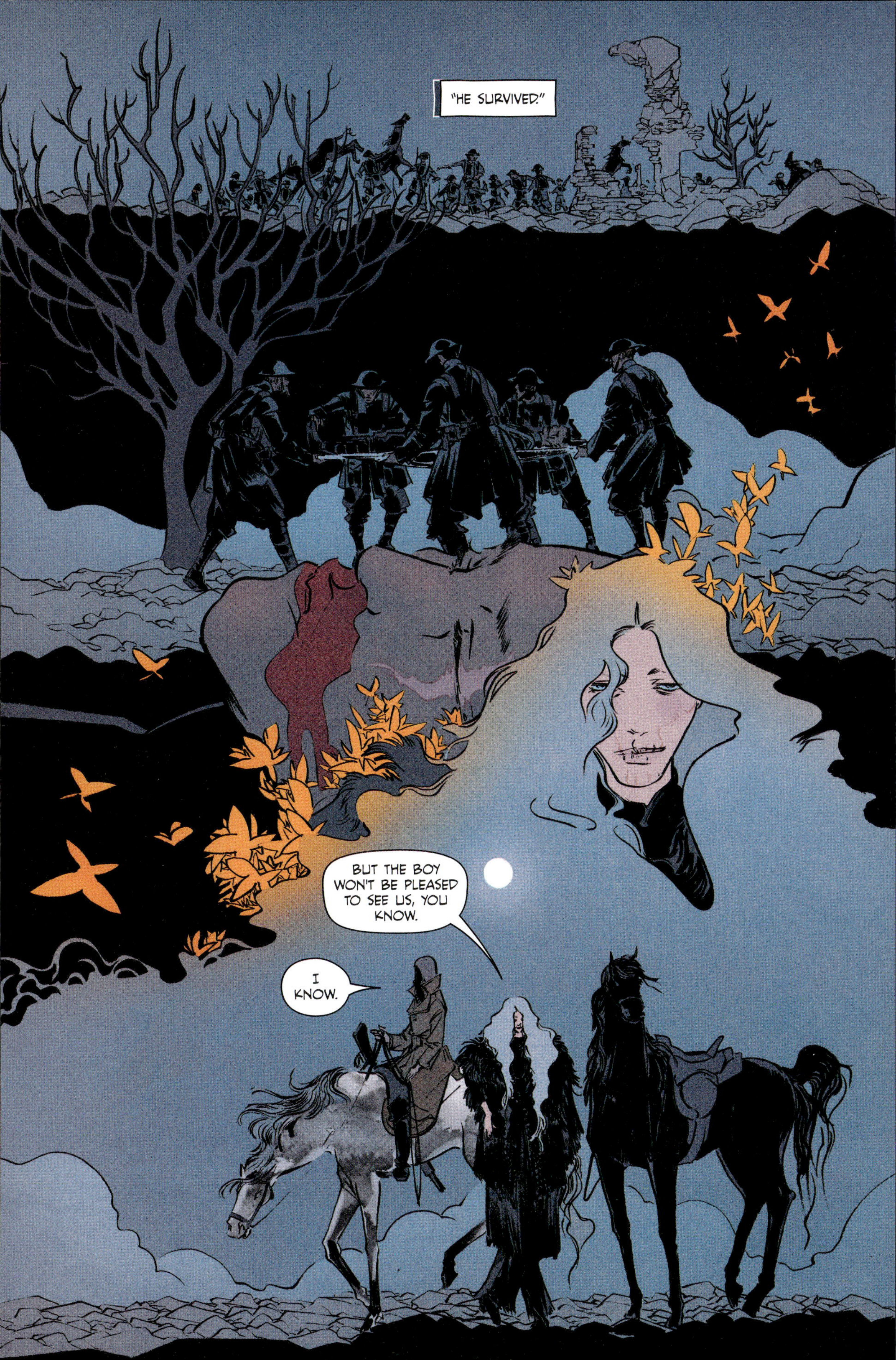
"HE SURVIVED."
BUT THE BOY WON'T BE PLEASED TO SEE US, YOU KNOW.
I KNOW.

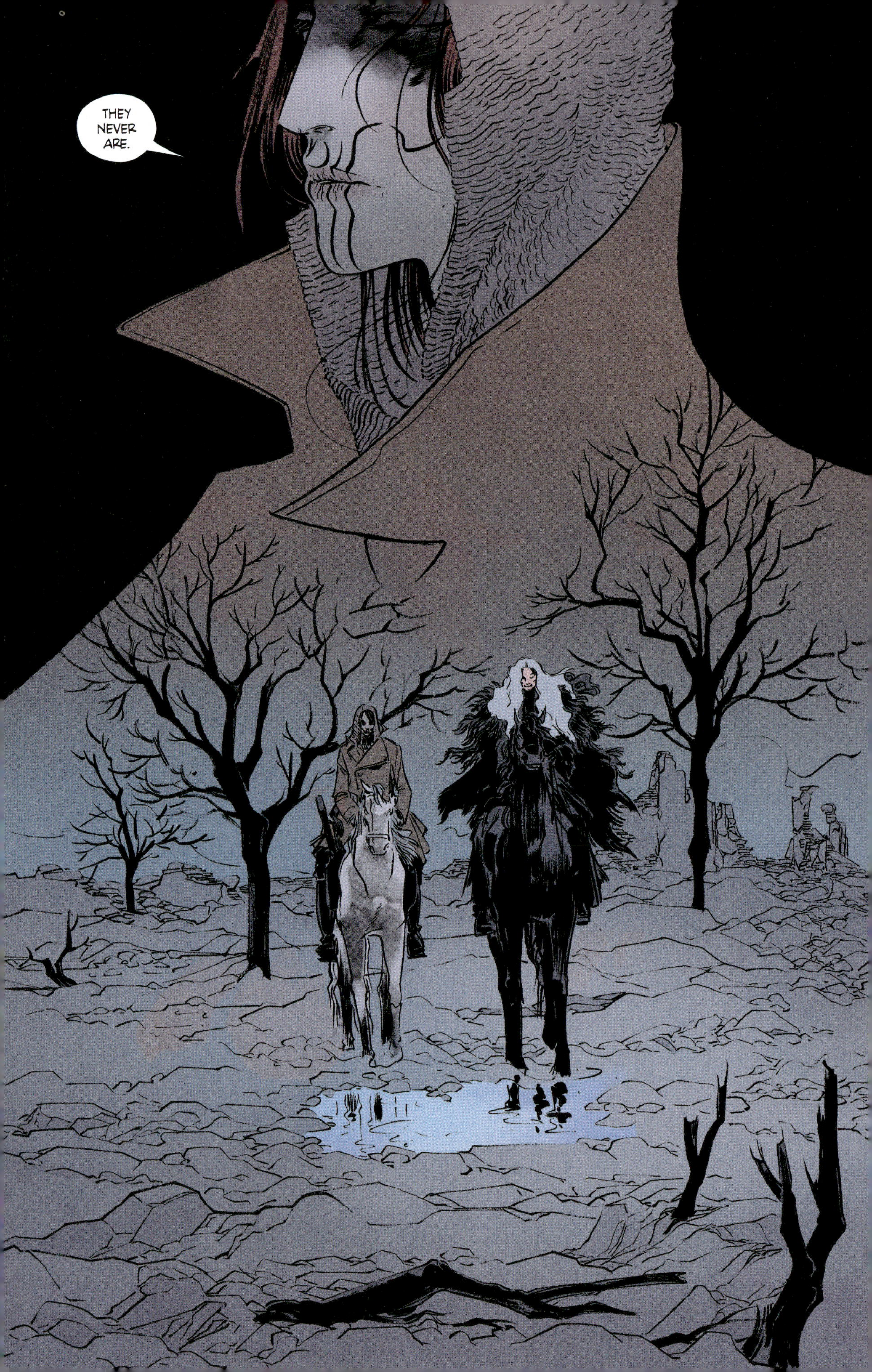
THEY NEVER ARE.

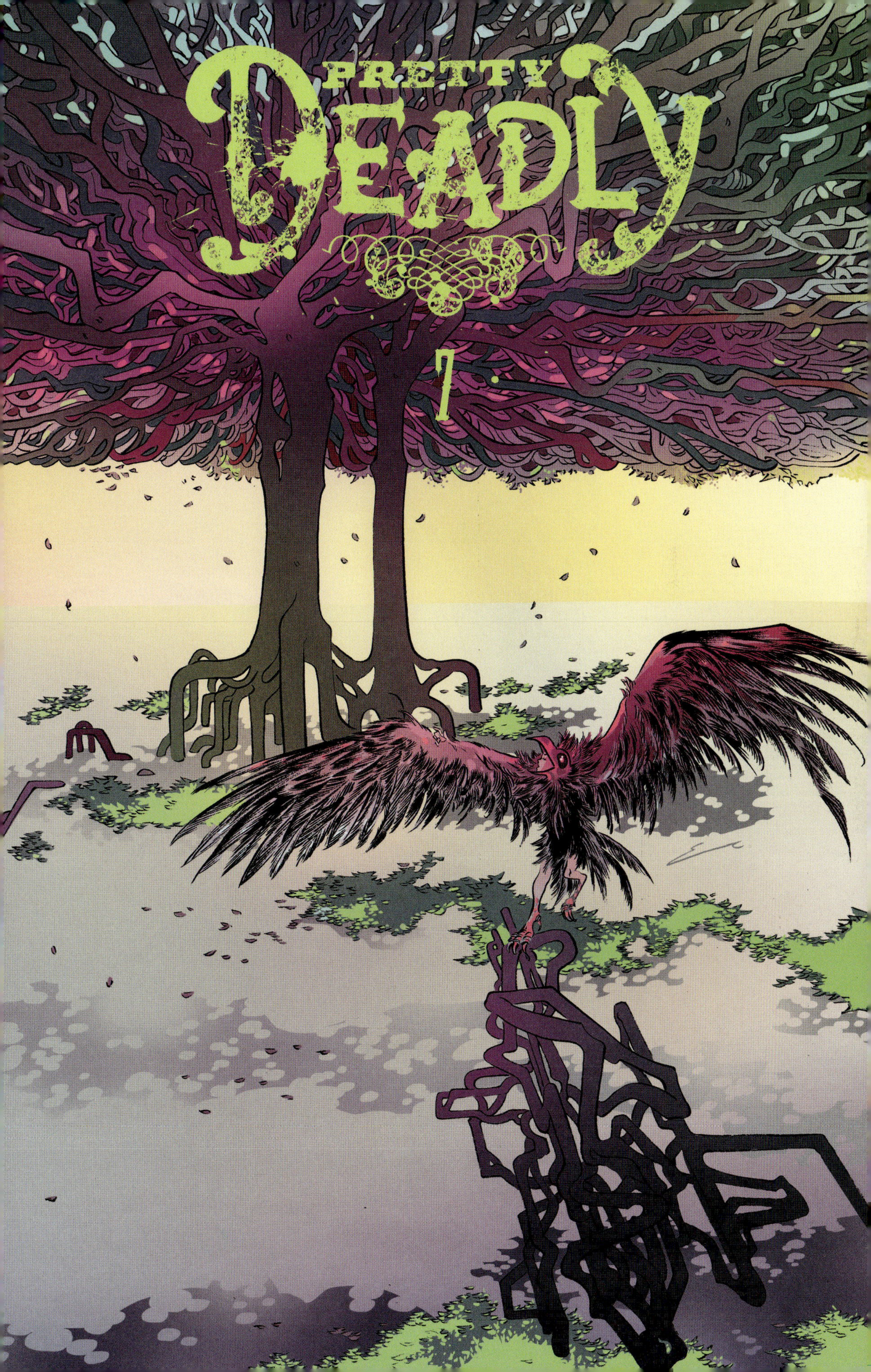
PRETTY
DEADLY
7

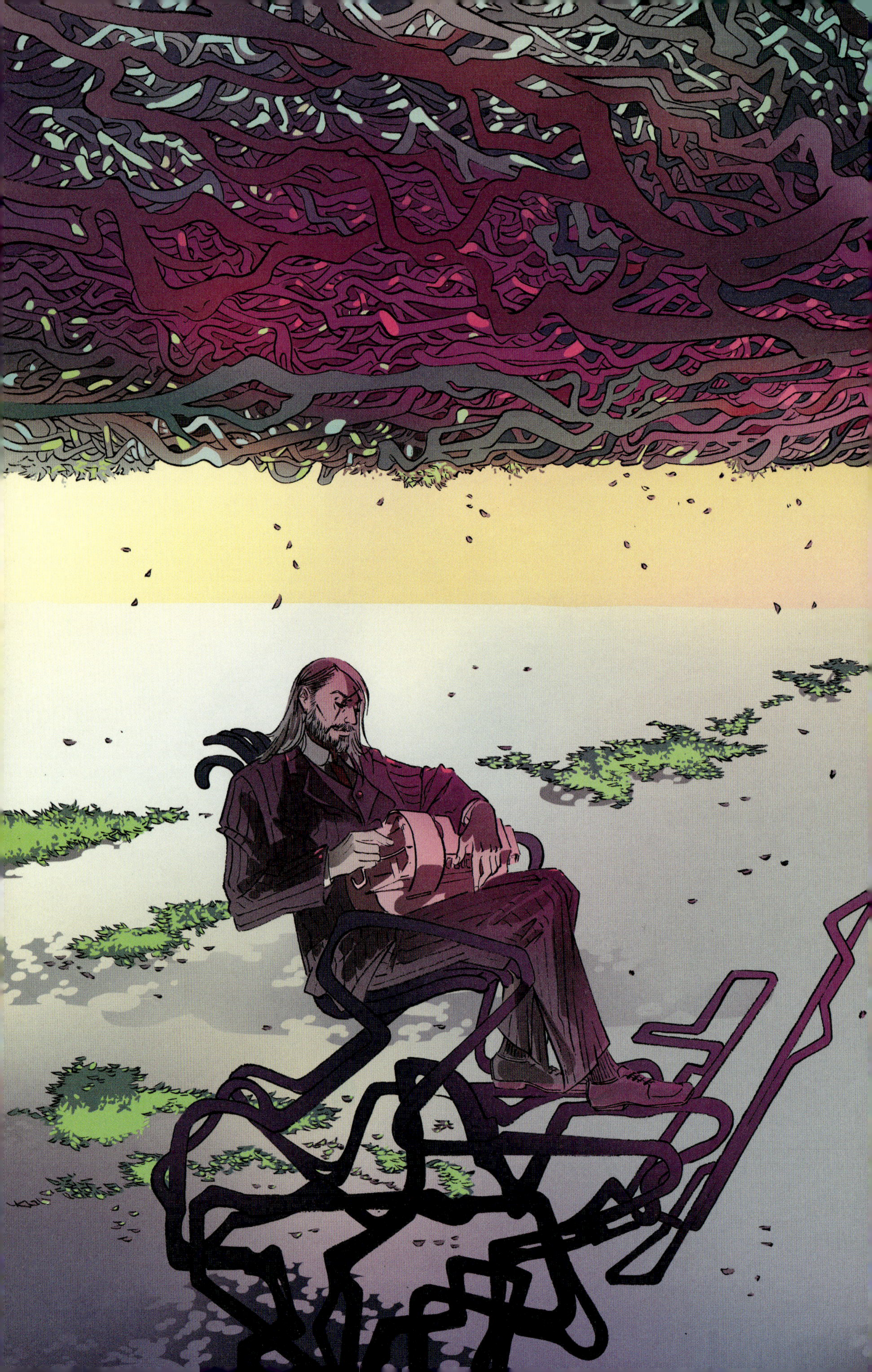

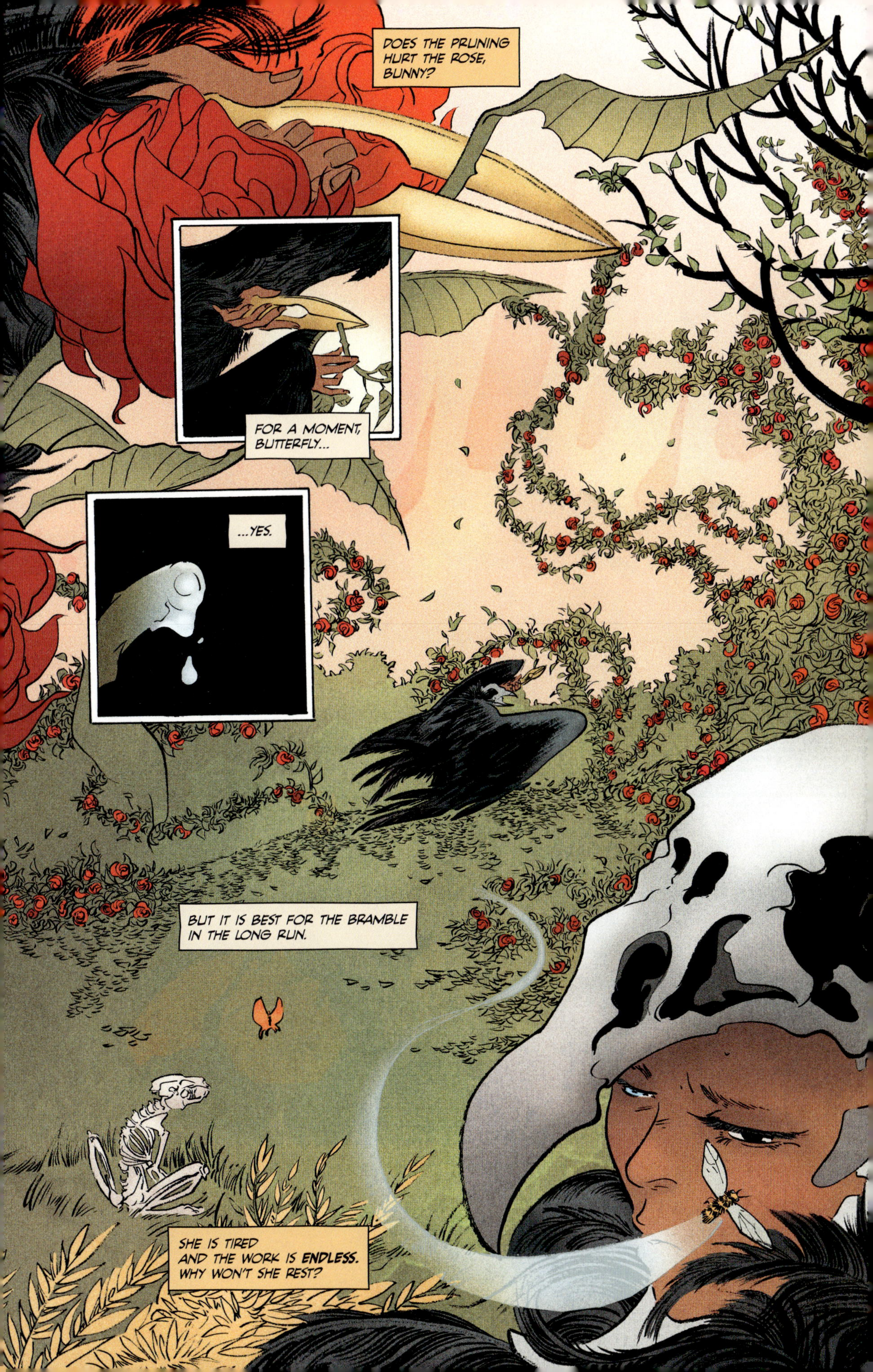
DOES THE PRUNING HURT THE ROSE, BUNNY?
FOR A MOMENT, BUTTERFLY...
...YES.
BUT IT IS BEST FOR THE BRAMBLE IN THE LONG RUN.
SHE IS TIRED AND THE WORK IS **ENDLESS.** WHY WON'T SHE REST?

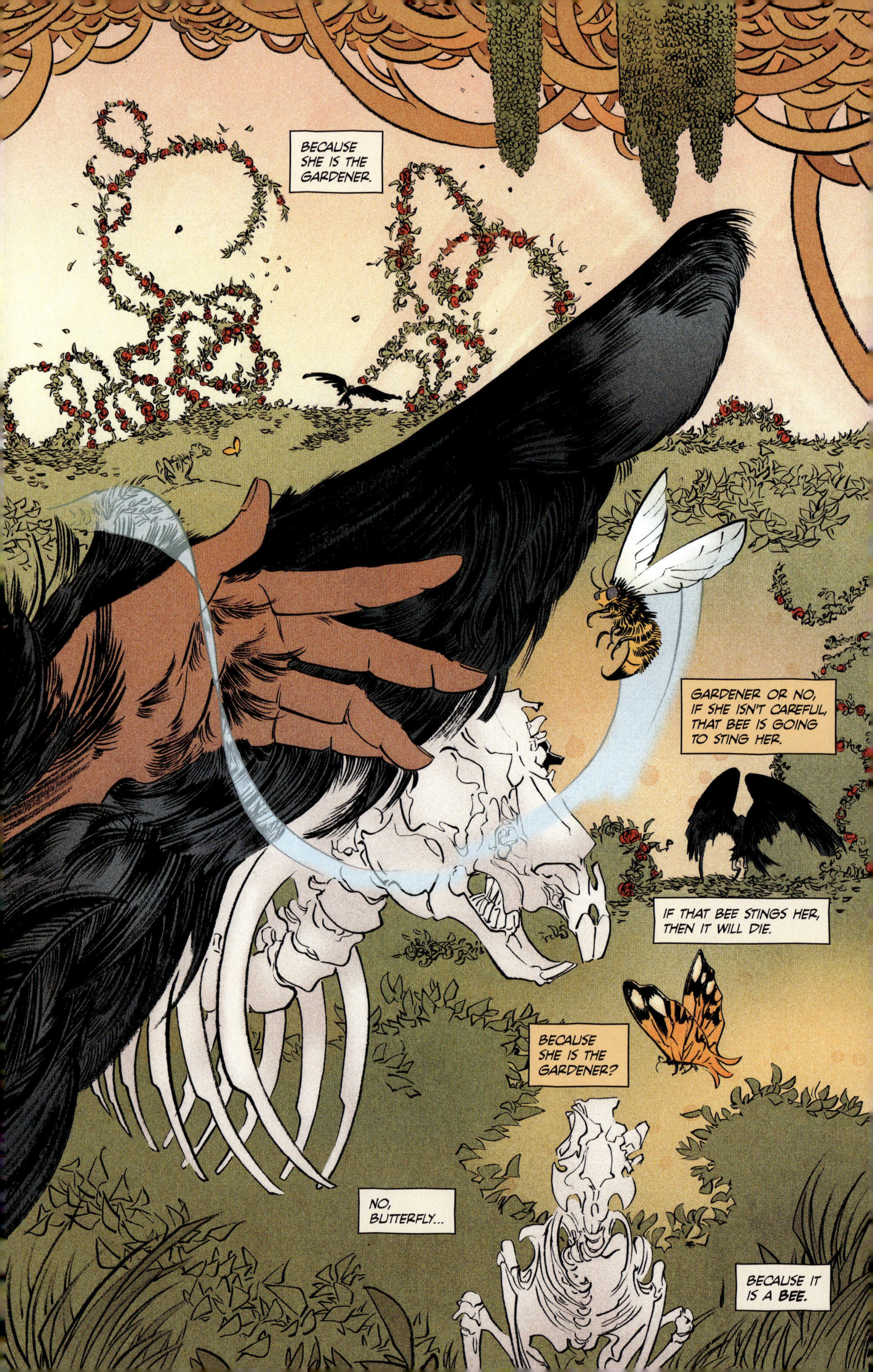

BECAUSE SHE IS THE GARDENER.
GARDENER OR NO, IF SHE ISN'T CAREFUL, THAT BEE IS GOING TO STING HER.
IF THAT BEE STINGS HER, THEN IT WILL DIE.
BECAUSE SHE IS THE GARDENER?
NO, BUTTERFLY...
BECAUSE IT IS A **BEE.**

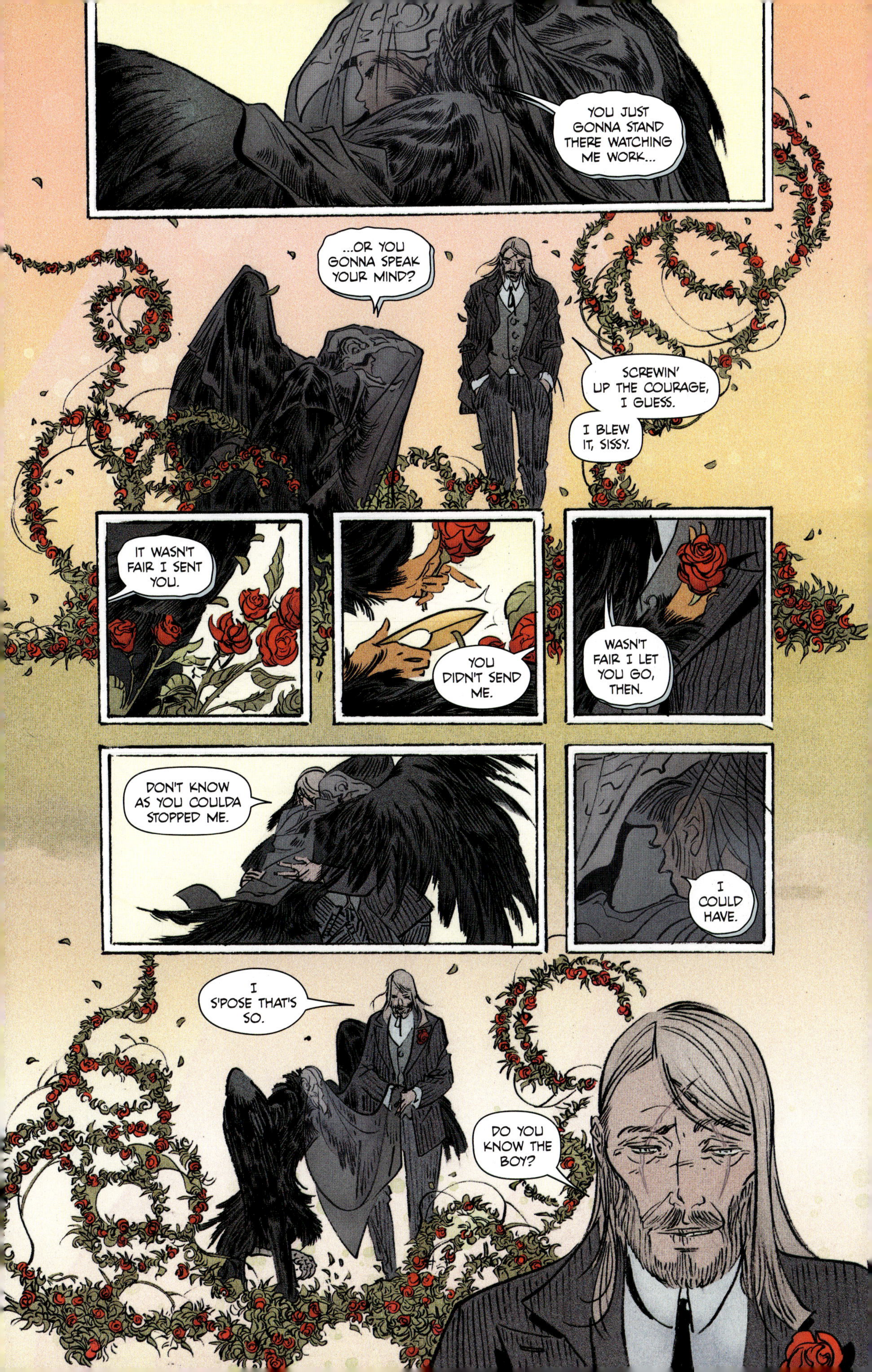
YOU JUST GONNA STAND THERE WATCHING ME WORK...
...OR YOU GONNA SPEAK YOUR MIND?
SCREWIN' UP THE COURAGE, I GUESS.
I BLEW IT, SISSY.
IT WASN'T FAIR I SENT YOU.
YOU DIDN'T SEND ME.
WASN'T FAIR I LET YOU GO, THEN.
DON'T KNOW AS YOU COULDA STOPPED ME.
I COULD HAVE.
I S'POSE THAT'S SO.
DO YOU KNOW THE BOY?

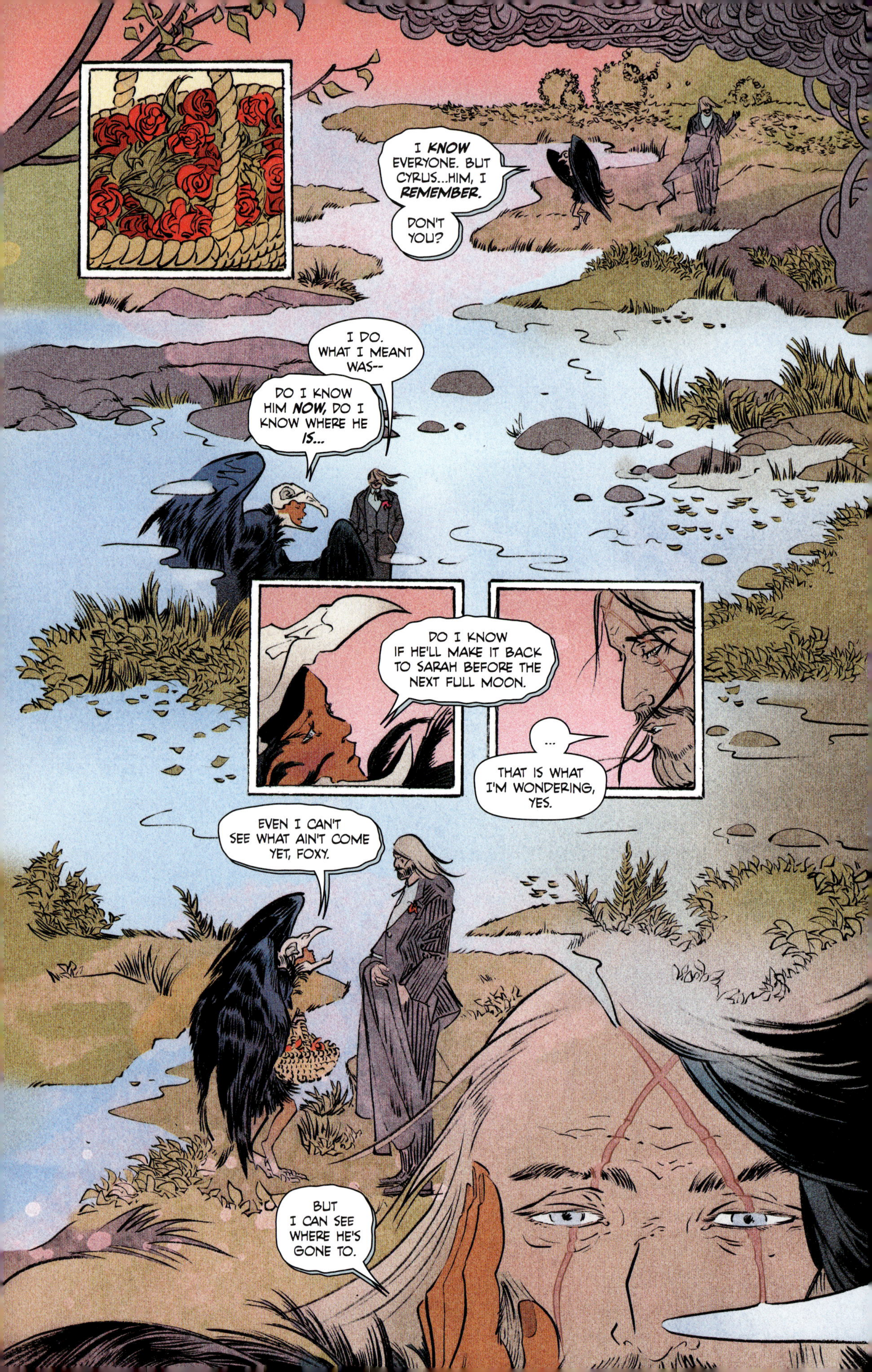
I KNOW EVERYONE. BUT CYRUS...HIM, I REMEMBER.
DON'T YOU?
I DO. WHAT I MEANT WAS--
DO I KNOW HIM NOW, DO I KNOW WHERE HE IS...
DO I KNOW IF HE'LL MAKE IT BACK TO SARAH BEFORE THE NEXT FULL MOON.
...
THAT IS WHAT I'M WONDERING, YES.
EVEN I CAN'T SEE WHAT AIN'T COME YET, FOXY.
BUT I CAN SEE WHERE HE'S GONE TO.

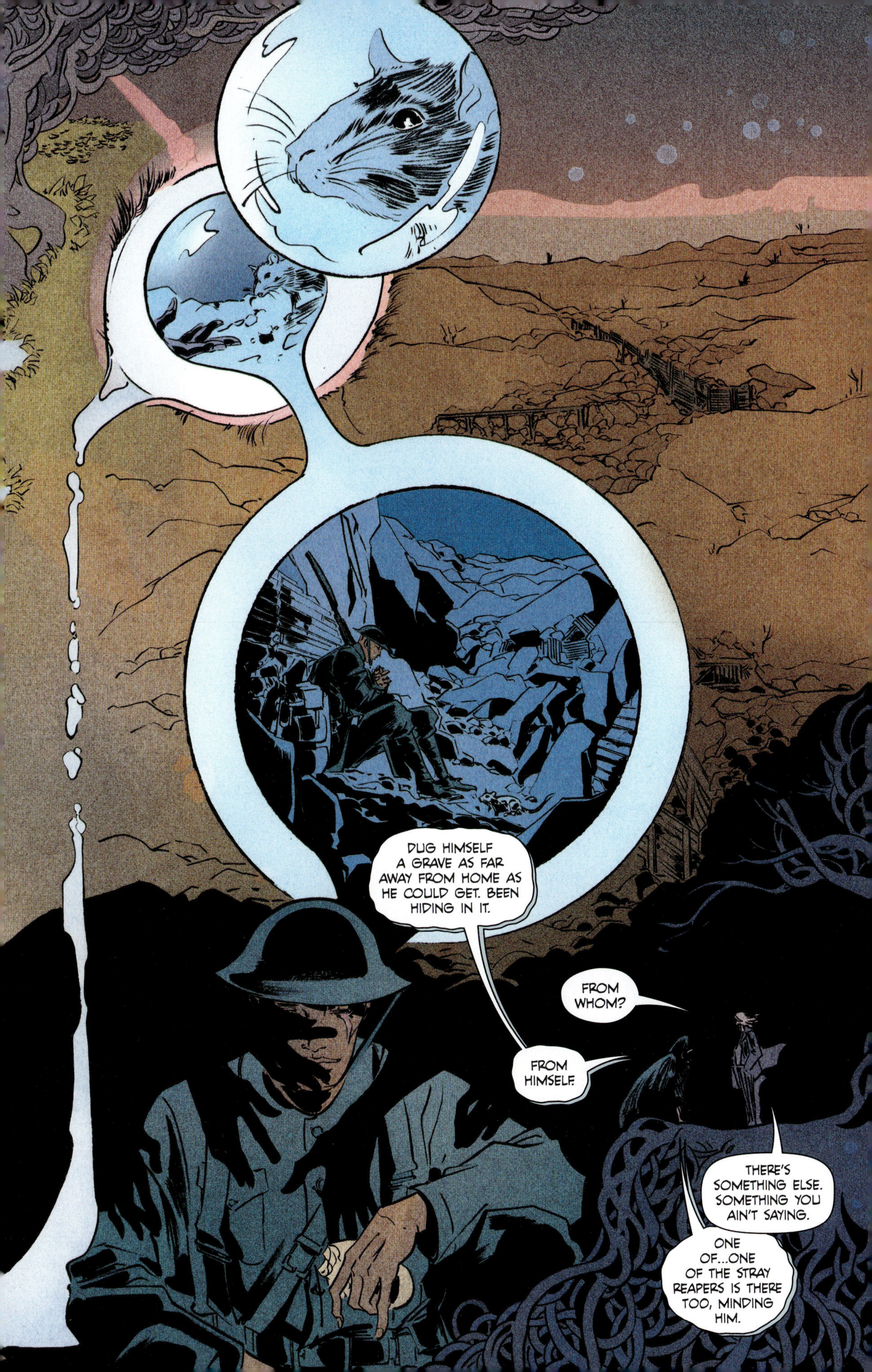
DUG HIMSELF A GRAVE AS FAR AWAY FROM HOME AS HE COULD GET. BEEN HIDING IN IT.
FROM WHOM?
FROM HIMSELF.
THERE'S SOMETHING ELSE. SOMETHING YOU AIN'T SAYING.
ONE OF...ONE OF THE STRAY REAPERS IS THERE TOO, MINDING HIM.

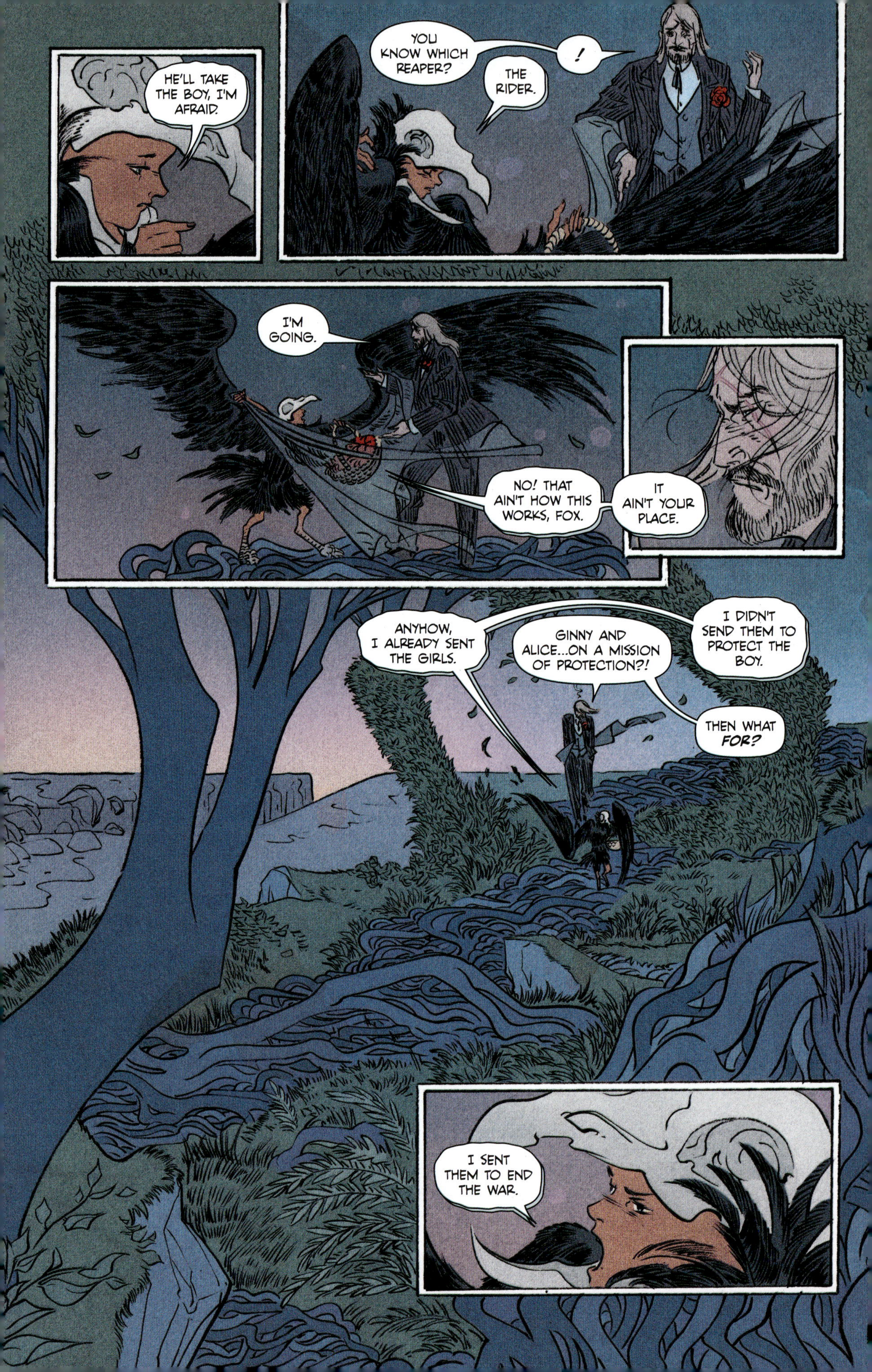
HE'LL TAKE THE BOY, I'M AFRAID.
YOU KNOW WHICH REAPER?
!
THE RIDER.
I'M GOING.
NO! THAT AIN'T HOW THIS WORKS, FOX.
IT AIN'T YOUR PLACE.
ANYHOW, I ALREADY SENT THE GIRLS.
GINNY AND ALICE...ON A MISSION OF PROTECTION?!
I DIDN'T SEND THEM TO PROTECT THE BOY.
THEN WHAT *FOR?*
I SENT THEM TO END THE WAR.

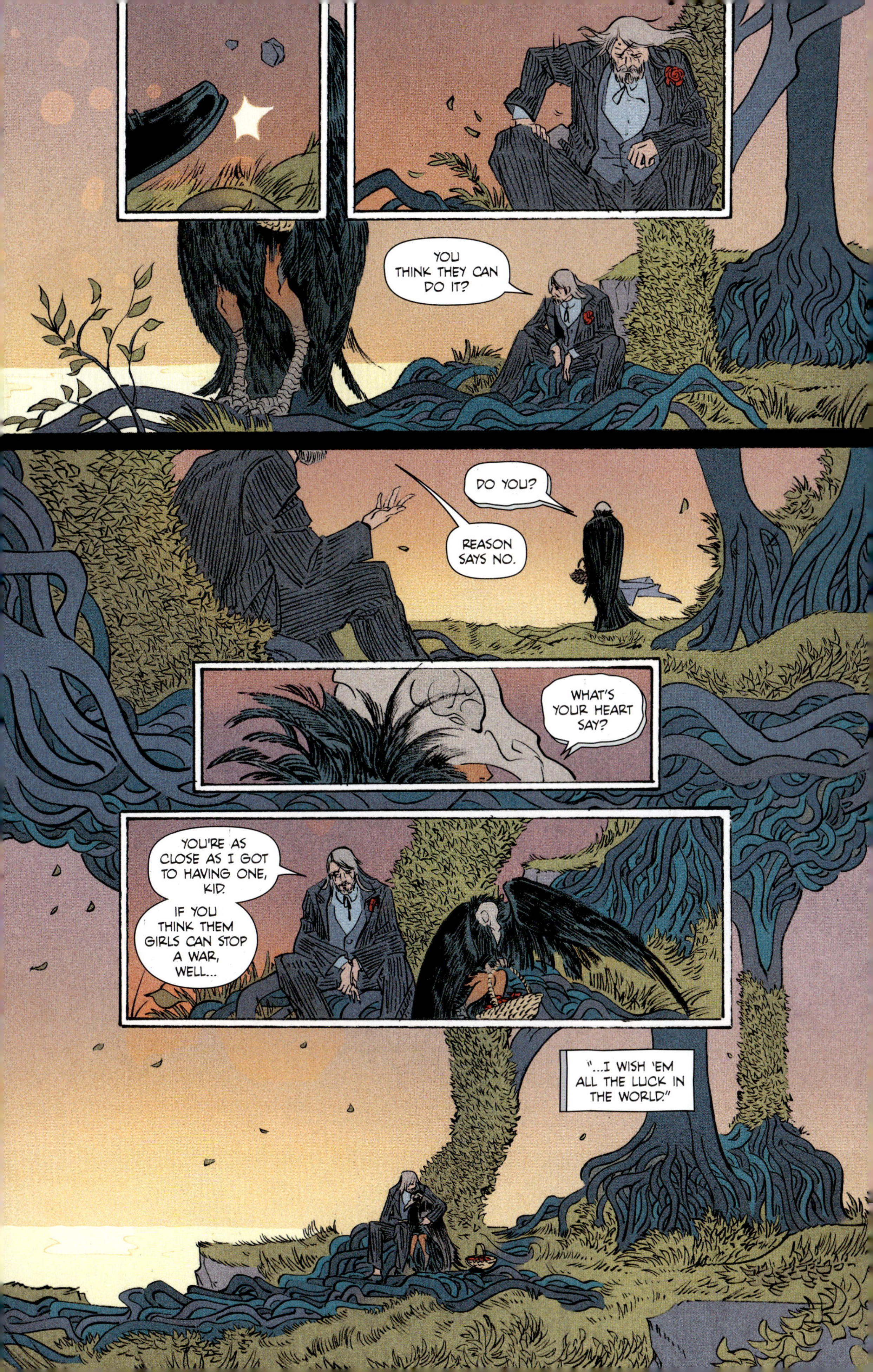
YOU THINK THEY CAN DO IT?
DO YOU?
REASON SAYS NO.
WHAT'S YOUR HEART SAY?
YOU'RE AS CLOSE AS I GOT TO HAVING ONE, KID.
IF YOU THINK THEM GIRLS CAN STOP A WAR, WELL...
"...I WISH 'EM ALL THE LUCK IN THE WORLD."

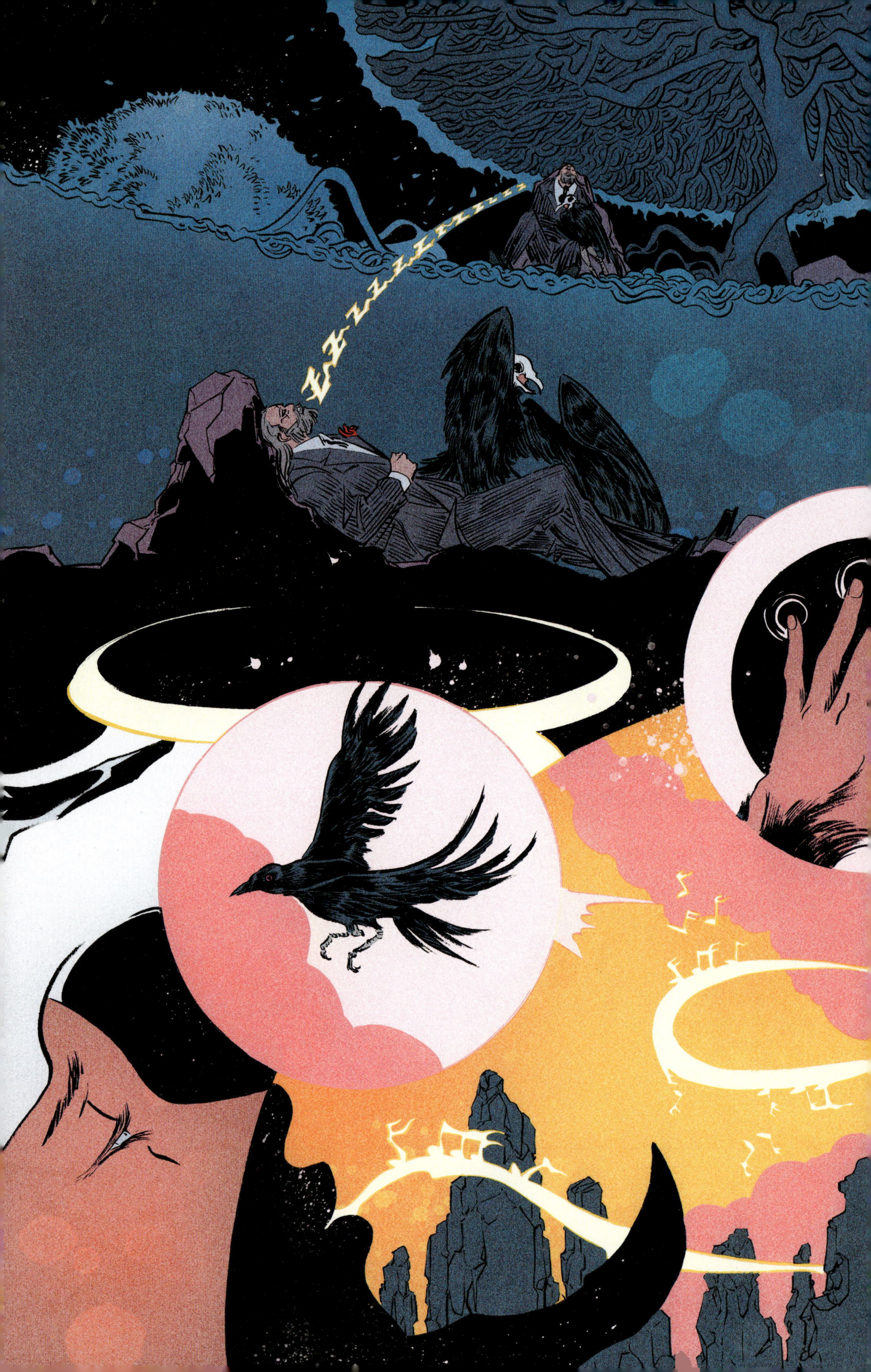

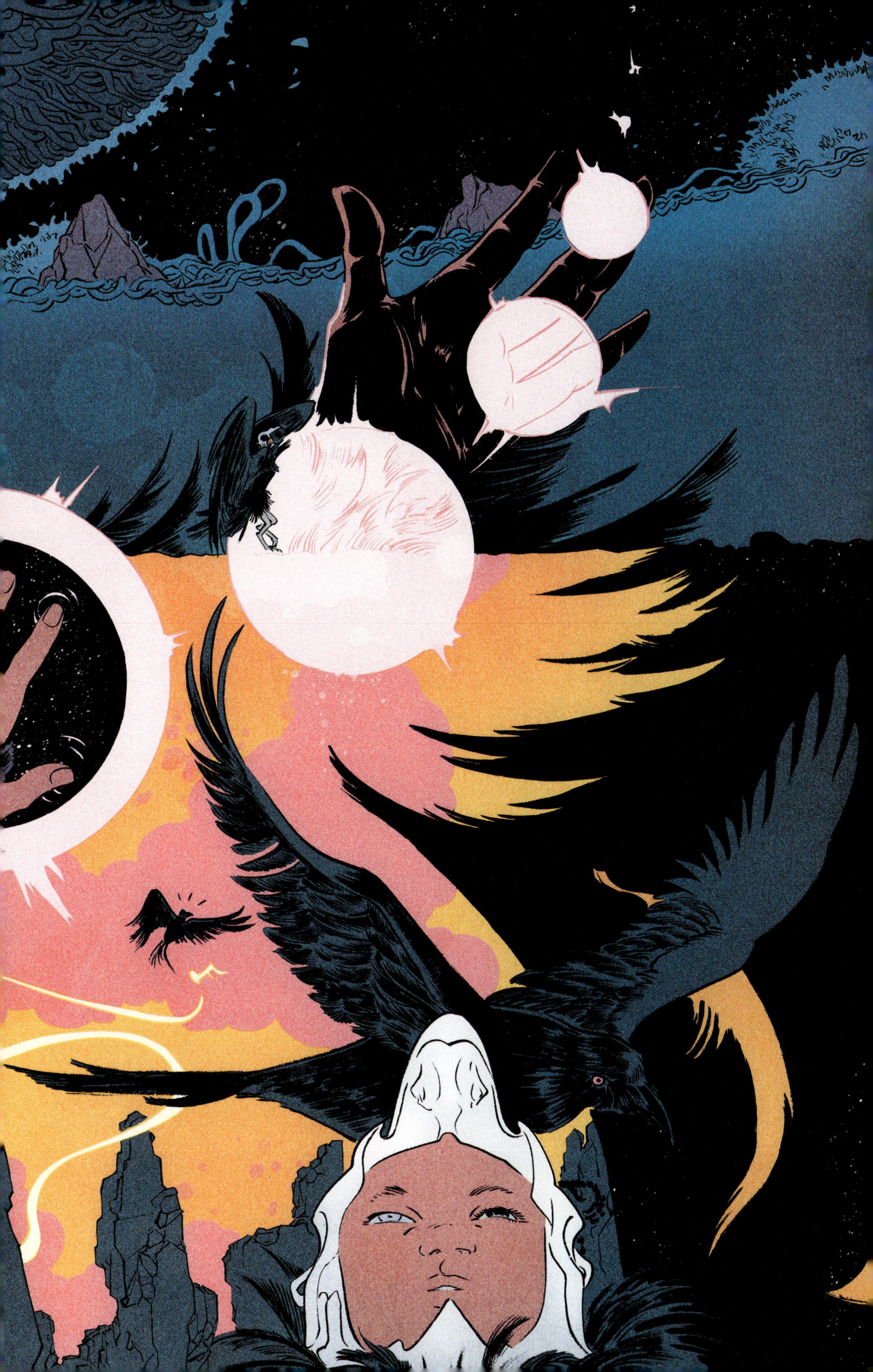

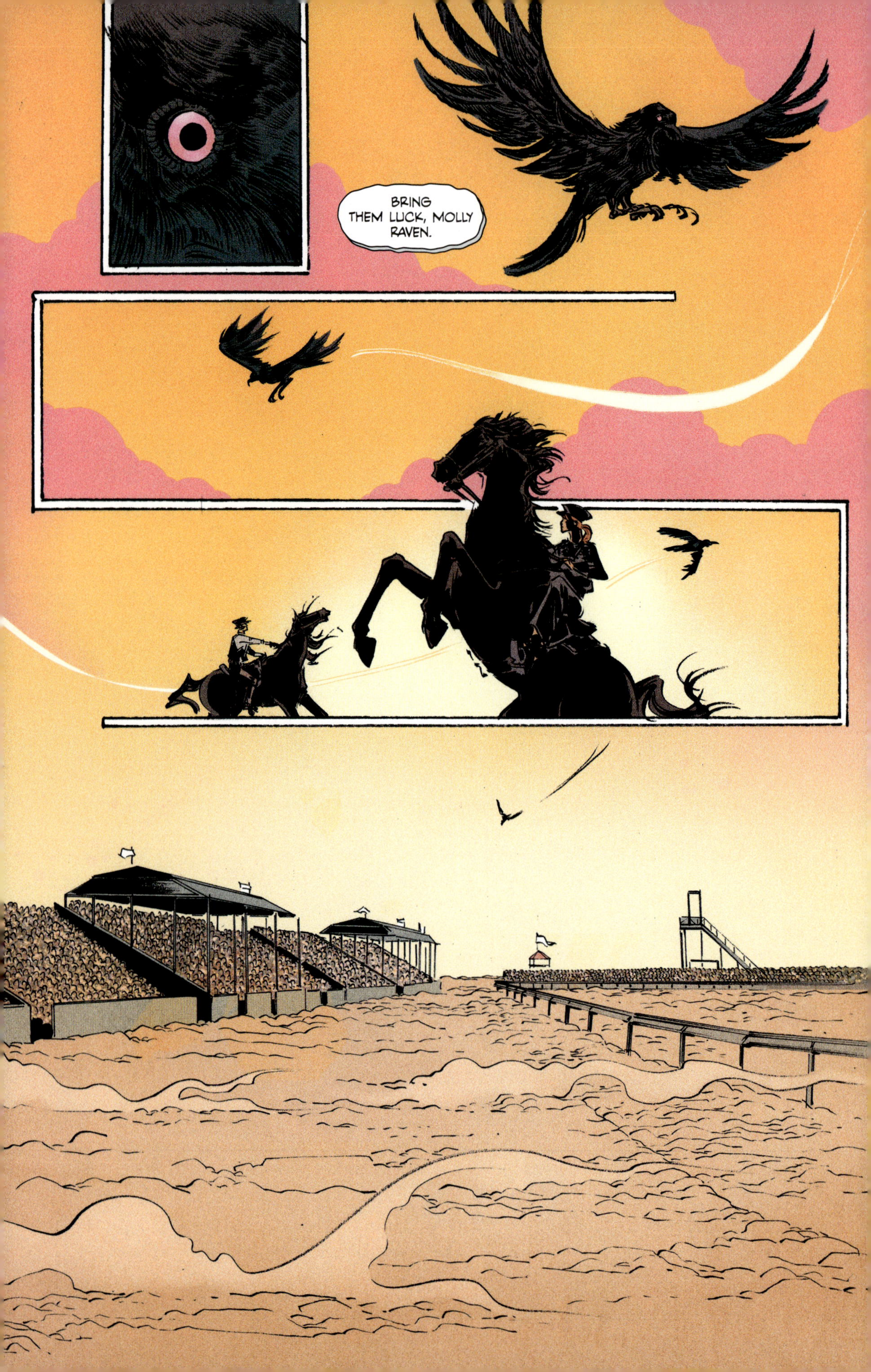
BRING THEM LUCK, MOLLY RAVEN.

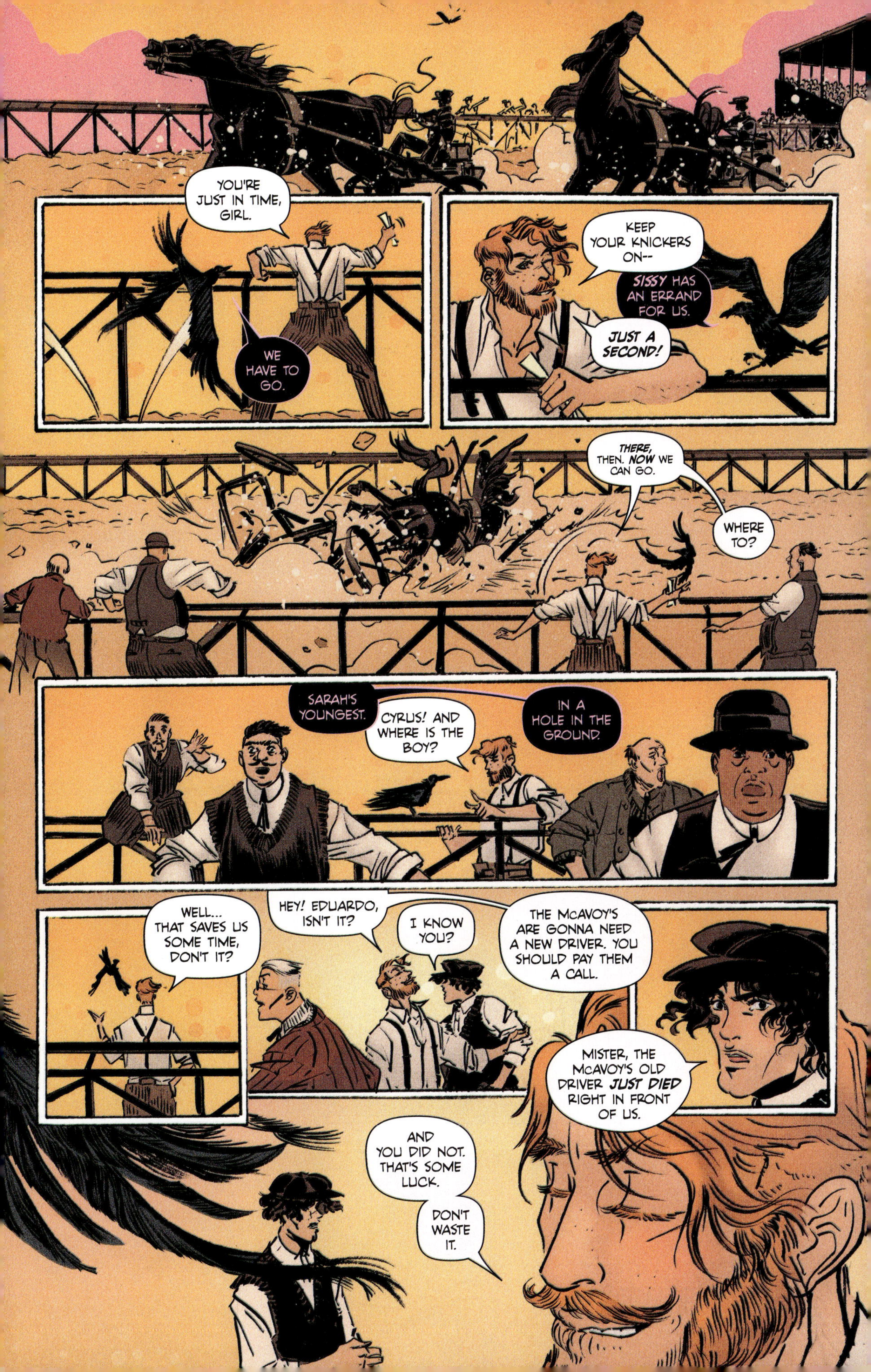
YOU'RE JUST IN TIME, GIRL.
WE HAVE TO GO.
KEEP YOUR KNICKERS ON--
SISSY HAS AN ERRAND FOR US.
JUST A SECOND!
THERE, THEN. NOW WE CAN GO.
WHERE TO?
SARAH'S YOUNGEST.
CYRUS! AND WHERE IS THE BOY?
IN A HOLE IN THE GROUND.
WELL... THAT SAVES US SOME TIME, DON'T IT?
HEY! EDUARDO, ISN'T IT?
I KNOW YOU?
THE McAVOY'S ARE GONNA NEED A NEW DRIVER. YOU SHOULD PAY THEM A CALL.
MISTER, THE McAVOY'S OLD DRIVER JUST DIED RIGHT IN FRONT OF US.
AND YOU DID NOT. THAT'S SOME LUCK.
DON'T WASTE IT.

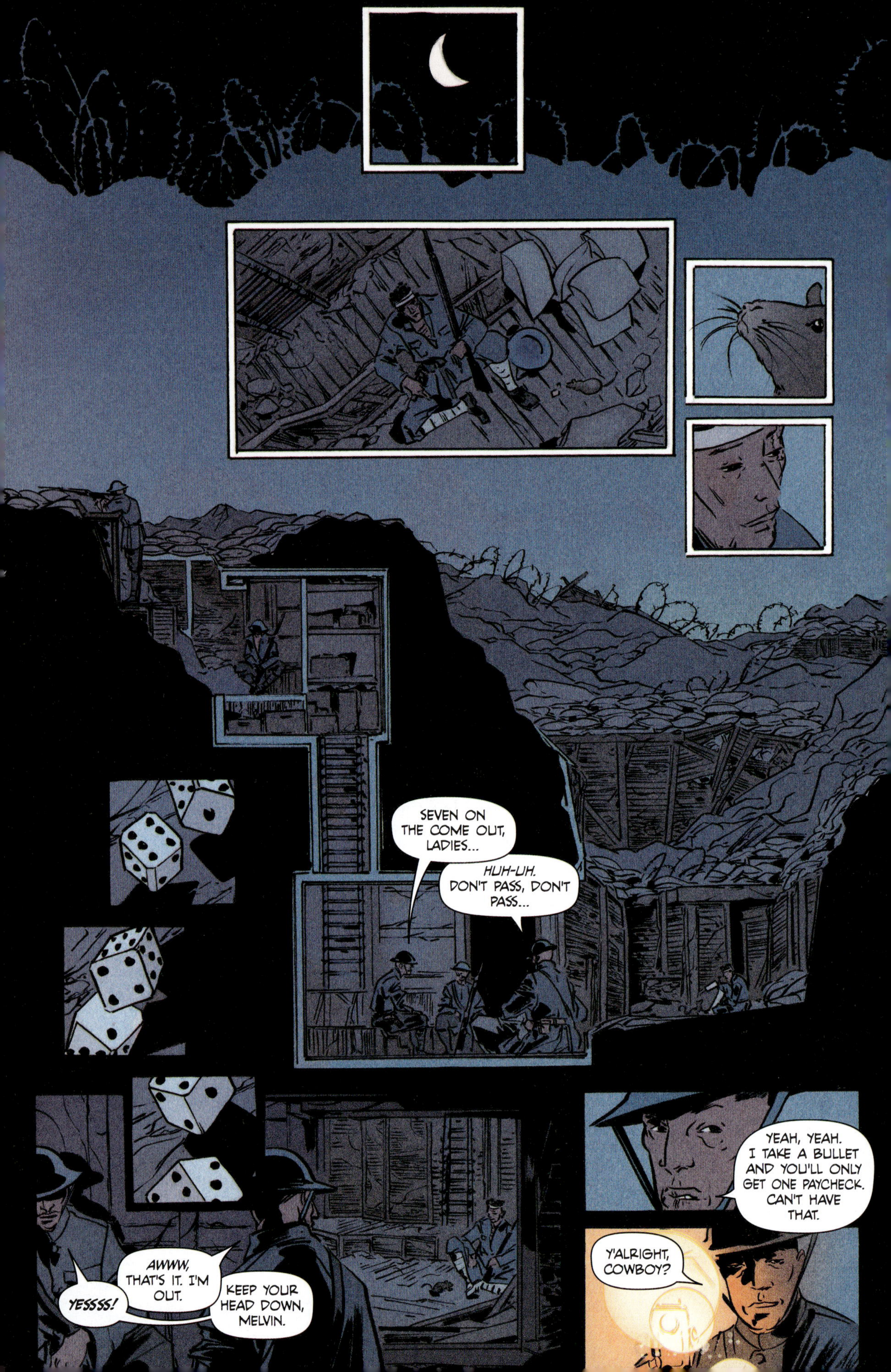
SEVEN ON THE COME OUT, LADIES...
HUH-UH. DON'T PASS, DON'T PASS...
YESSSS!
AWWW, THAT'S IT. I'M OUT.
KEEP YOUR HEAD DOWN, MELVIN.
YEAH, YEAH. I TAKE A BULLET AND YOU'LL ONLY GET ONE PAYCHECK. CAN'T HAVE THAT.
Y'ALRIGHT, COWBOY?

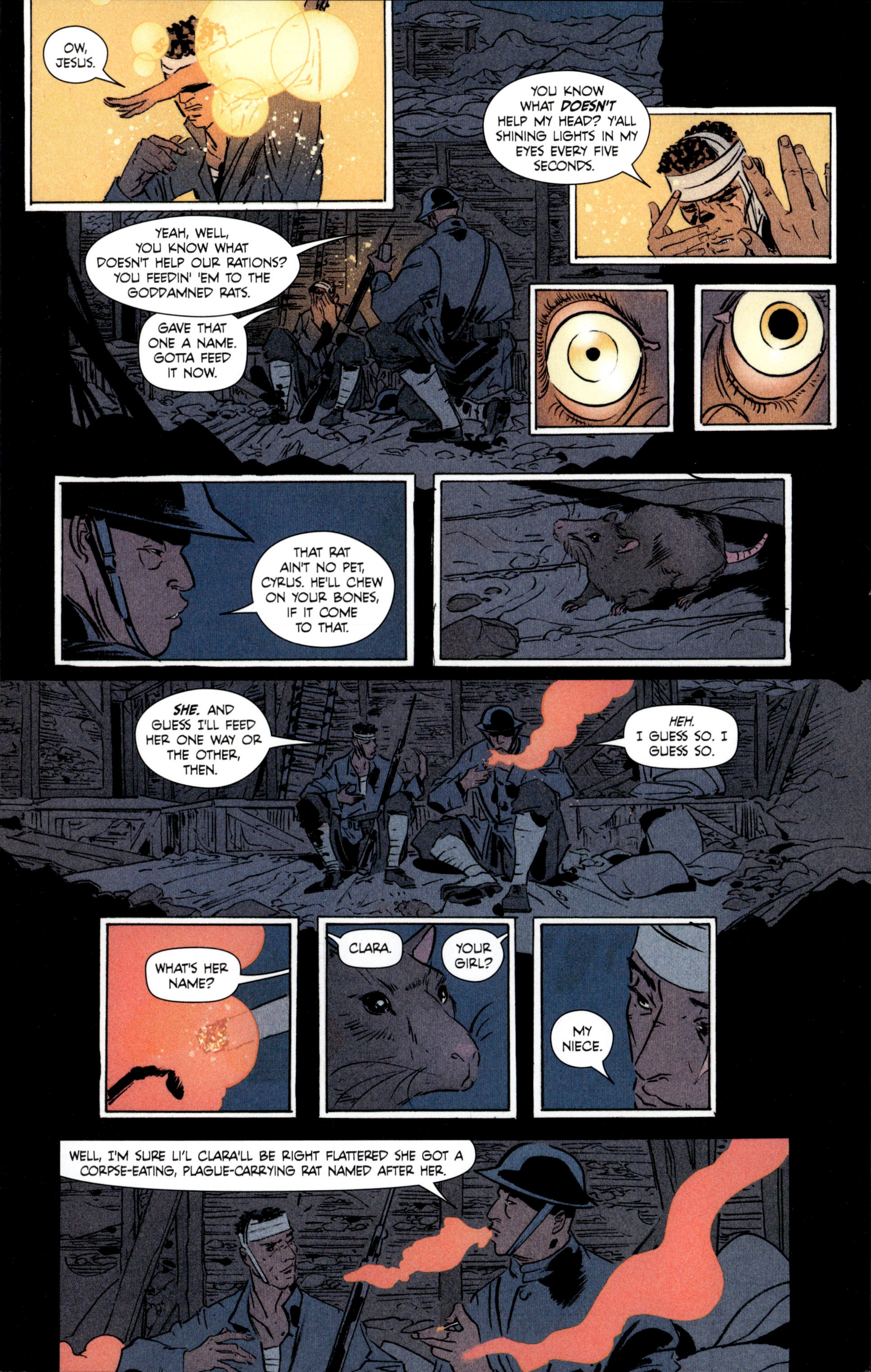
OW, JESUS.
YOU KNOW WHAT DOESN'T HELP MY HEAD? Y'ALL SHINING LIGHTS IN MY EYES EVERY FIVE SECONDS.
YEAH, WELL, YOU KNOW WHAT DOESN'T HELP OUR RATIONS? YOU FEEDIN' 'EM TO THE GODDAMNED RATS.
GAVE THAT ONE A NAME. GOTTA FEED IT NOW.
THAT RAT AIN'T NO PET, CYRUS. HE'LL CHEW ON YOUR BONES, IF IT COME TO THAT.
SHE. AND GUESS I'LL FEED HER ONE WAY OR THE OTHER, THEN.
HEH. I GUESS SO. I GUESS SO.
WHAT'S HER NAME?
CLARA.
YOUR GIRL?
MY NIECE.
WELL, I'M SURE LI'L CLARA'LL BE RIGHT FLATTERED SHE GOT A CORPSE-EATING, PLAGUE-CARRYING RAT NAMED AFTER HER.

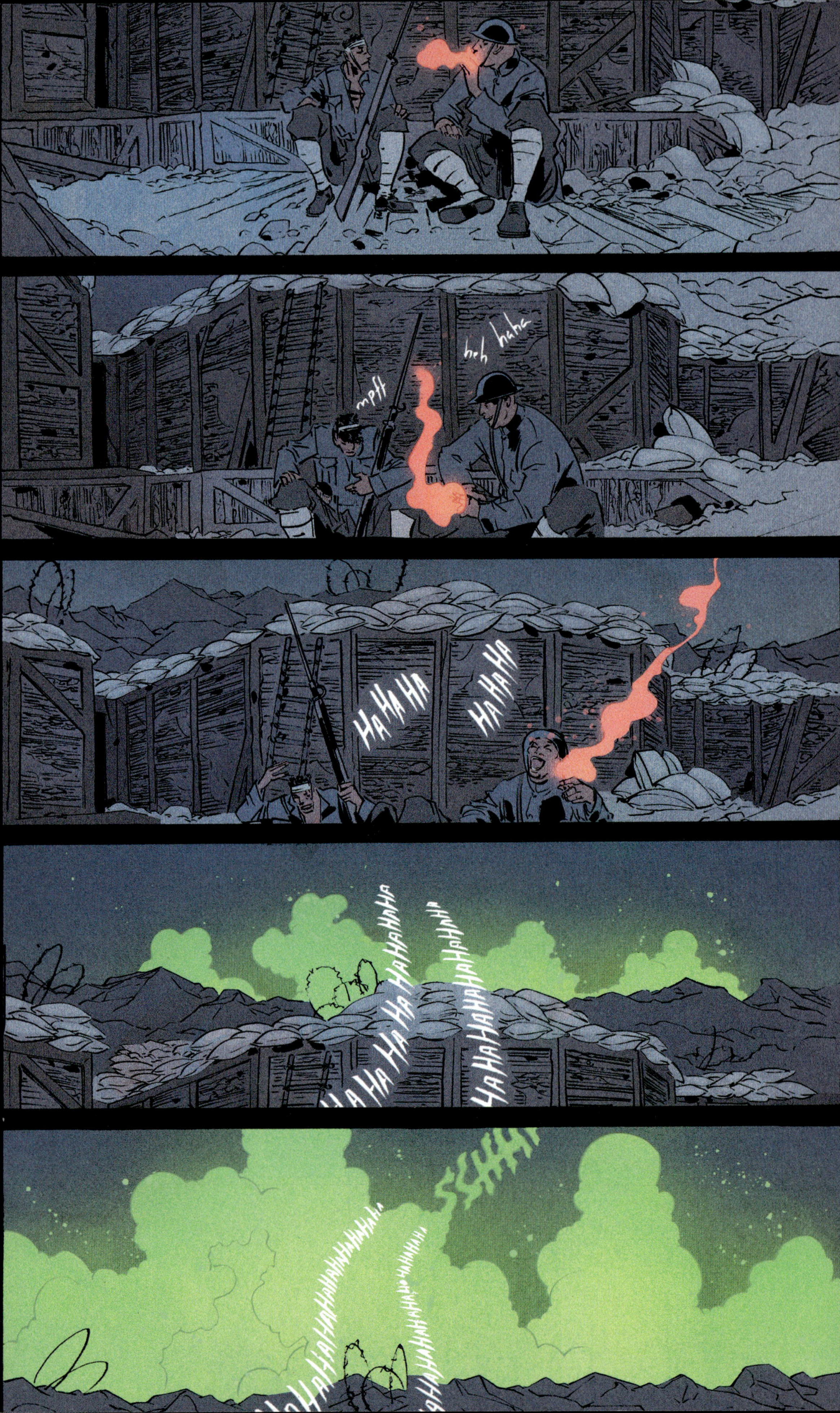
mpft
heh haha
HA HA HA
HA HA HA

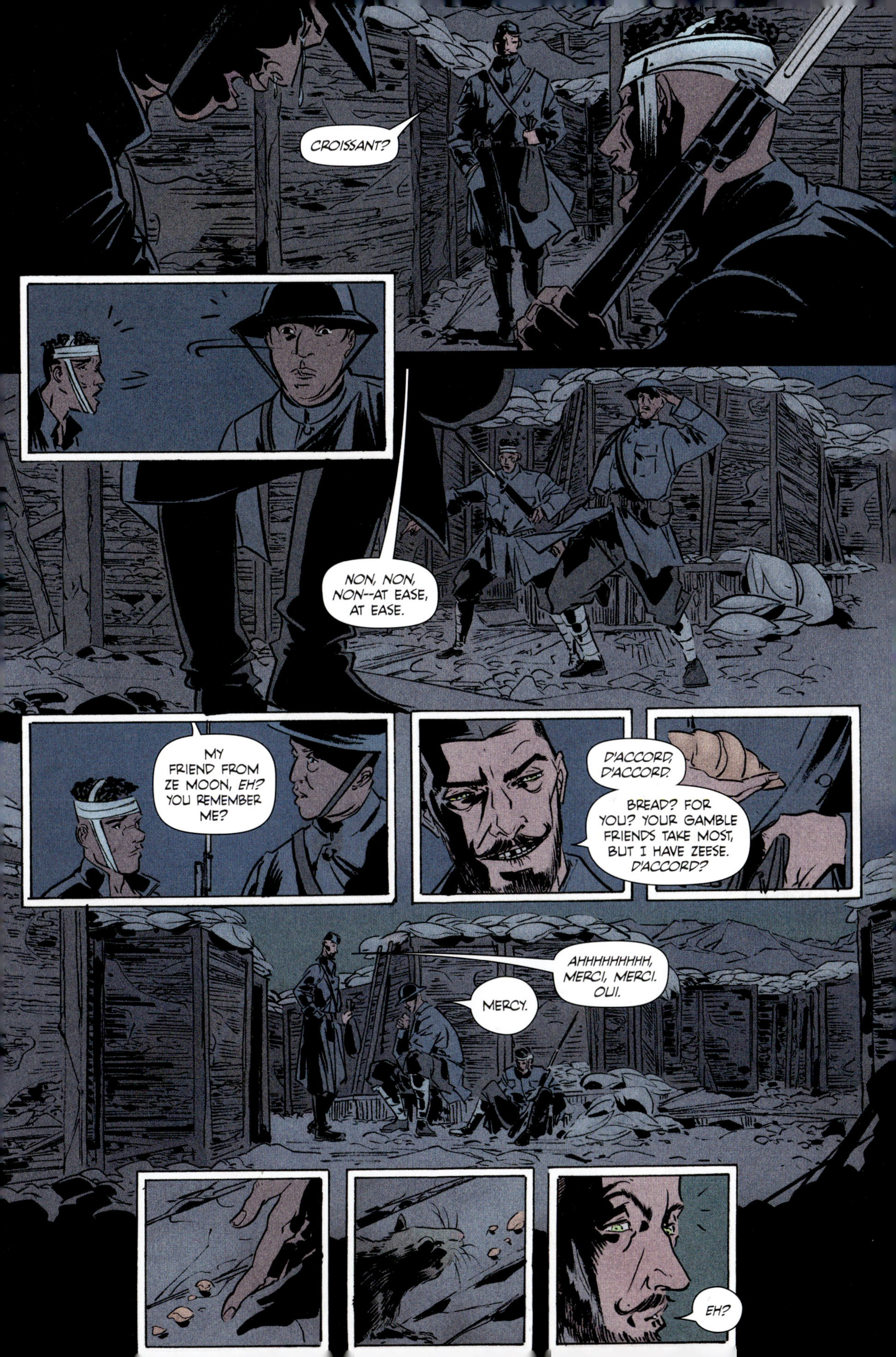
CROISSANT?
NON, NON, NON--AT EASE, AT EASE.
MY FRIEND FROM ZE MOON, *EH?* YOU REMEMBER ME?
D'ACCORD, D'ACCORD.
BREAD? FOR YOU? YOUR GAMBLE FRIENDS TAKE MOST, BUT I HAVE ZEESE. *D'ACCORD?*
AHHHHHHHHH, MERCI, MERCI. OUI.
MERCY.
EH?

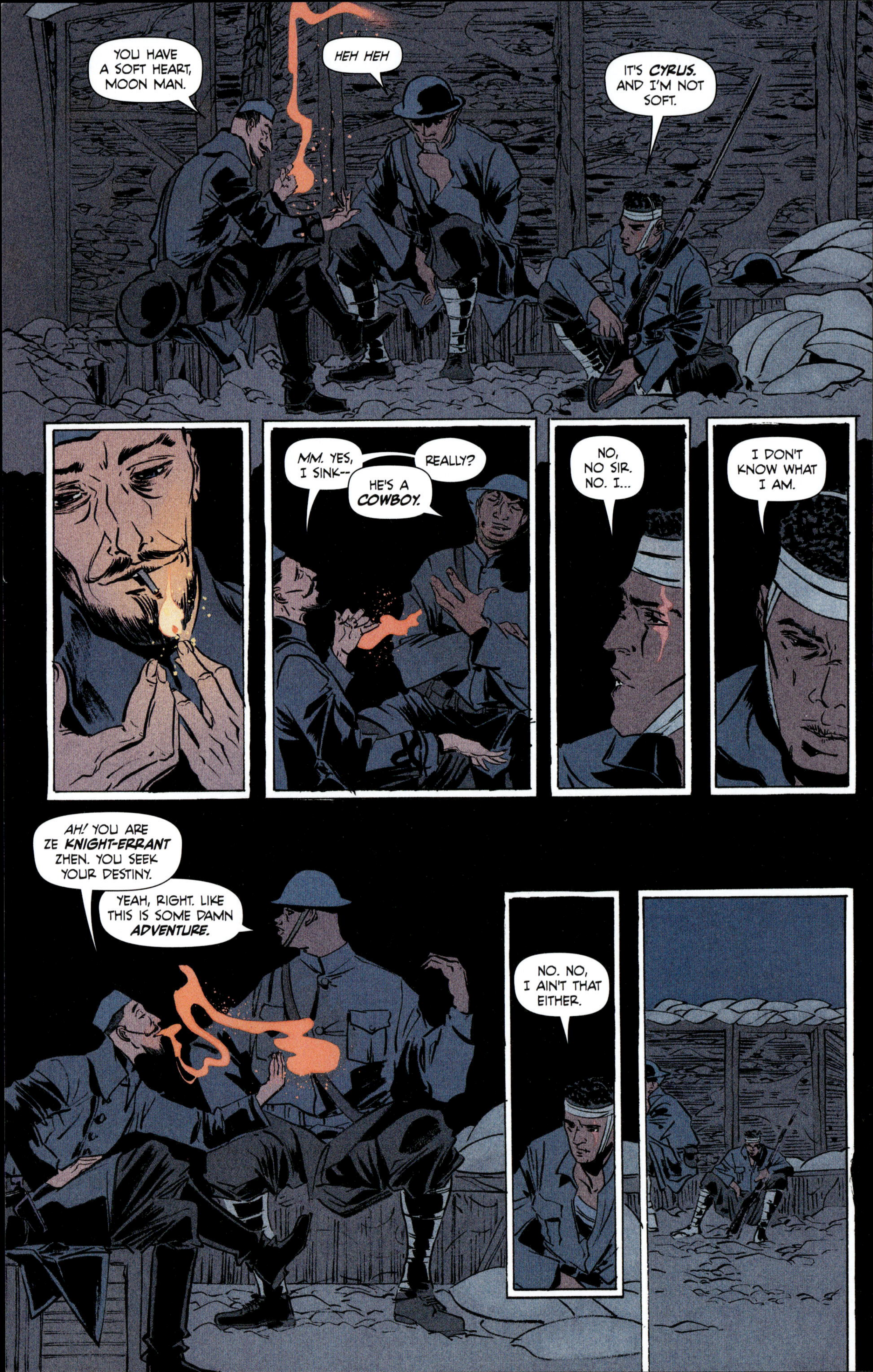
YOU HAVE A SOFT HEART, MOON MAN.
HEH HEH
IT'S **CYRUS.** AND I'M NOT SOFT.
MM. YES, I SINK--
REALLY?
HE'S A **COWBOY.**
NO, NO SIR. NO. I...
I DON'T KNOW WHAT I AM.
AH! YOU ARE ZE **KNIGHT-ERRANT** ZHEN. YOU SEEK YOUR DESTINY.
YEAH, RIGHT. LIKE THIS IS SOME DAMN ***ADVENTURE.***
NO. NO, I AIN'T THAT EITHER.

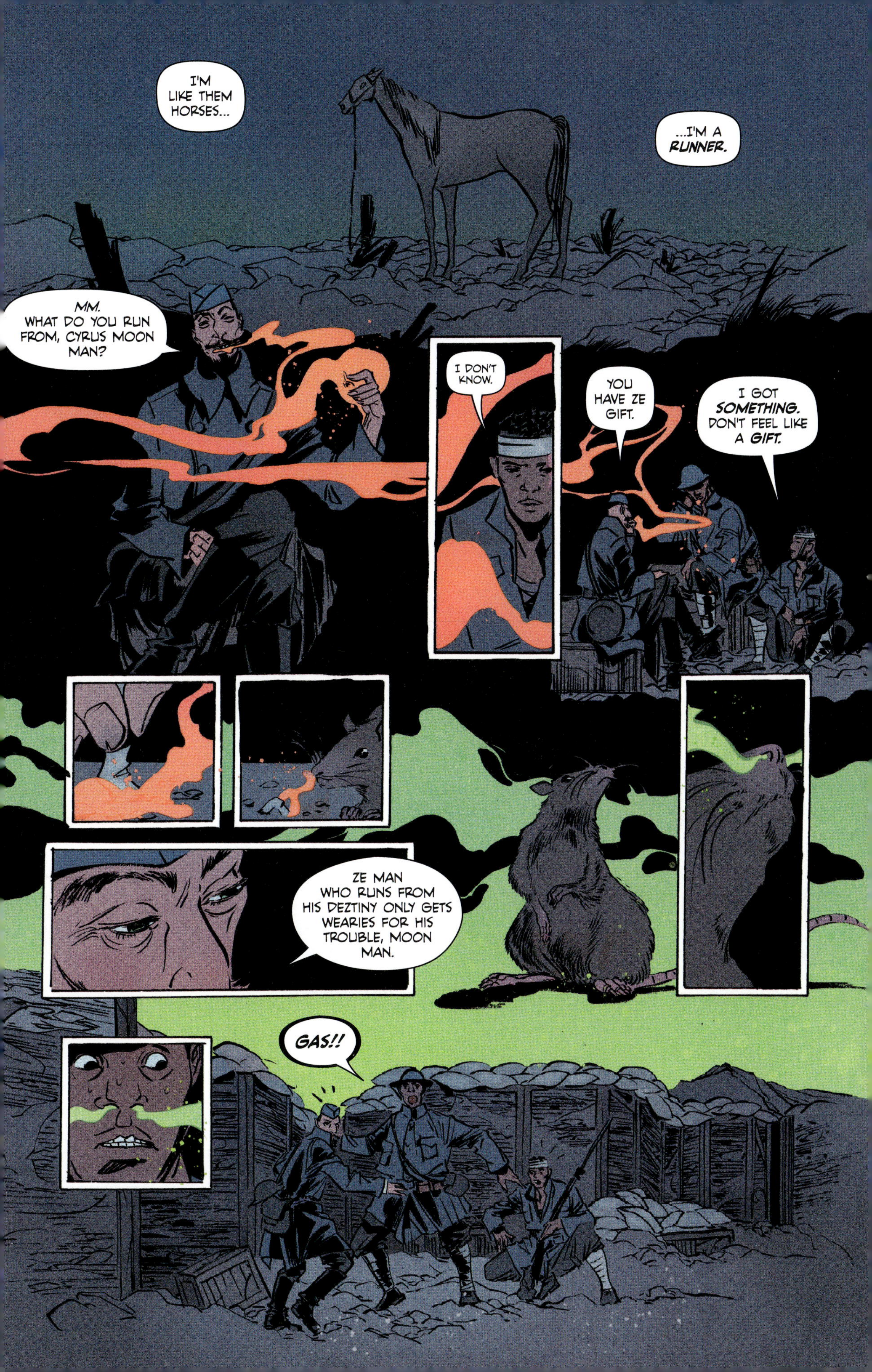
I'M LIKE THEM HORSES...
...I'M A RUNNER.
MM. WHAT DO YOU RUN FROM, CYRUS MOON MAN?
I DON'T KNOW.
YOU HAVE ZE GIFT.
I GOT SOMETHING. DON'T FEEL LIKE A GIFT.
ZE MAN WHO RUNS FROM HIS DEZTINY ONLY GETS WEARIES FOR HIS TROUBLE, MOON MAN.
GAS!!

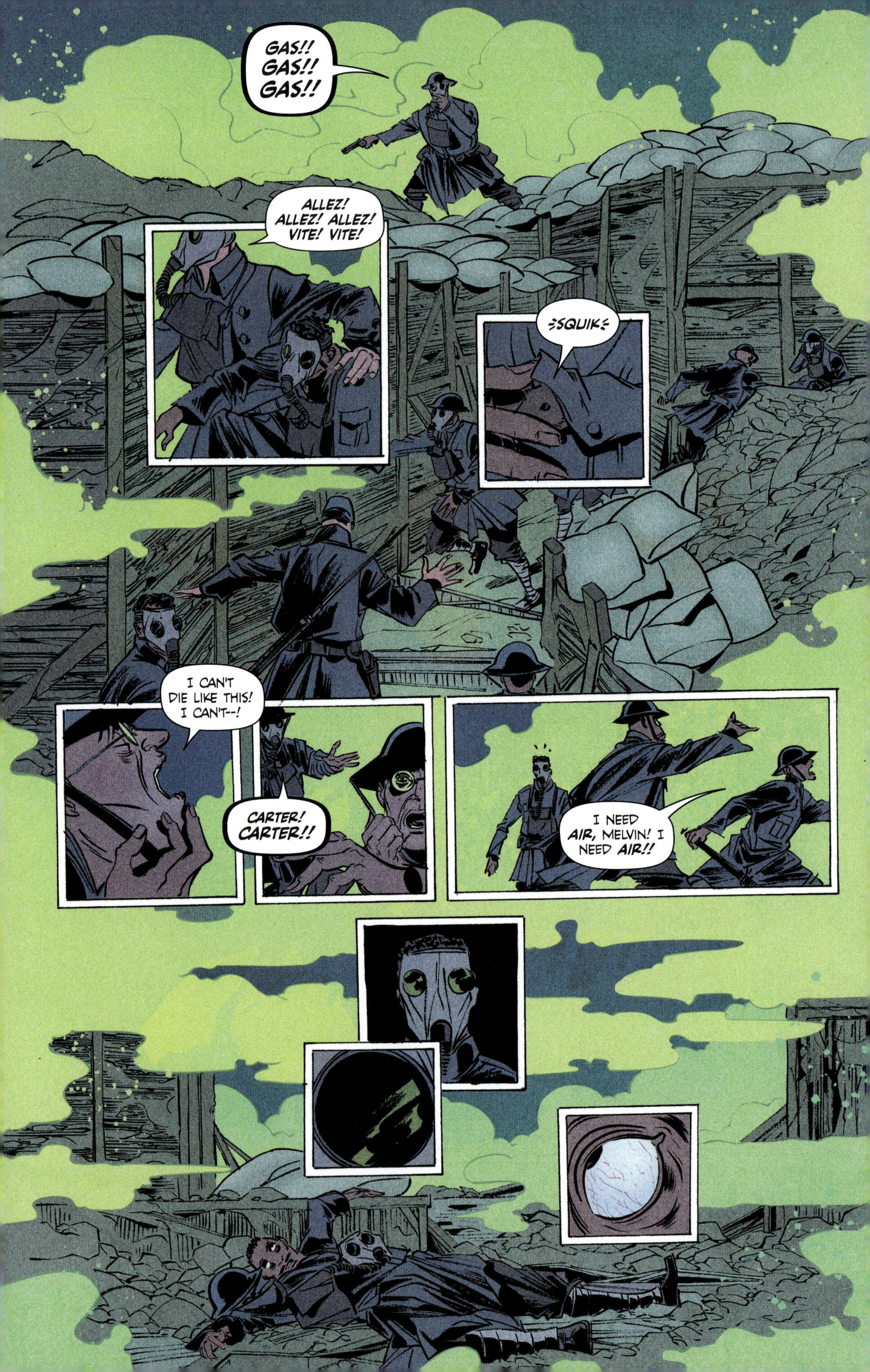
GAS!! GAS!! GAS!!
ALLEZ! ALLEZ! ALLEZ! VITE! VITE!
SQUIK
I CAN'T DIE LIKE THIS! I CAN'T--!
CARTER! CARTER!!
I NEED AIR, MELVIN! I NEED AIR!!

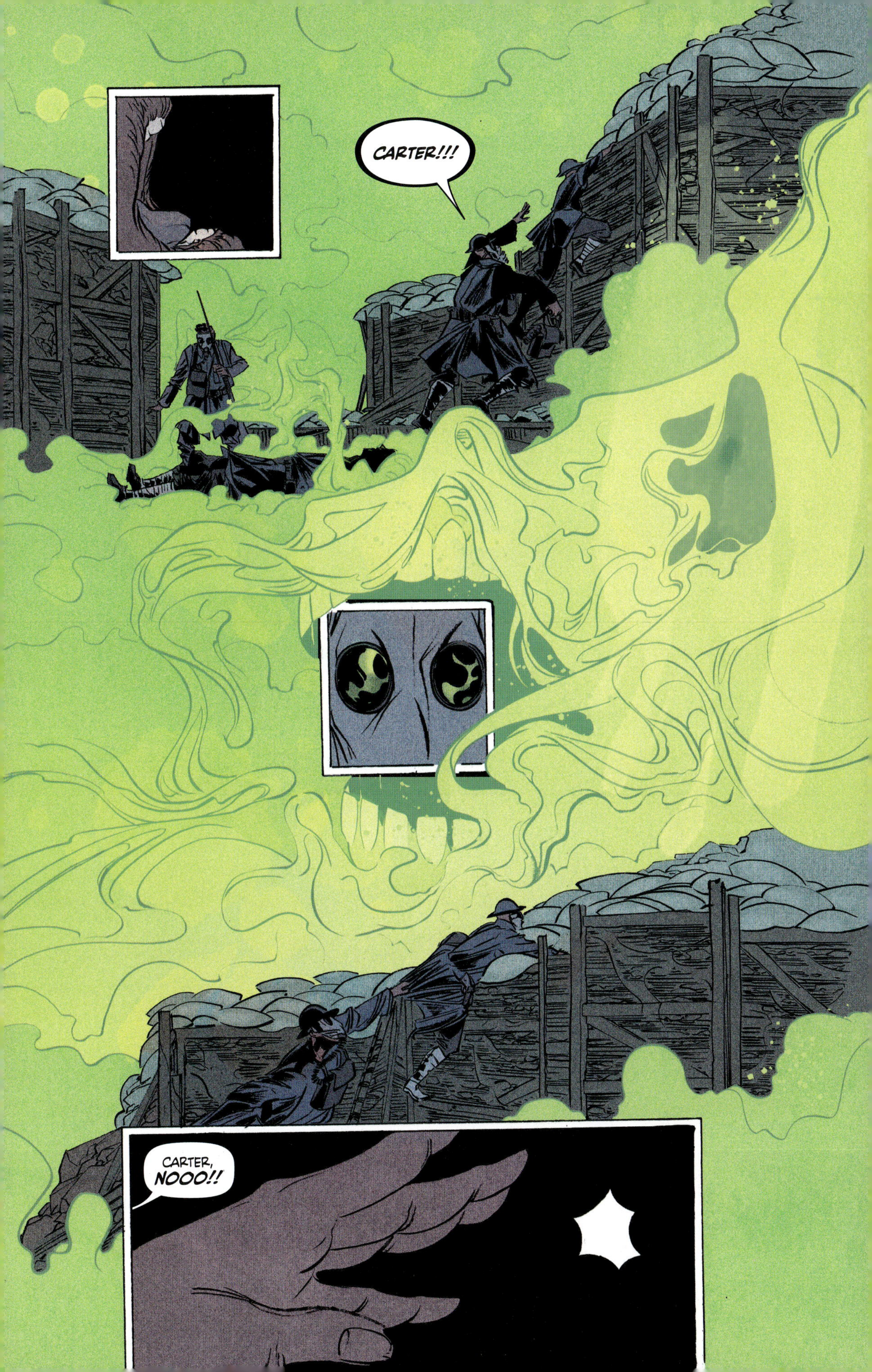
CARTER!!!
CARTER, NOOO!!

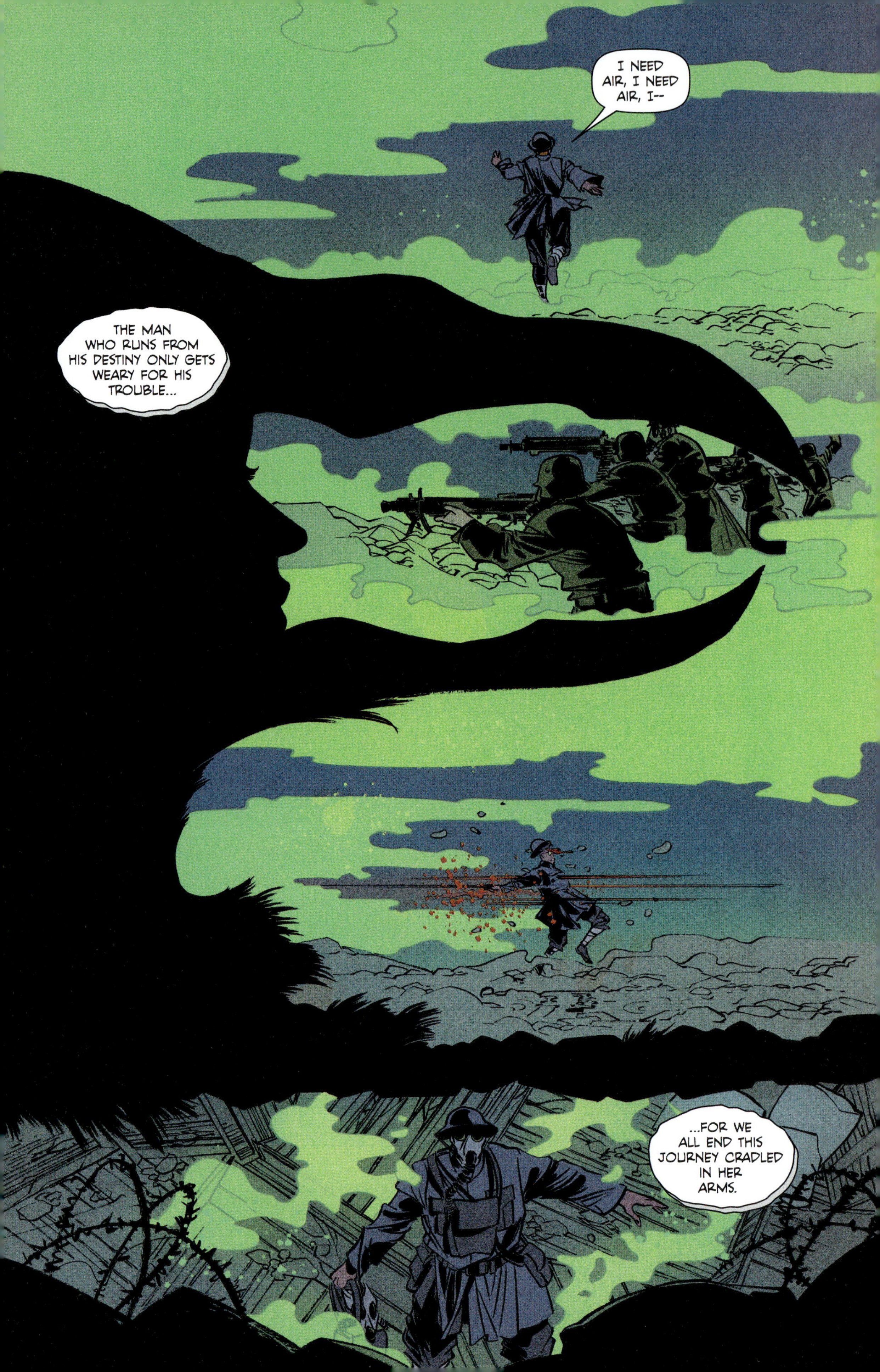
I NEED AIR, I NEED AIR, I--
THE MAN WHO RUNS FROM HIS DESTINY ONLY GETS WEARY FOR HIS TROUBLE...
...FOR WE ALL END THIS JOURNEY CRADLED IN HER ARMS.

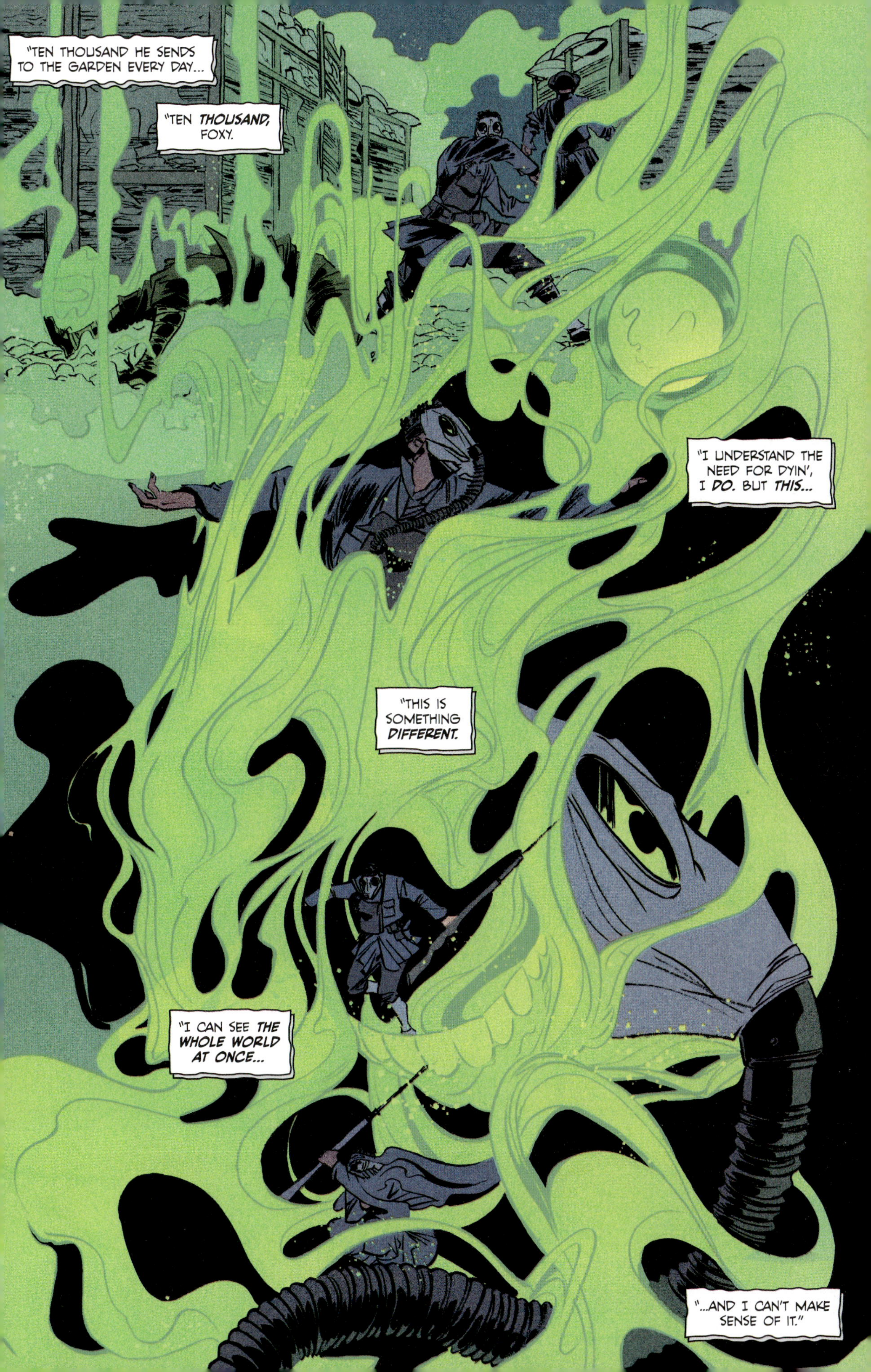
"TEN THOUSAND HE SENDS TO THE GARDEN EVERY DAY...
"TEN *THOUSAND,* FOXY.
"I UNDERSTAND THE NEED FOR DYIN', I *DO.* BUT *THIS...*
"THIS IS SOMETHING *DIFFERENT.*
"I CAN SEE *THE WHOLE WORLD AT ONCE...*
"...AND I CAN'T MAKE SENSE OF IT."

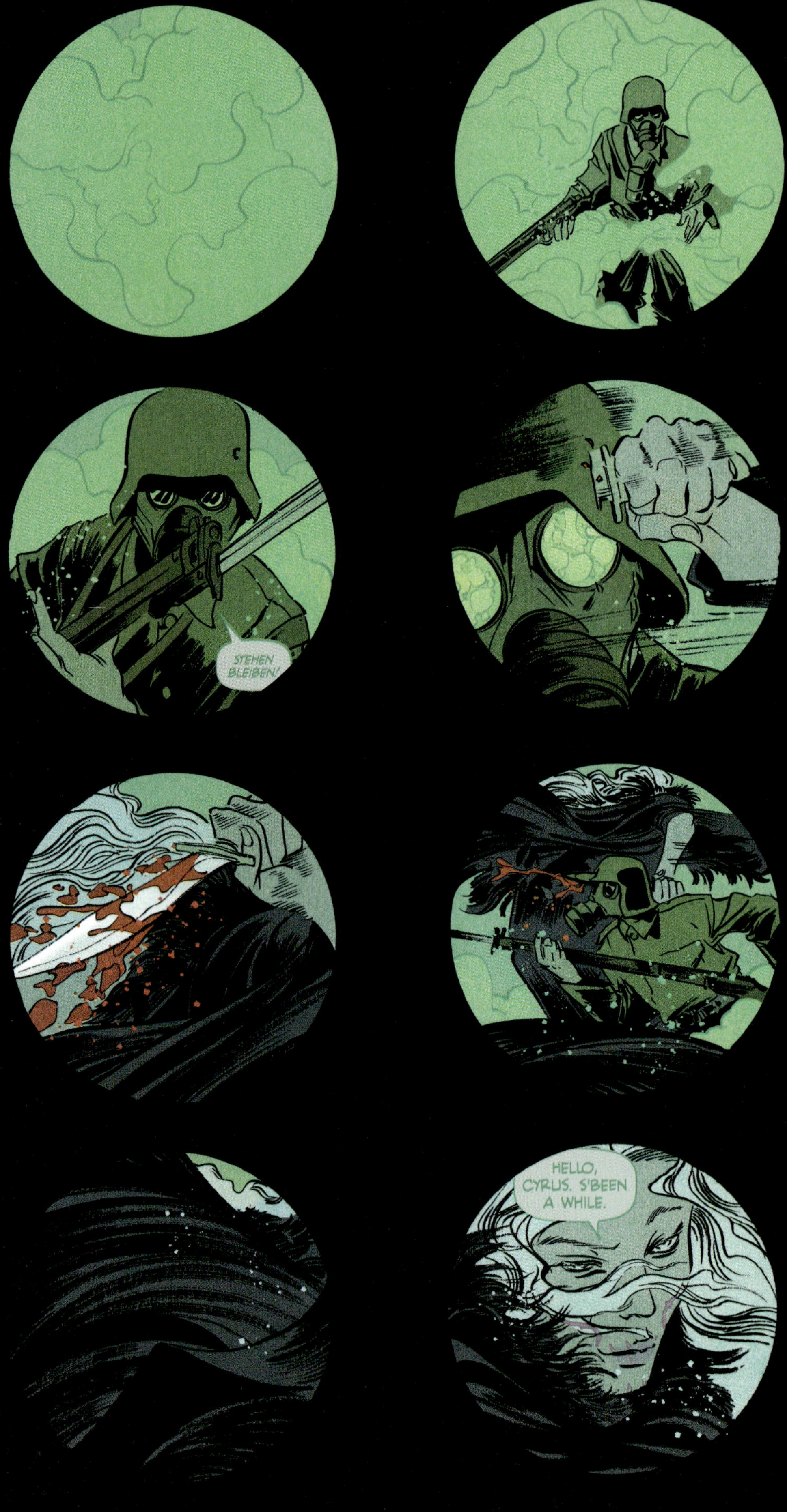
STEHEN BLEIBEN!
HELLO, CYRUS. S'BEEN A WHILE.

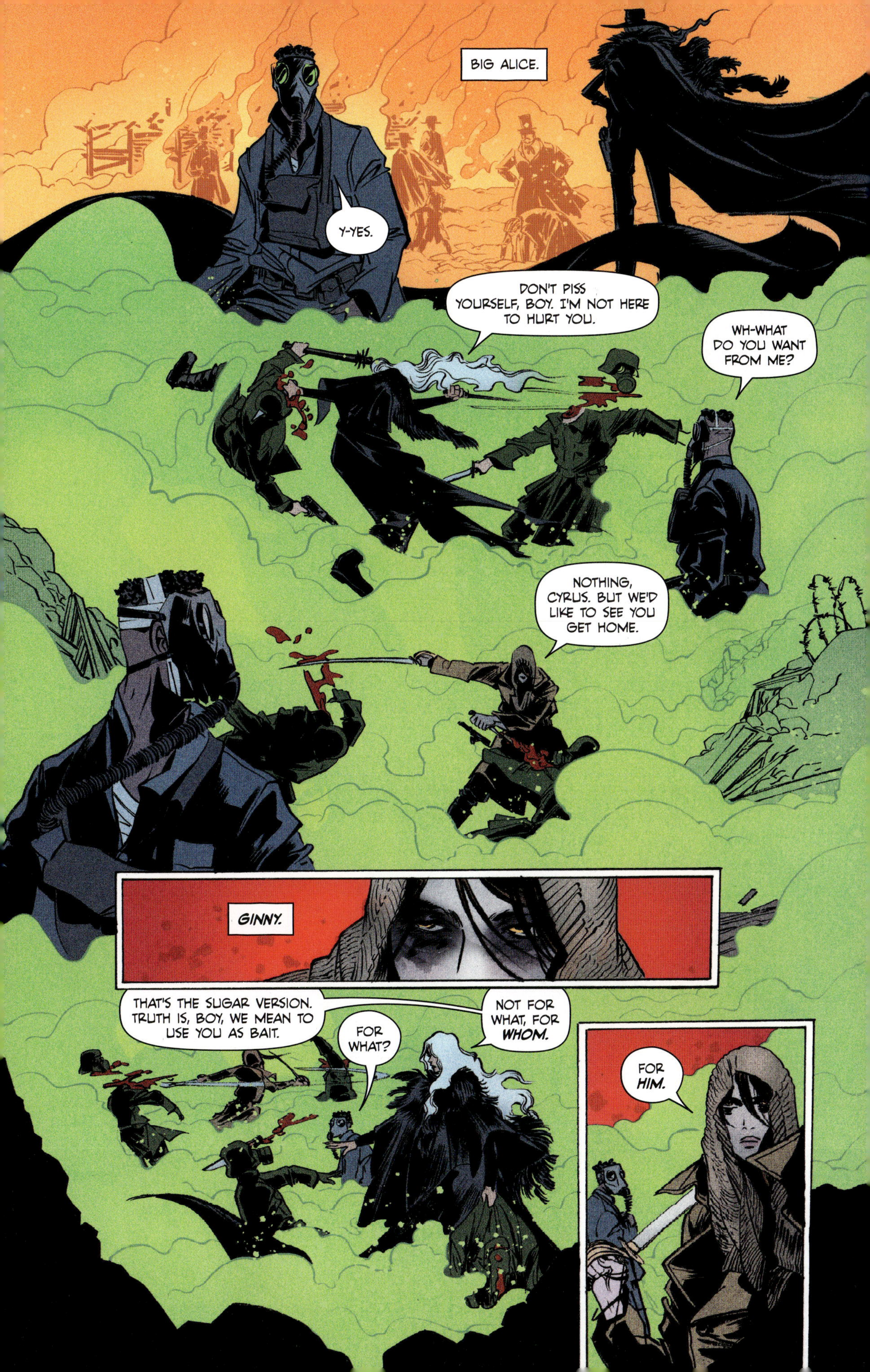
BIG ALICE.
Y-YES.
DON'T PISS YOURSELF, BOY. I'M NOT HERE TO HURT YOU.
WH-WHAT DO YOU WANT FROM ME?
NOTHING, CYRUS. BUT WE'D LIKE TO SEE YOU GET HOME.
GINNY.
THAT'S THE SUGAR VERSION. TRUTH IS, BOY, WE MEAN TO USE YOU AS BAIT.
FOR WHAT?
NOT FOR WHAT, FOR *WHOM.*
FOR *HIM.*

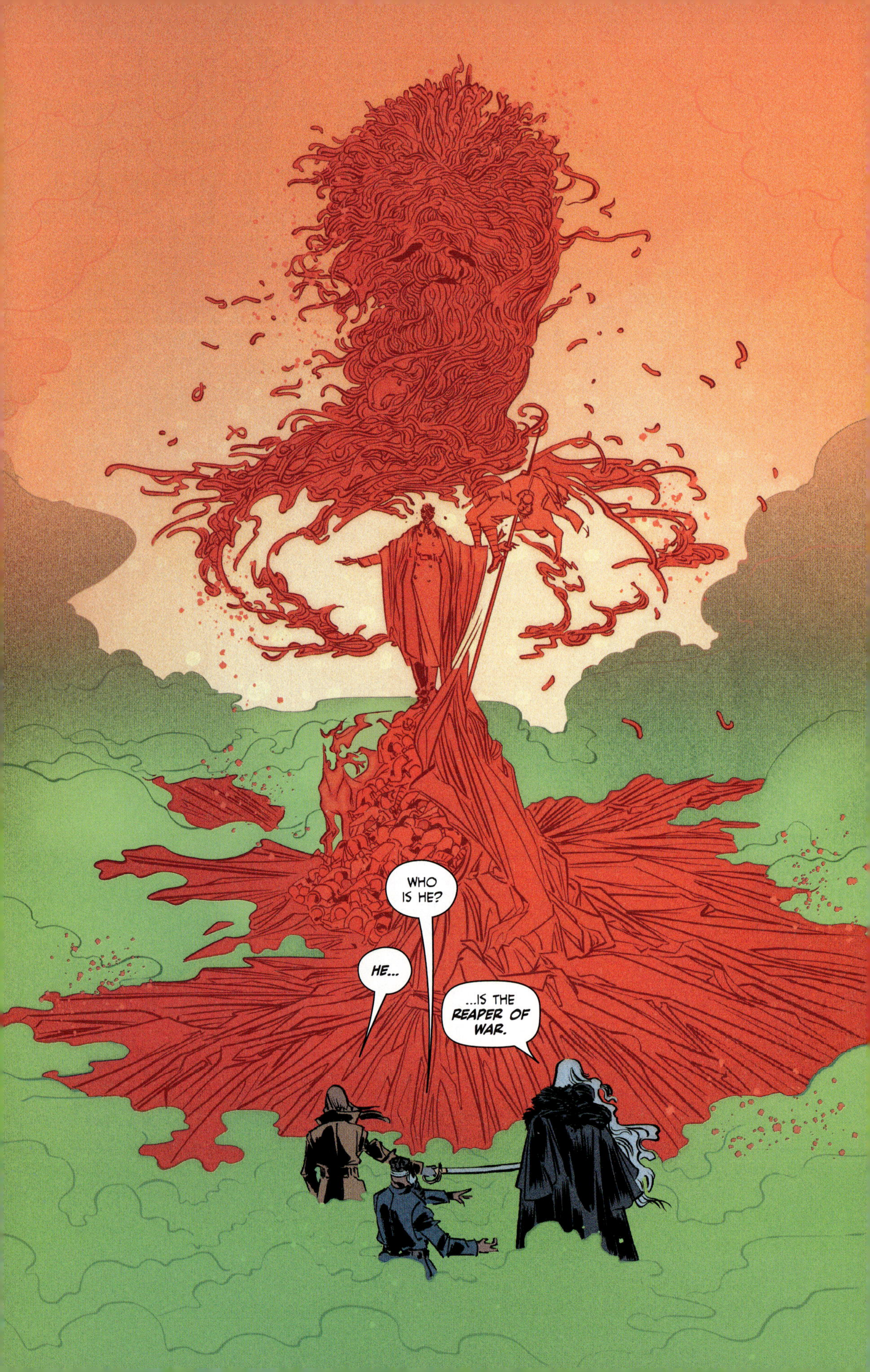
WHO IS HE?
HE...
...IS THE REAPER OF WAR.

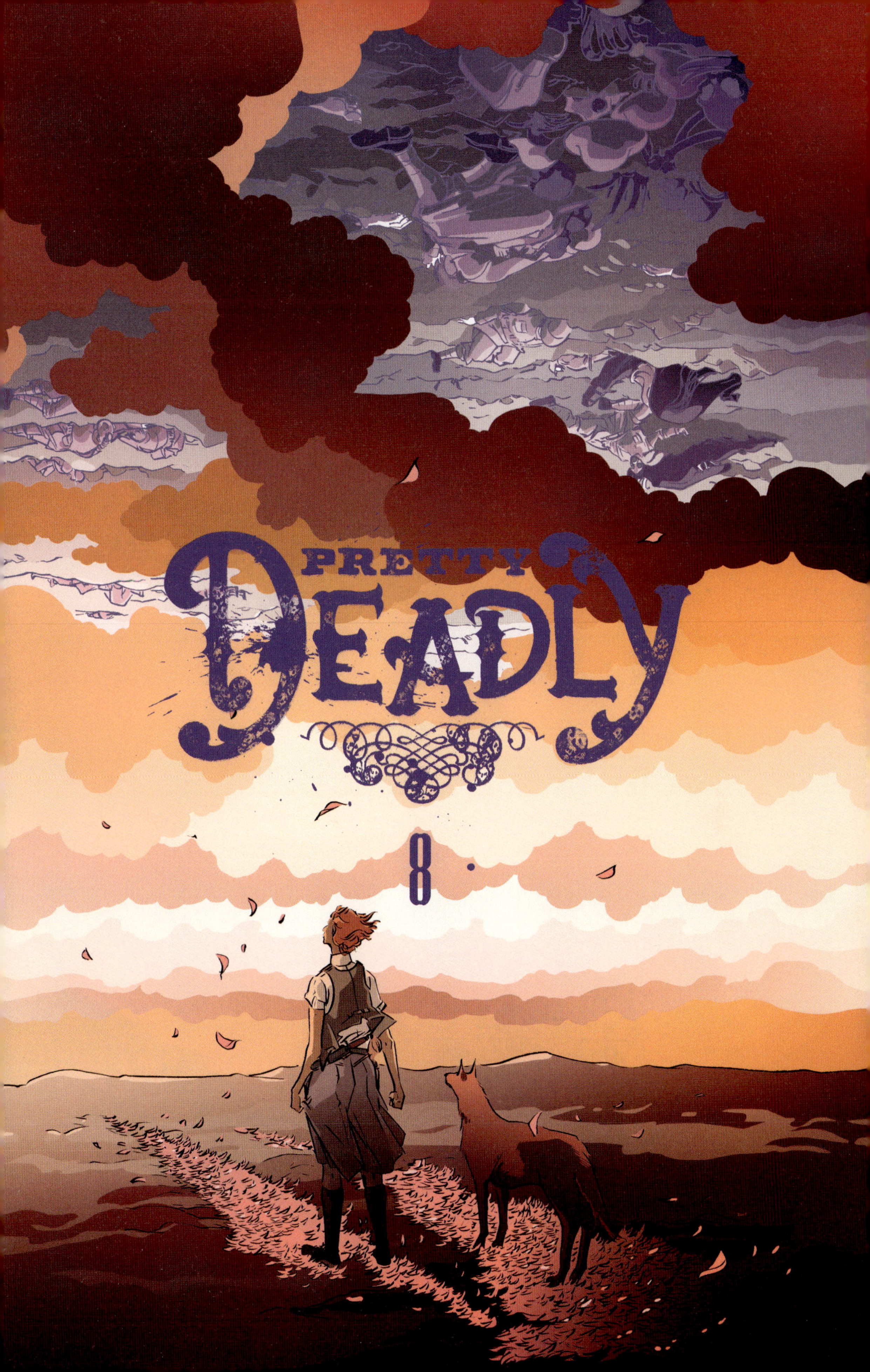
PRETTY
DEADLY
8

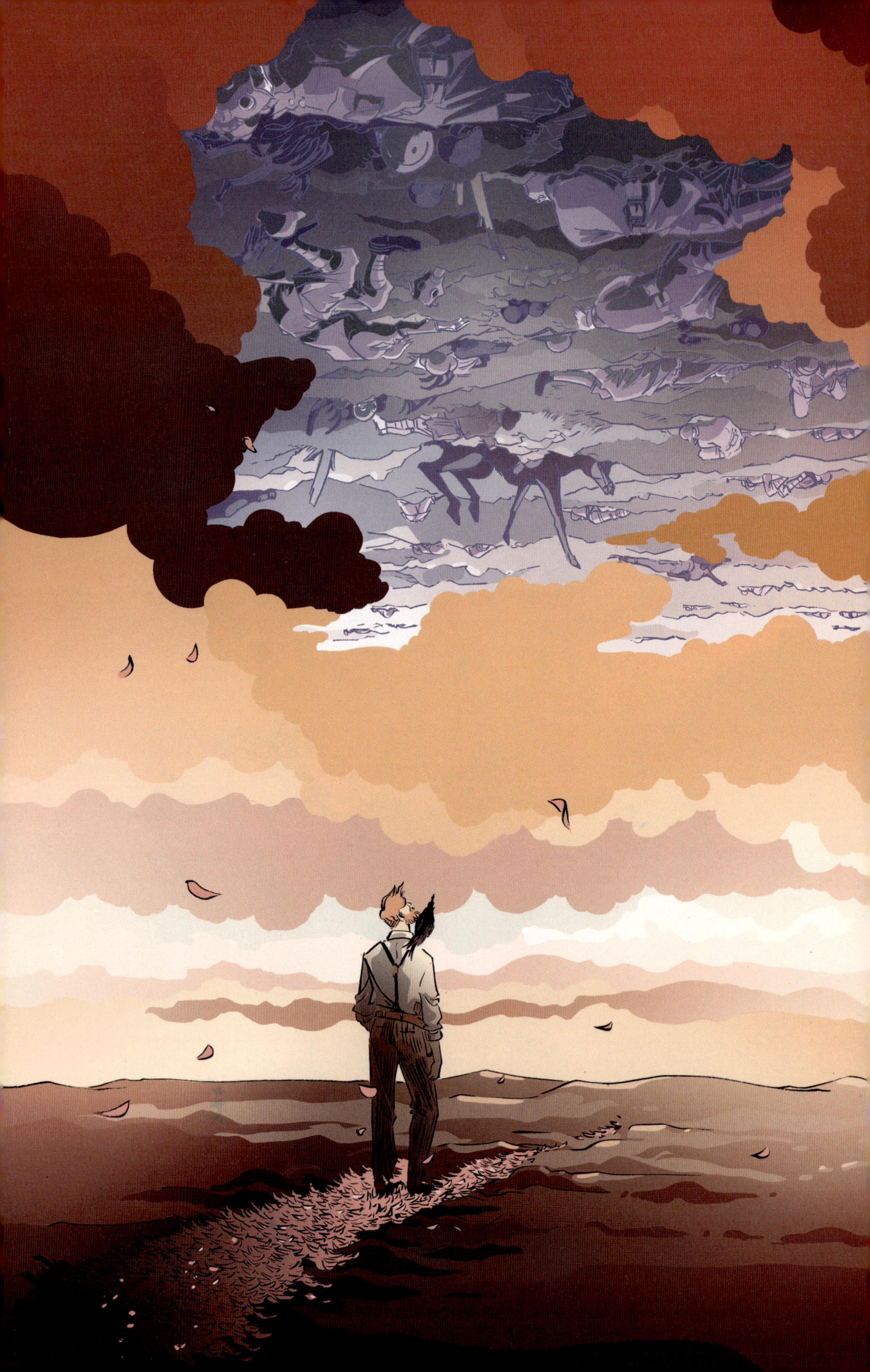

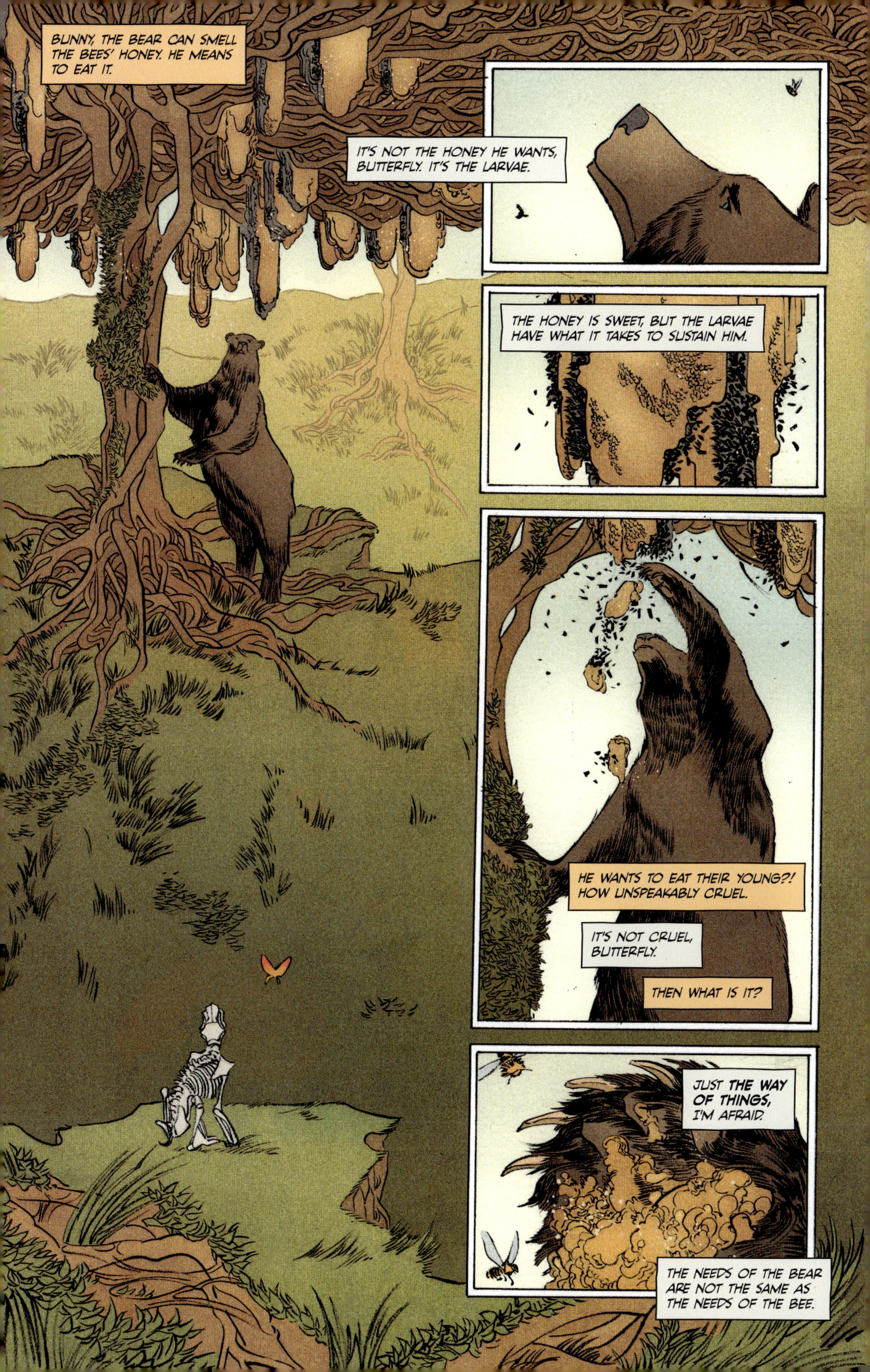
BUNNY, THE BEAR CAN SMELL THE BEES' HONEY. HE MEANS TO EAT IT.
IT'S NOT THE HONEY HE WANTS, BUTTERFLY. IT'S THE LARVAE.
THE HONEY IS SWEET, BUT THE LARVAE HAVE WHAT IT TAKES TO SUSTAIN HIM.
HE WANTS TO EAT THEIR YOUNG?! HOW UNSPEAKABLY CRUEL.
IT'S NOT CRUEL, BUTTERFLY.
THEN WHAT IS IT?
JUST **THE WAY OF THINGS,** I'M AFRAID.
THE NEEDS OF THE BEAR ARE NOT THE SAME AS THE NEEDS OF THE BEE.

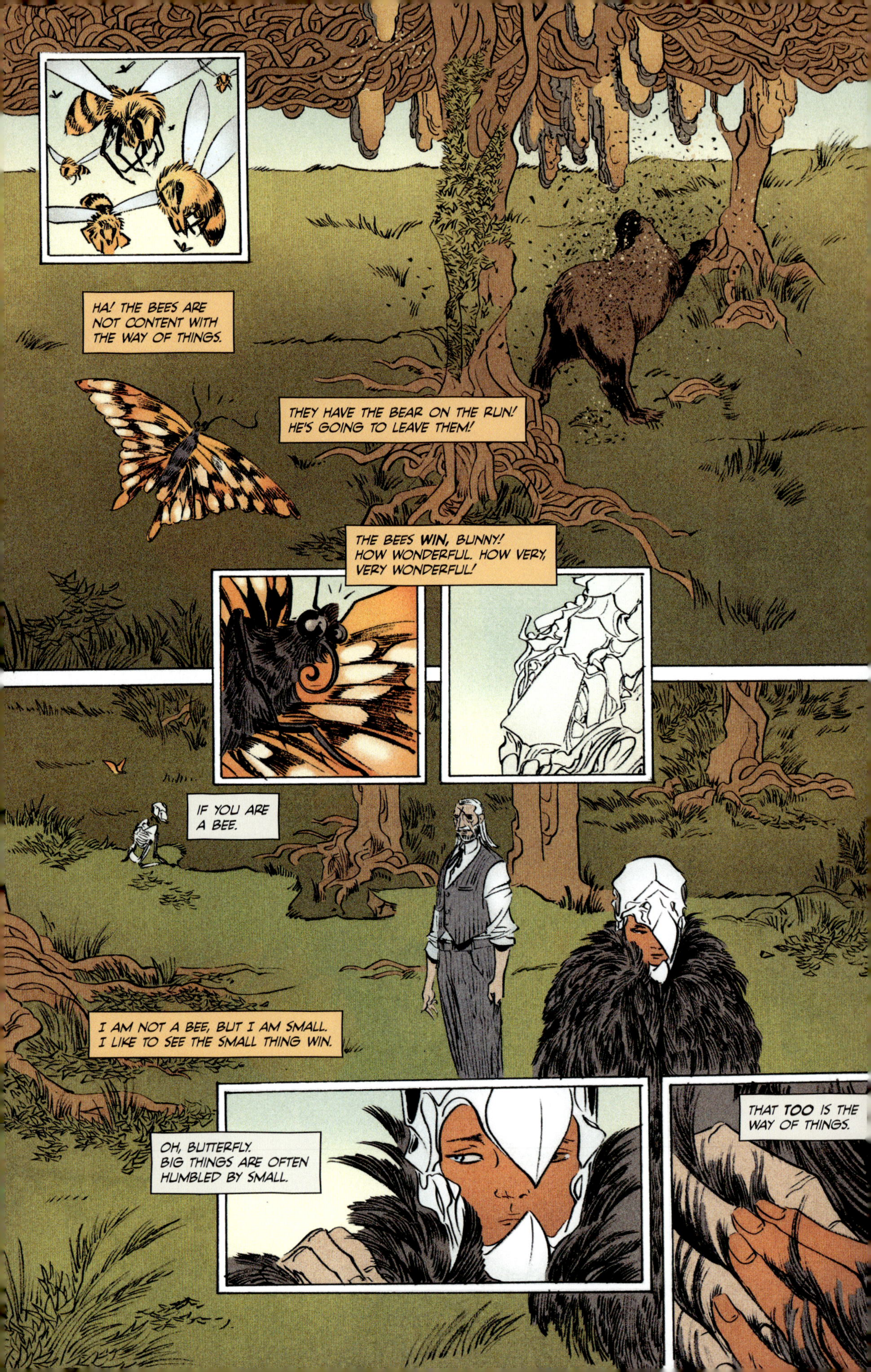
HA! THE BEES ARE NOT CONTENT WITH THE WAY OF THINGS.
THEY HAVE THE BEAR ON THE RUN! HE'S GOING TO LEAVE THEM!
THE BEES **WIN,** BUNNY! HOW WONDERFUL. HOW VERY, VERY WONDERFUL!
IF YOU ARE A BEE.
I AM NOT A BEE, BUT I AM SMALL. I LIKE TO SEE THE SMALL THING WIN.
OH, BUTTERFLY. BIG THINGS ARE OFTEN HUMBLED BY SMALL.
THAT **TOO** IS THE WAY OF THINGS.

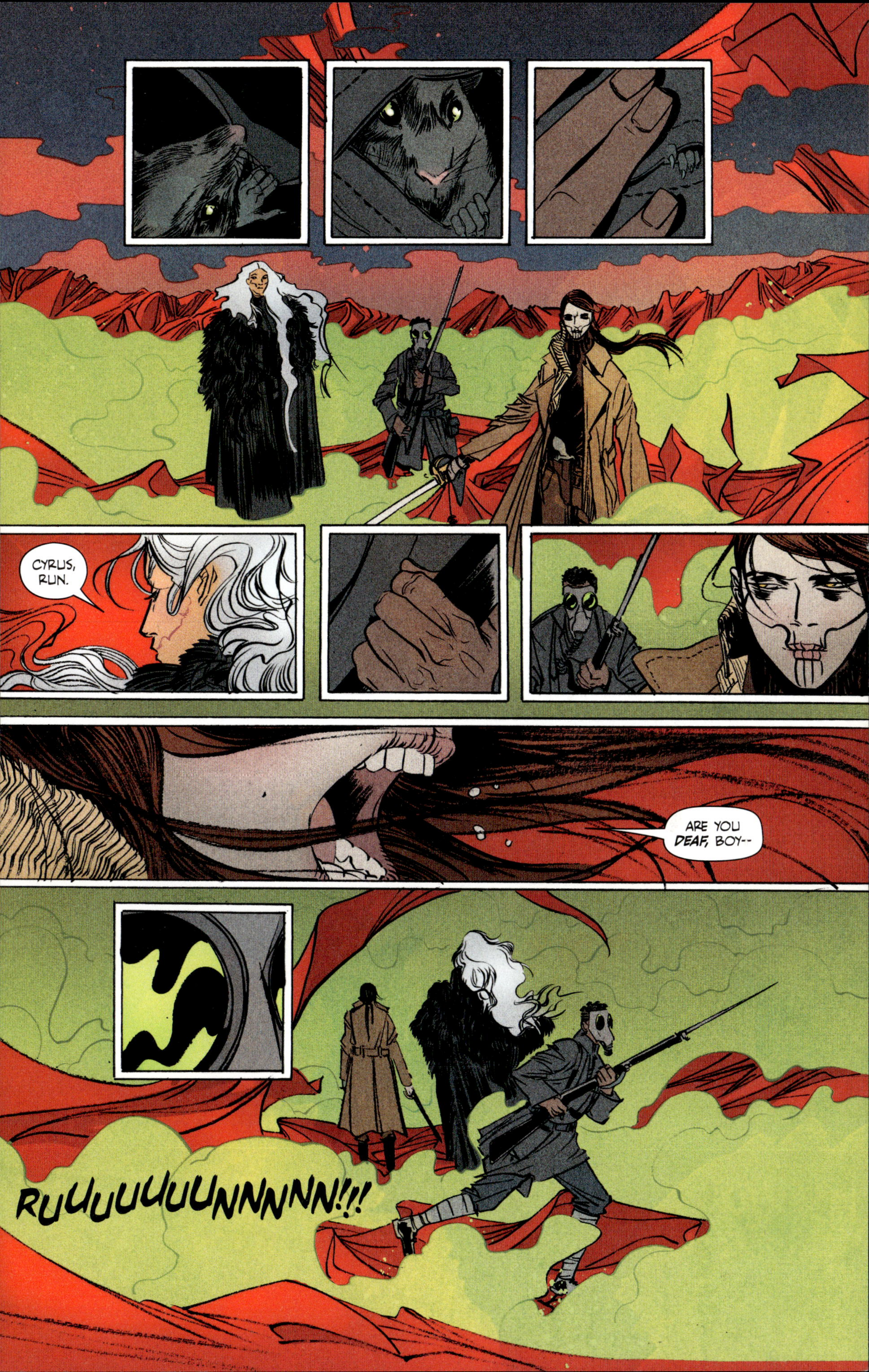
CYRUS, RUN.
ARE YOU DEAF, BOY--
RUUUUUUUNNNNN!!!

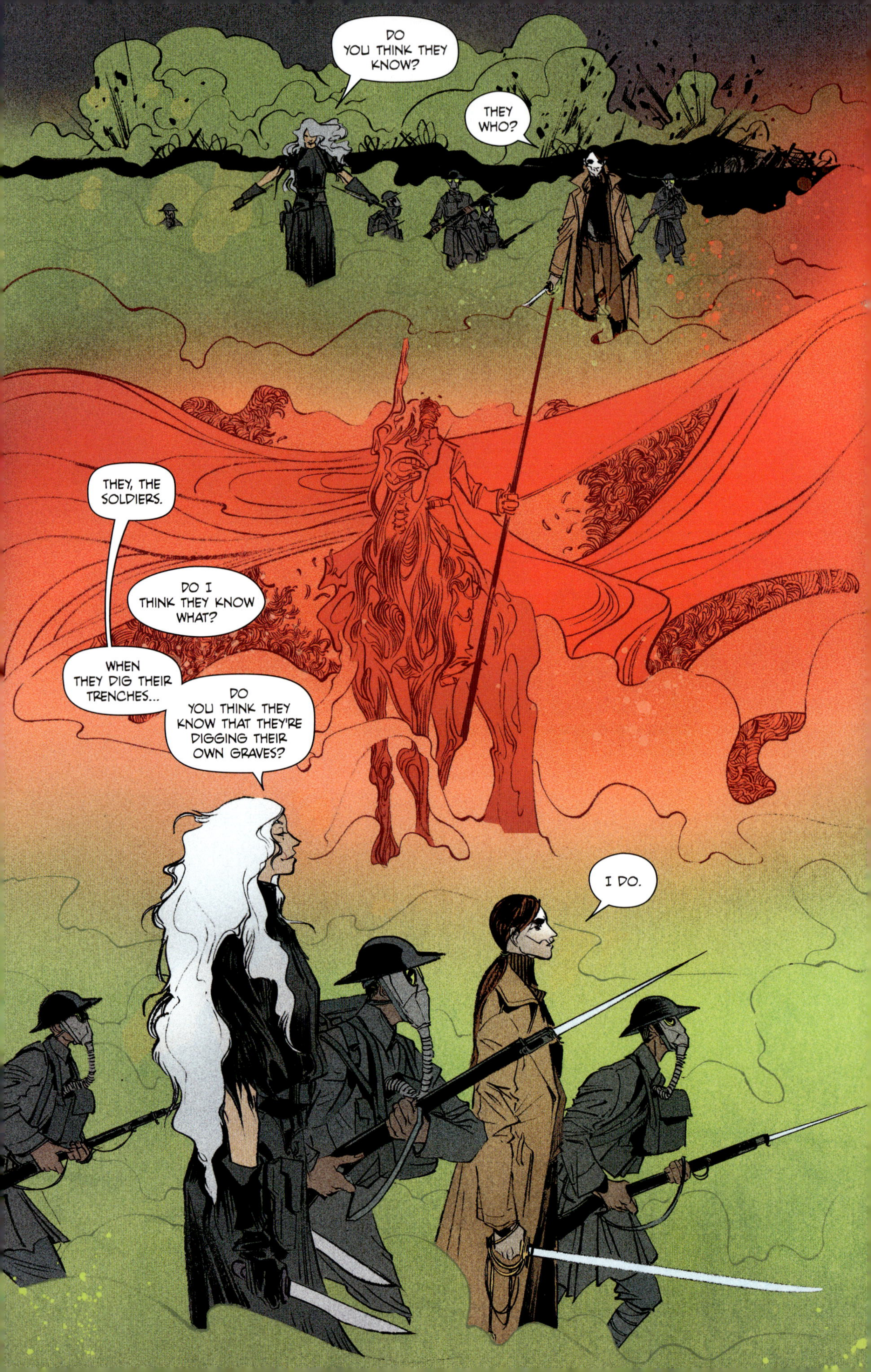
DO YOU THINK THEY KNOW?
THEY WHO?
THEY, THE SOLDIERS.
DO I THINK THEY KNOW WHAT?
WHEN THEY DIG THEIR TRENCHES...
DO YOU THINK THEY KNOW THAT THEY'RE DIGGING THEIR OWN GRAVES?
I DO.

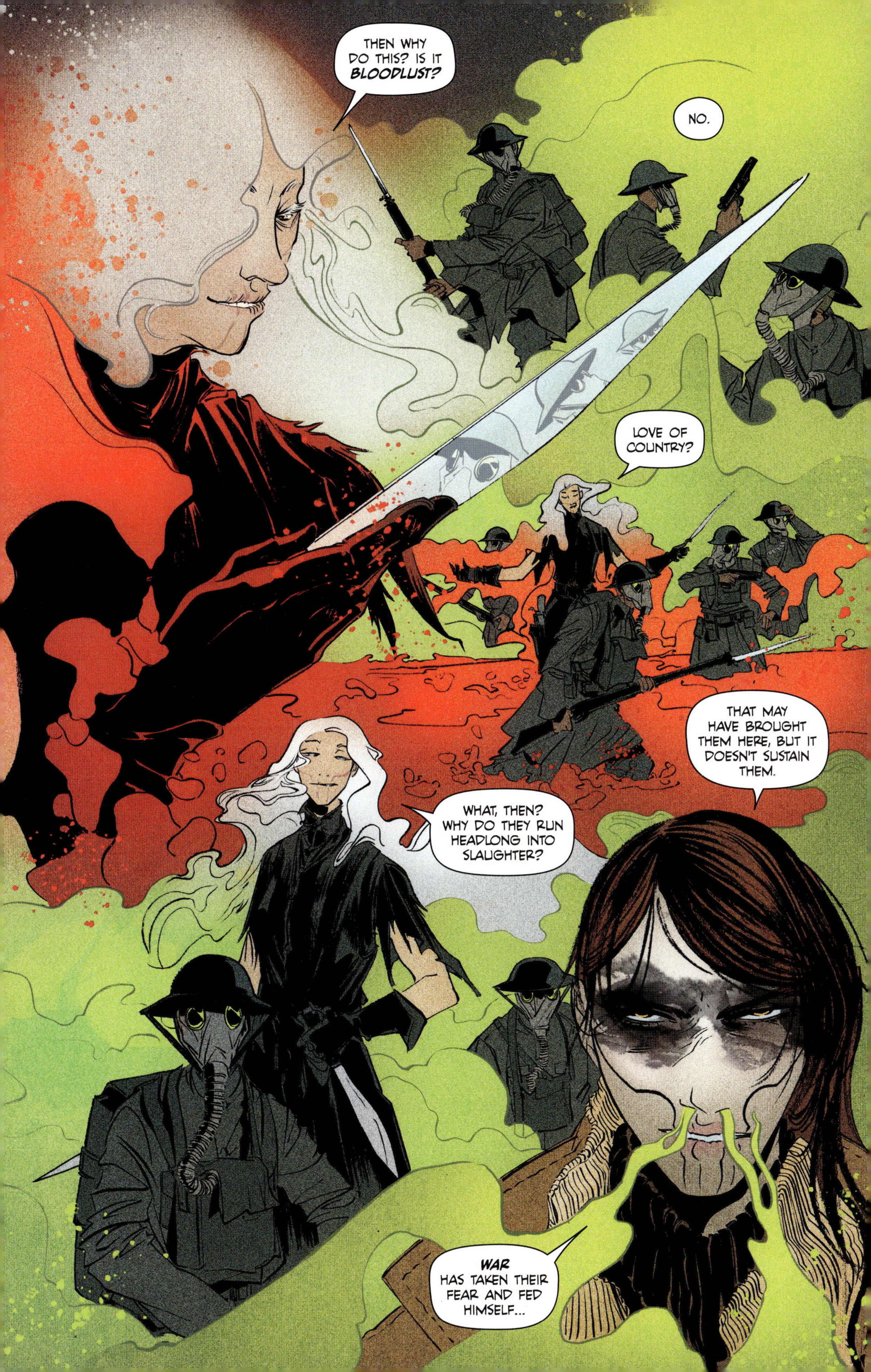
THEN WHY DO THIS? IS IT *BLOODLUST?*
NO.
LOVE OF COUNTRY?
THAT MAY HAVE BROUGHT THEM HERE, BUT IT DOESN'T SUSTAIN THEM.
WHAT, THEN? WHY DO THEY RUN HEADLONG INTO SLAUGHTER?
WAR HAS TAKEN THEIR FEAR AND FED HIMSELF...

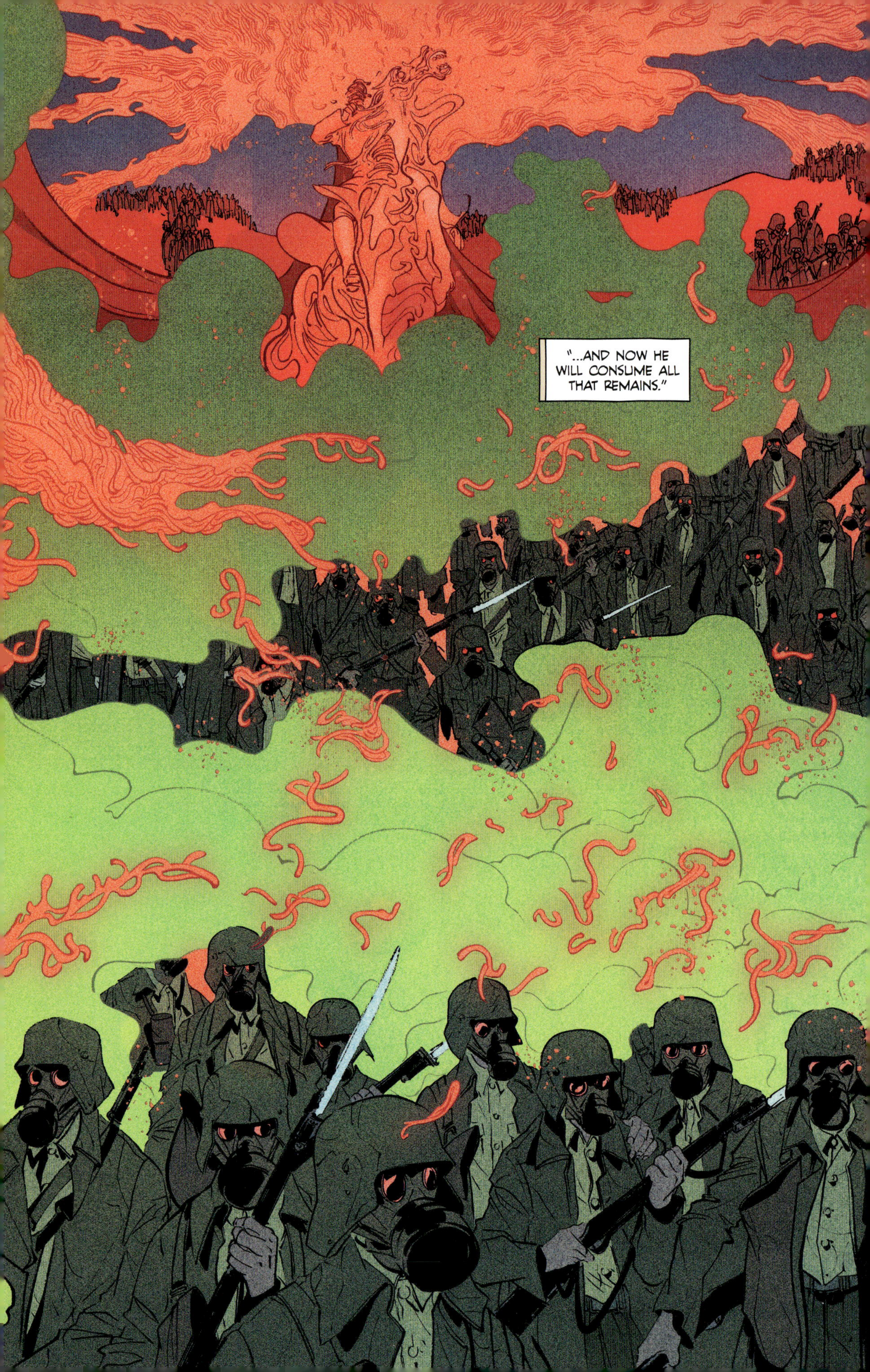
"...AND NOW HE WILL CONSUME ALL THAT REMAINS."

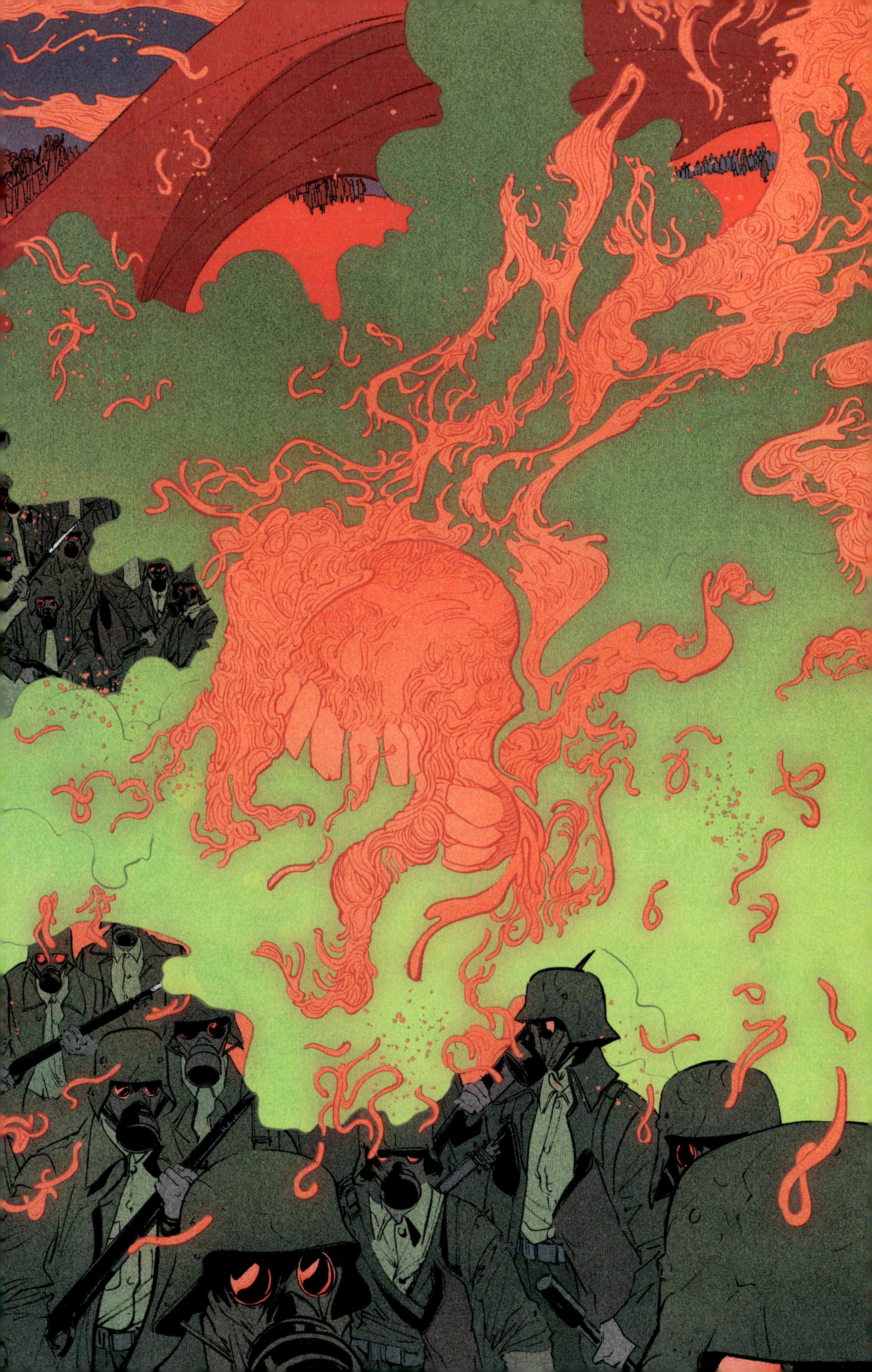

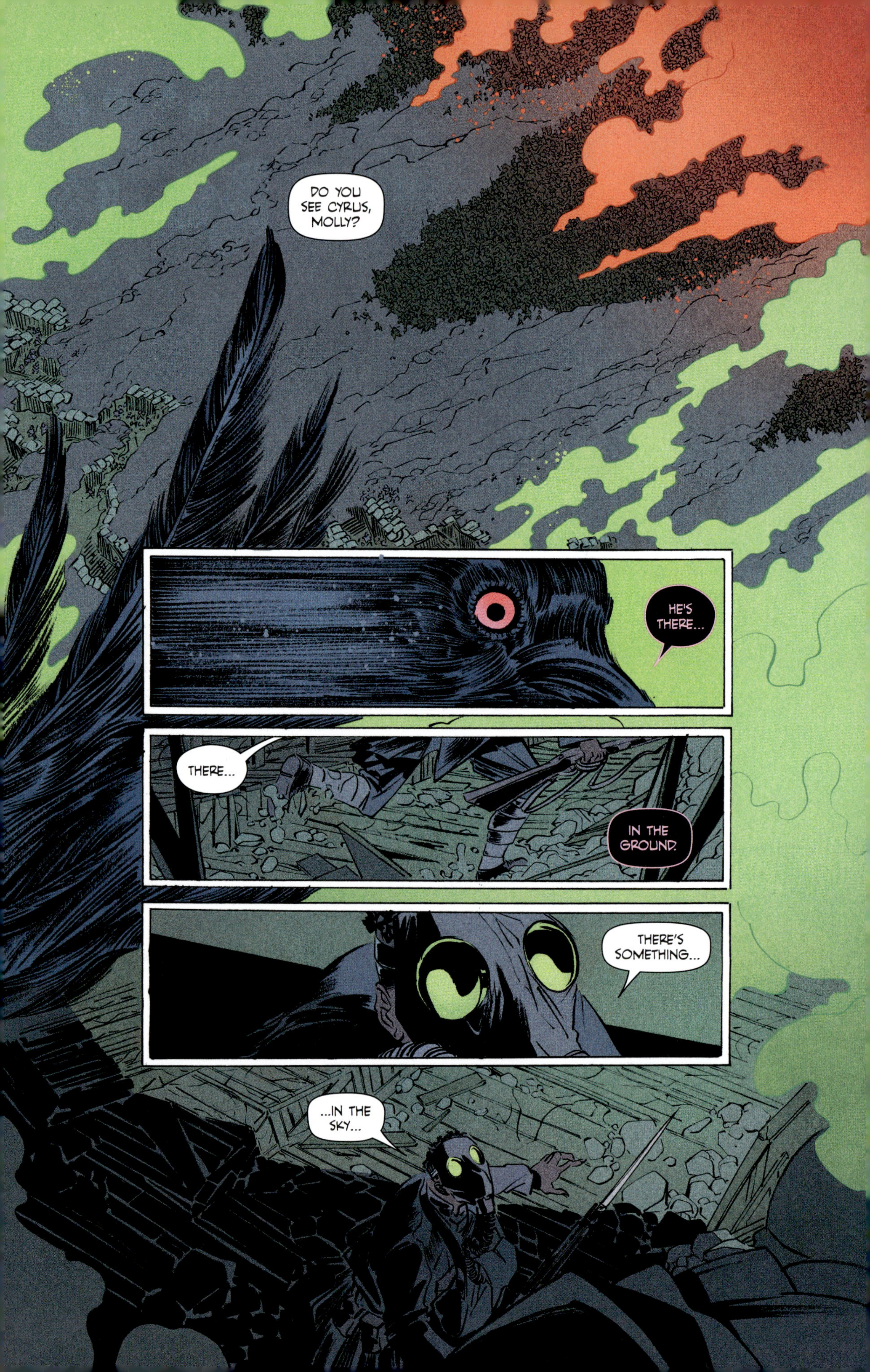
DO YOU SEE CYRUS, MOLLY?
HE'S THERE...
THERE...
IN THE GROUND.
THERE'S SOMETHING...
...IN THE SKY...

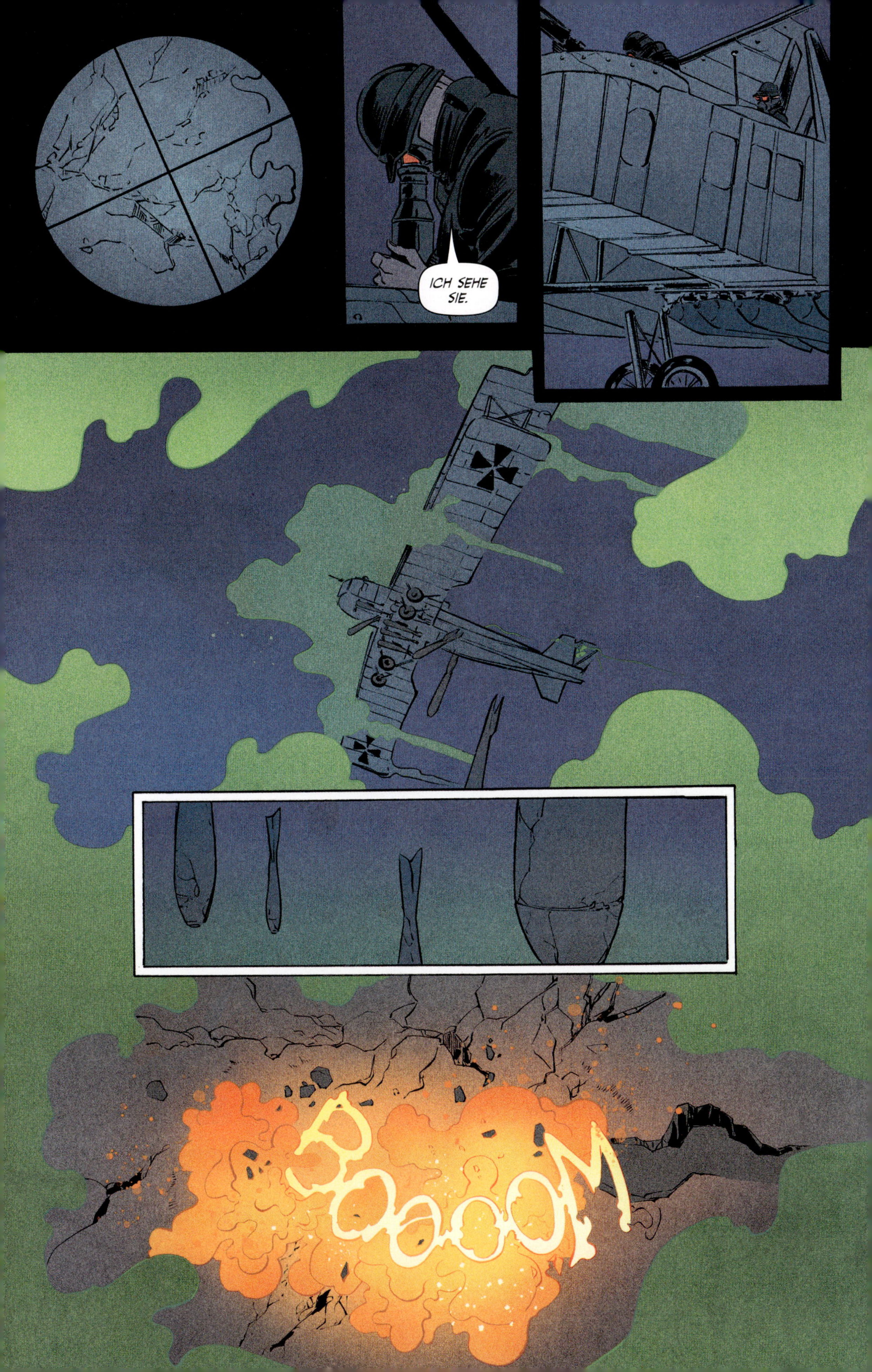
ICH SEHE SIE.
BOOOOM

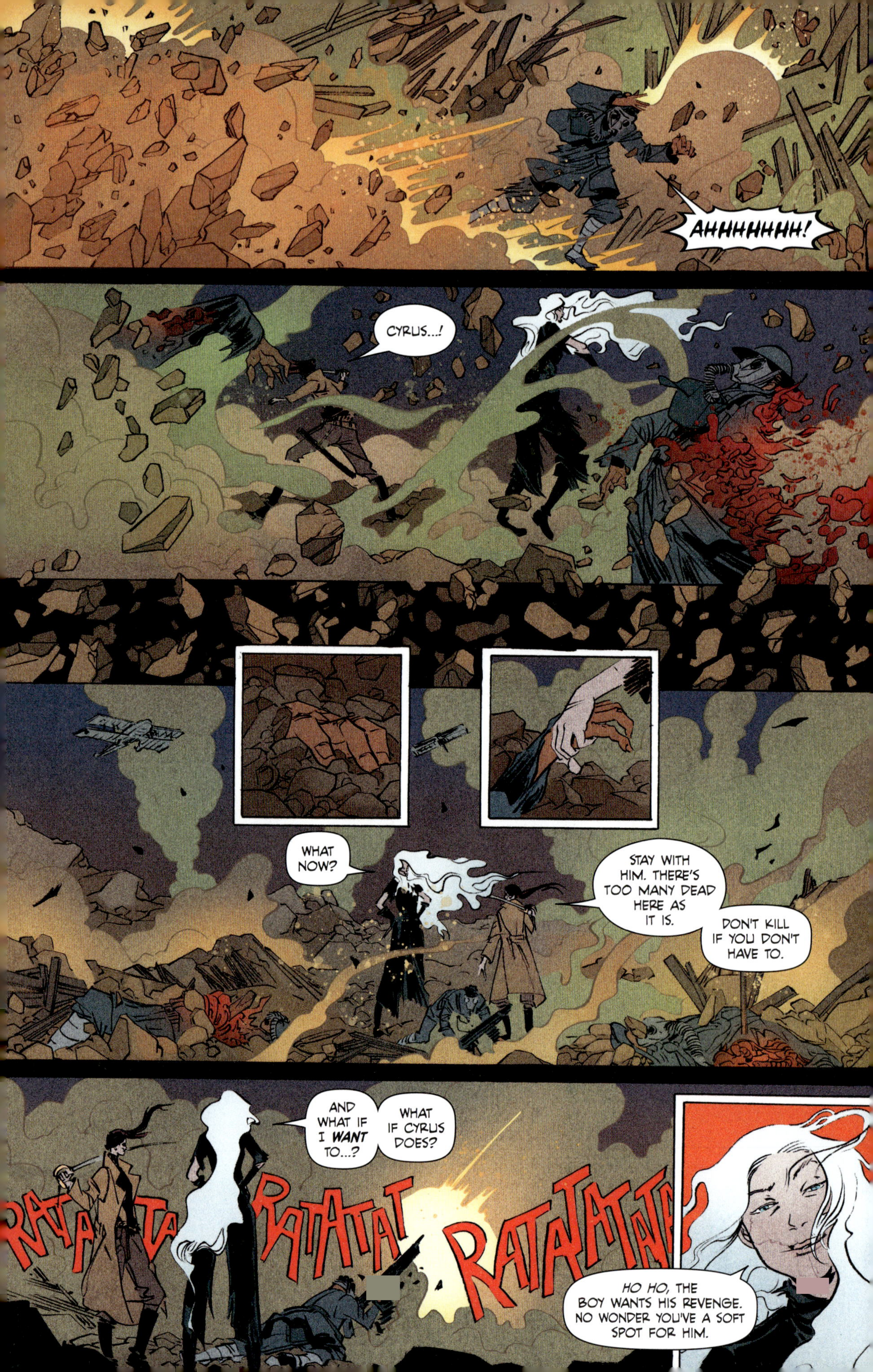
AHHHHHHH!
CYRUS...!
WHAT NOW?
STAY WITH HIM. THERE'S TOO MANY DEAD HERE AS IT IS.
DON'T KILL IF YOU DON'T HAVE TO.
RATATATAT
AND WHAT IF I **WANT** TO...?
WHAT IF CYRUS DOES?
RATATATAT
RATATATATAT
HO HO, THE BOY WANTS HIS REVENGE. NO WONDER YOU'VE A SOFT SPOT FOR HIM.

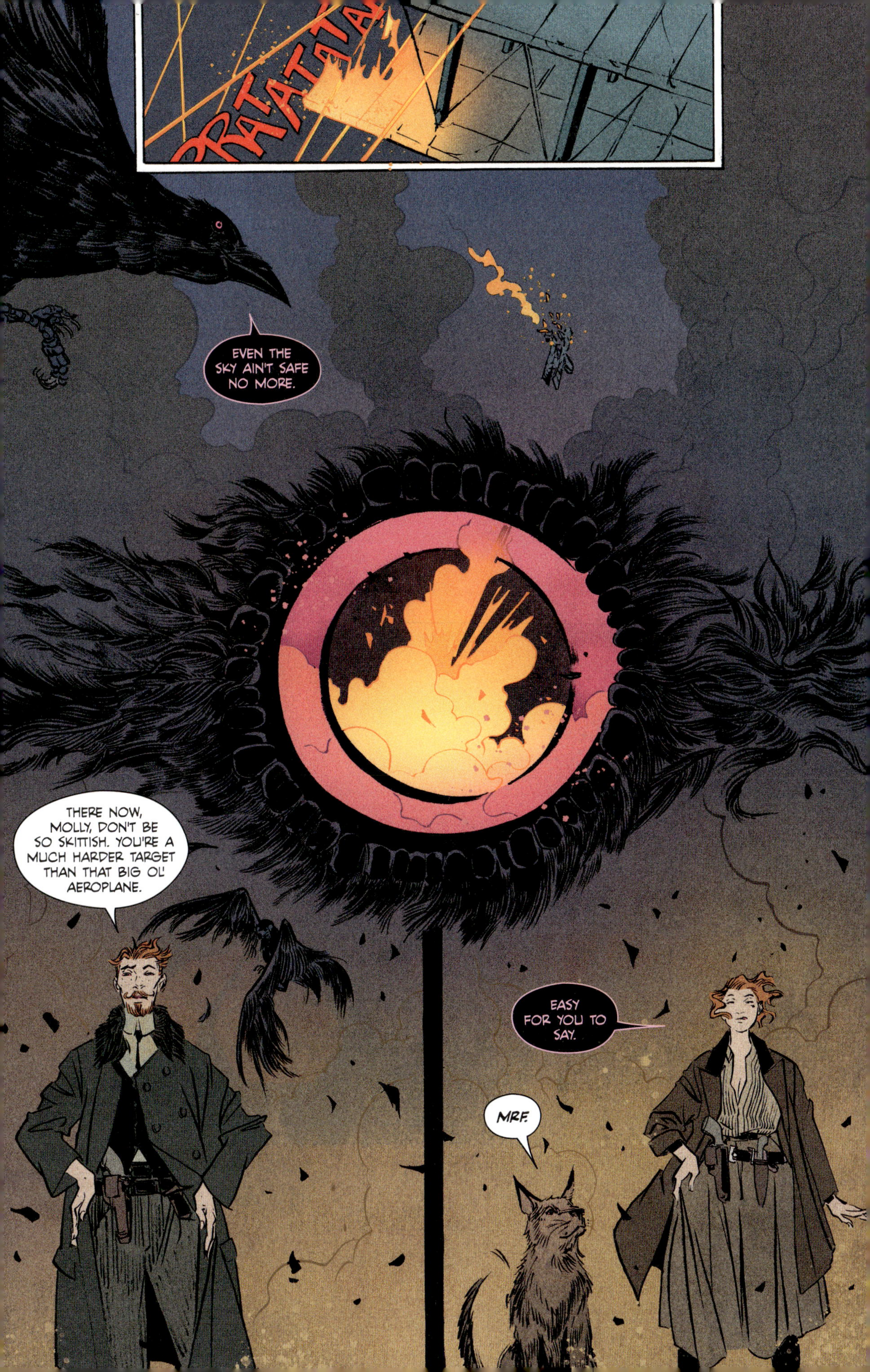
RATATATA
EVEN THE SKY AIN'T SAFE NO MORE.
THERE NOW, MOLLY, DON'T BE SO SKITTISH. YOU'RE A MUCH HARDER TARGET THAN THAT BIG OL' AEROPLANE.
EASY FOR YOU TO SAY.
MRF.

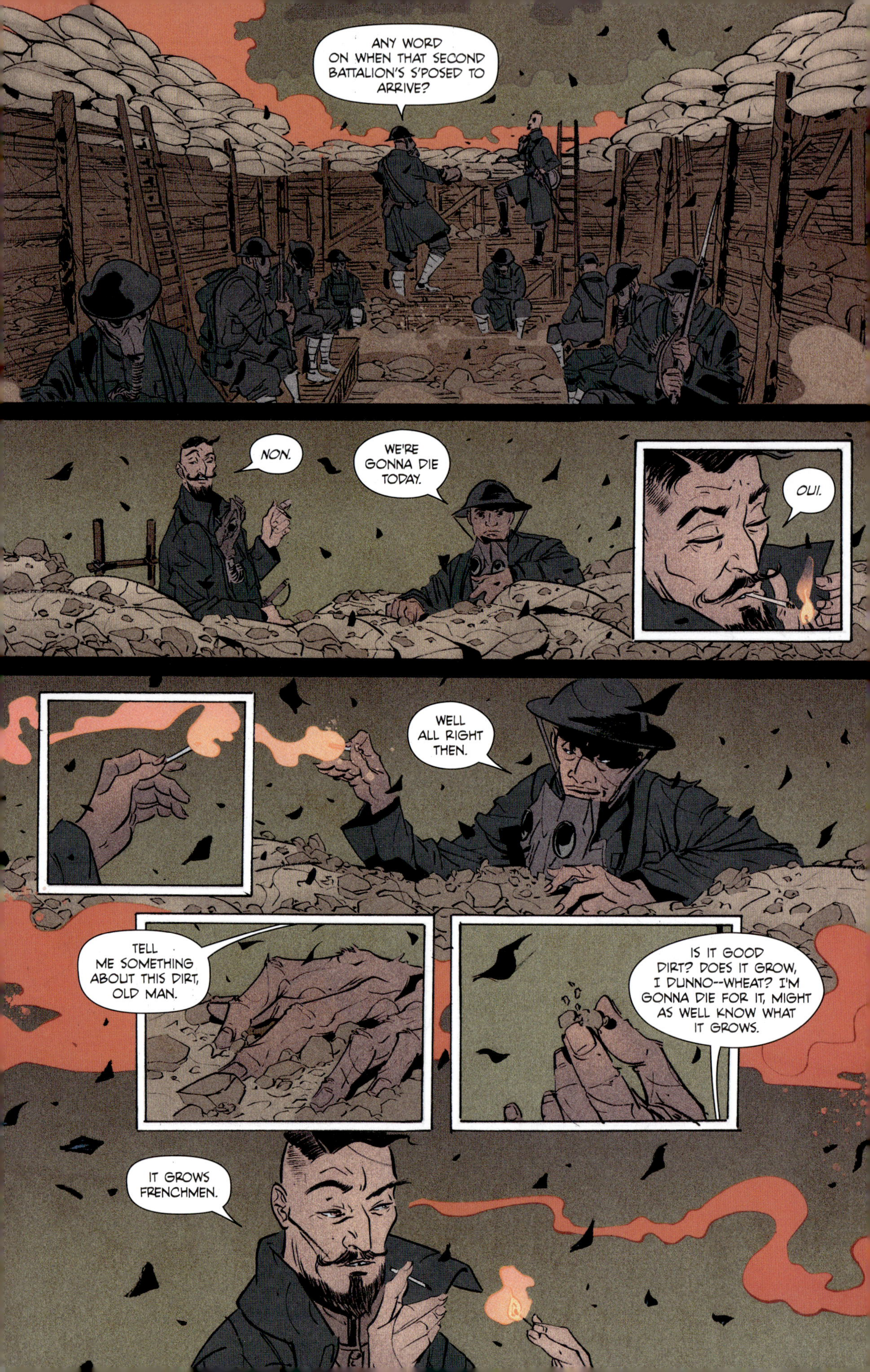
ANY WORD ON WHEN THAT SECOND BATTALION'S S'POSED TO ARRIVE?
NON.
WE'RE GONNA DIE TODAY.
OUI.
WELL ALL RIGHT THEN.
TELL ME SOMETHING ABOUT THIS DIRT, OLD MAN.
IS IT GOOD DIRT? DOES IT GROW, I DUNNO--WHEAT? I'M GONNA DIE FOR IT, MIGHT AS WELL KNOW WHAT IT GROWS.
IT GROWS FRENCHMEN.

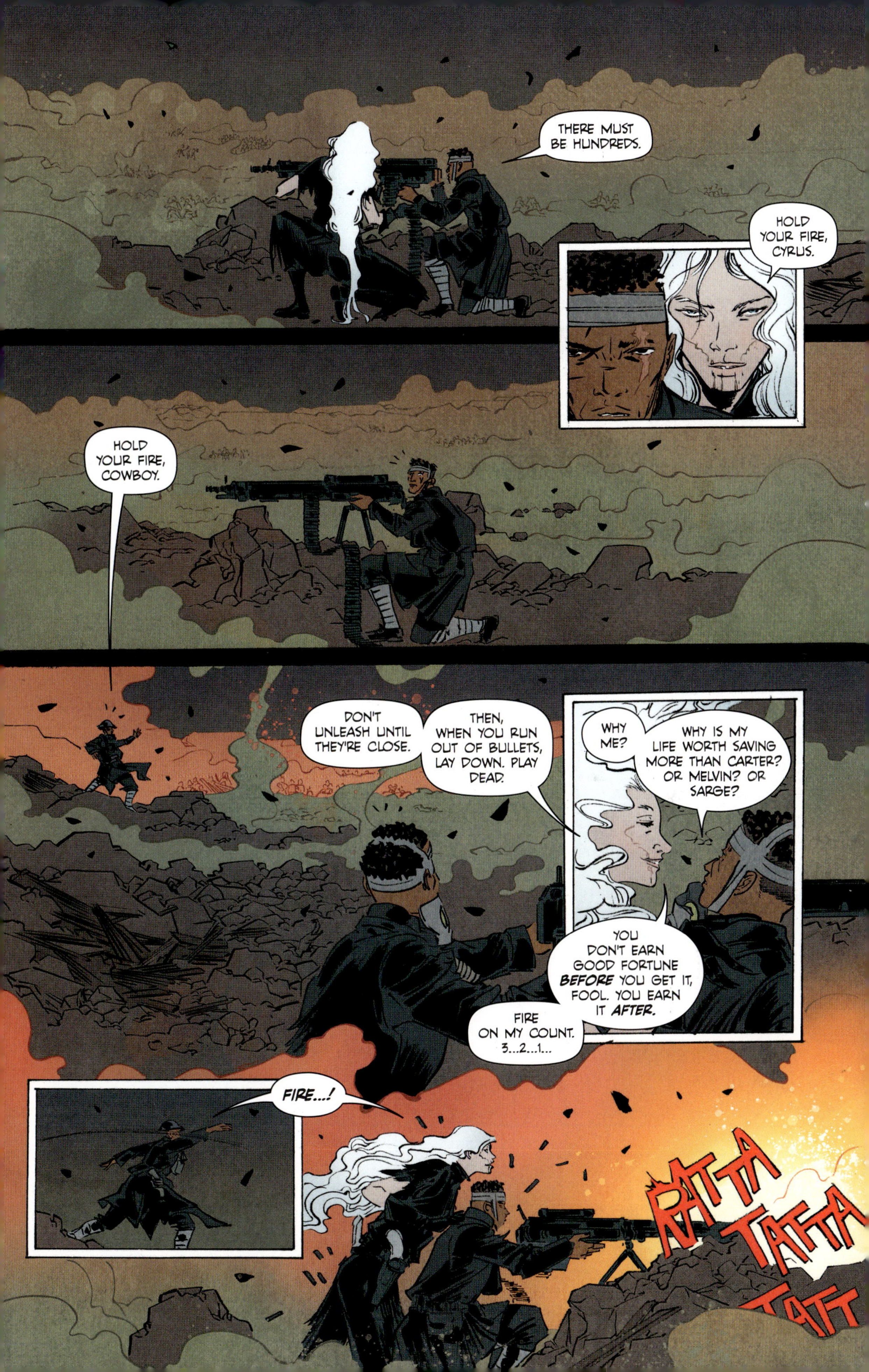
THERE MUST BE HUNDREDS.
HOLD YOUR FIRE, CYRUS.
HOLD YOUR FIRE, COWBOY.
DON'T UNLEASH UNTIL THEY'RE CLOSE.
THEN, WHEN YOU RUN OUT OF BULLETS, LAY DOWN. PLAY DEAD.
WHY ME?
WHY IS MY LIFE WORTH SAVING MORE THAN CARTER? OR MELVIN? OR SARGE?
YOU DON'T EARN GOOD FORTUNE **BEFORE** YOU GET IT, FOOL. YOU EARN IT **AFTER.**
FIRE ON MY COUNT. 3...2...1...
FIRE...!
RATTA TATTA TATT

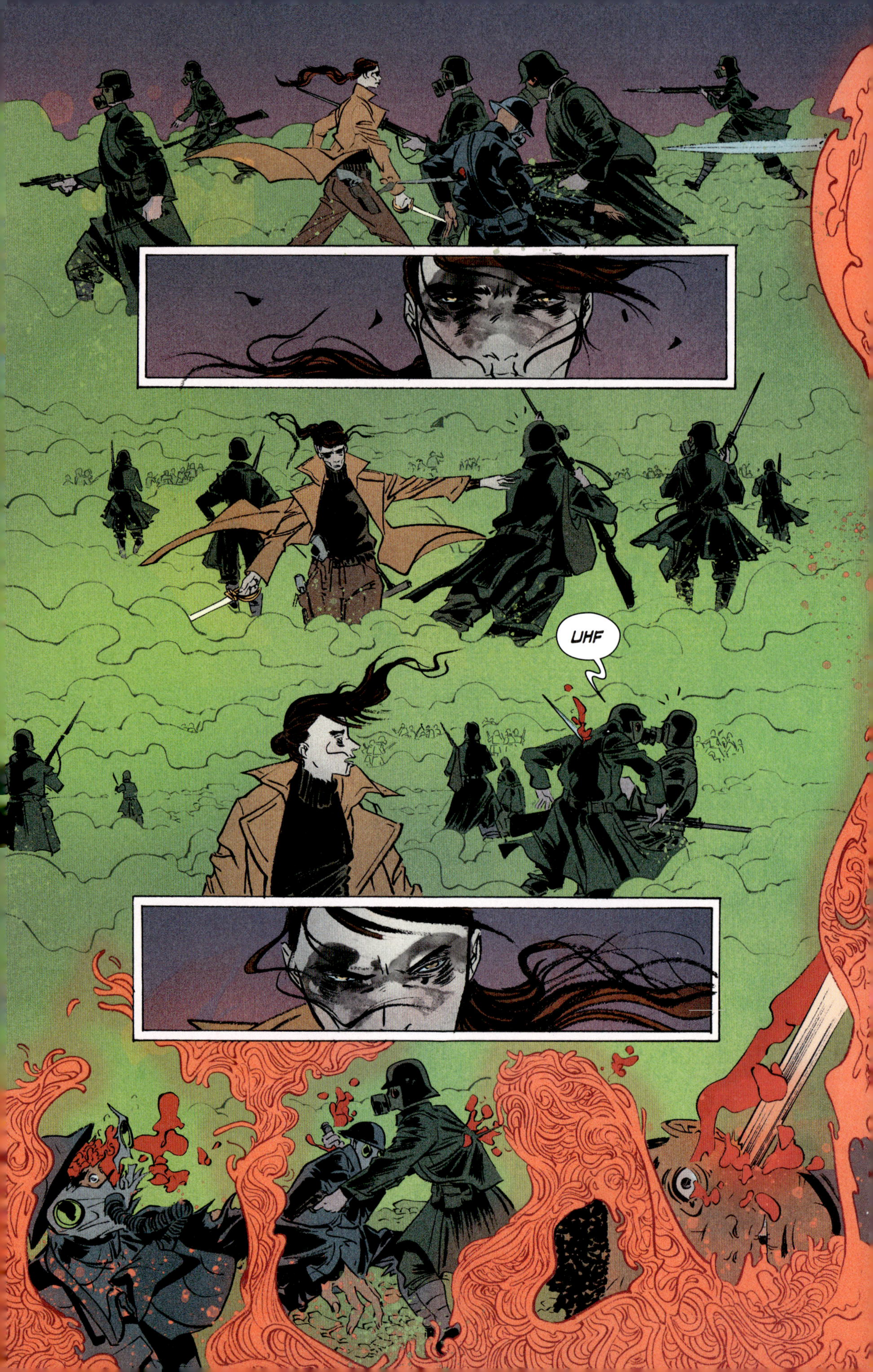
UHF

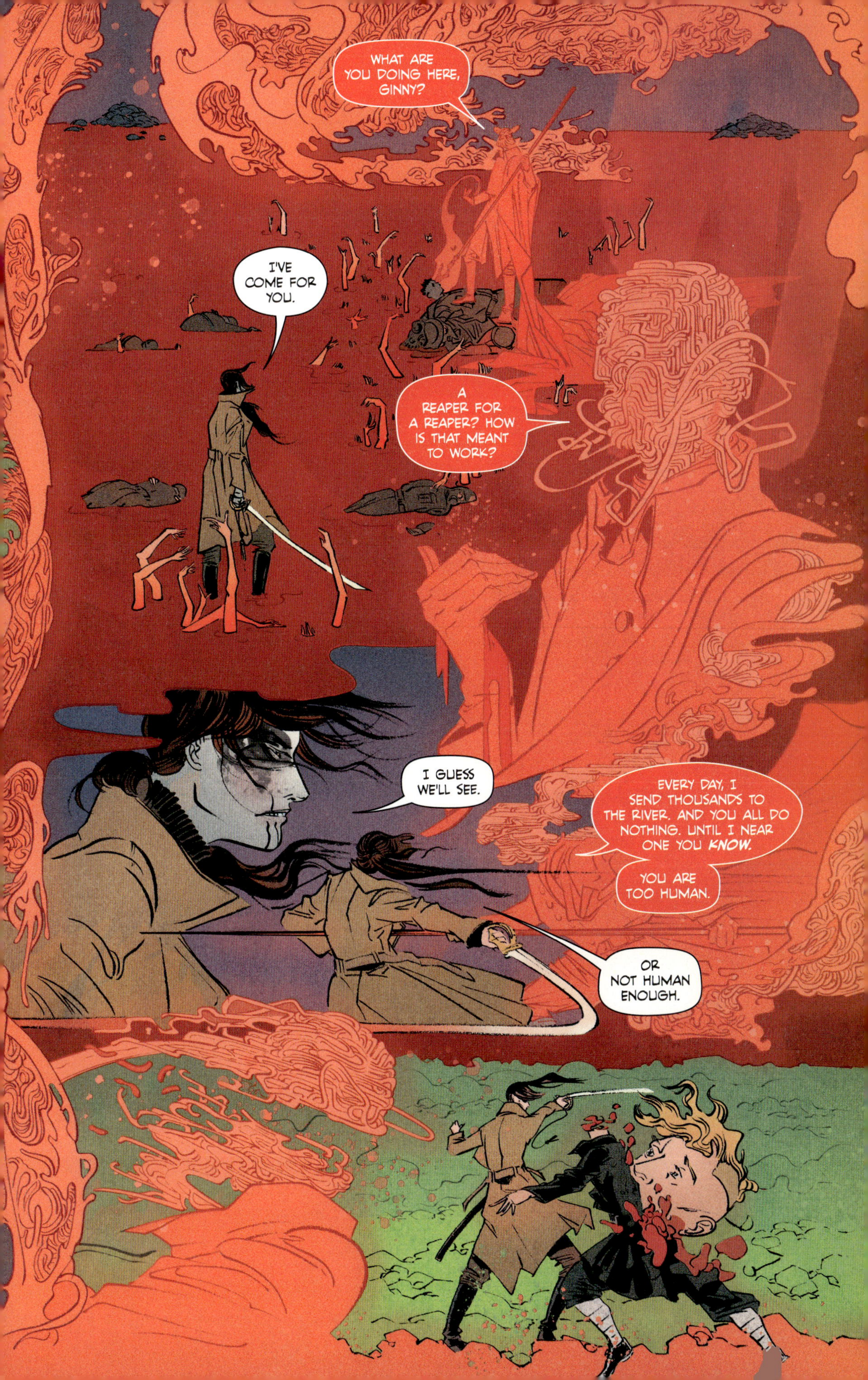
WHAT ARE YOU DOING HERE, GINNY?
I'VE COME FOR YOU.
A REAPER FOR A REAPER? HOW IS THAT MEANT TO WORK?
I GUESS WE'LL SEE.
EVERY DAY, I SEND THOUSANDS TO THE RIVER. AND YOU ALL DO NOTHING. UNTIL I NEAR ONE YOU *KNOW.*
YOU ARE TOO HUMAN.
OR NOT HUMAN ENOUGH.

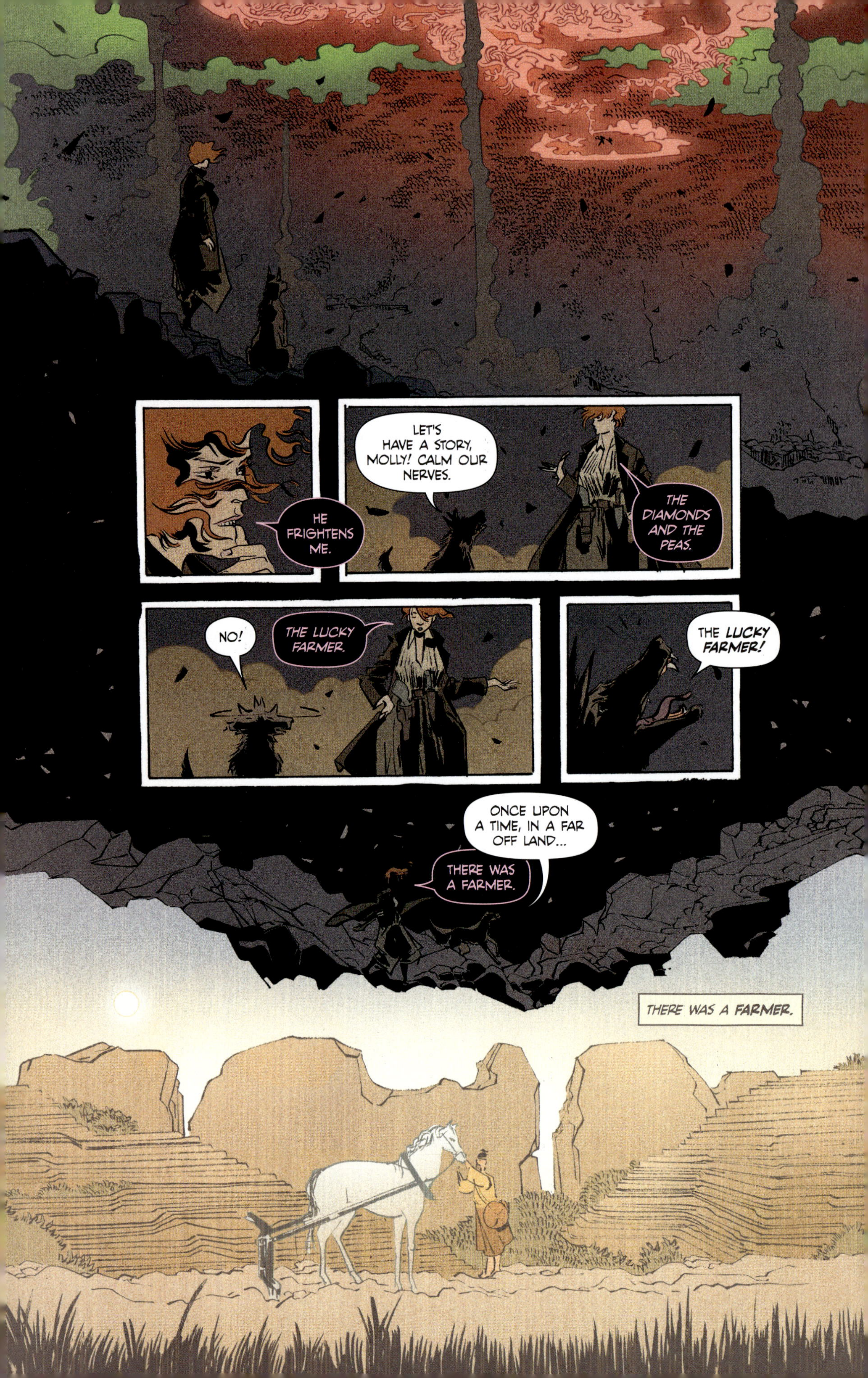
HE FRIGHTENS ME.
LET'S HAVE A STORY, MOLLY! CALM OUR NERVES.
THE DIAMONDS AND THE PEAS.
NO!
THE LUCKY FARMER.
THE LUCKY FARMER!
ONCE UPON A TIME, IN A FAR OFF LAND...
THERE WAS A FARMER.
THERE WAS A FARMER.

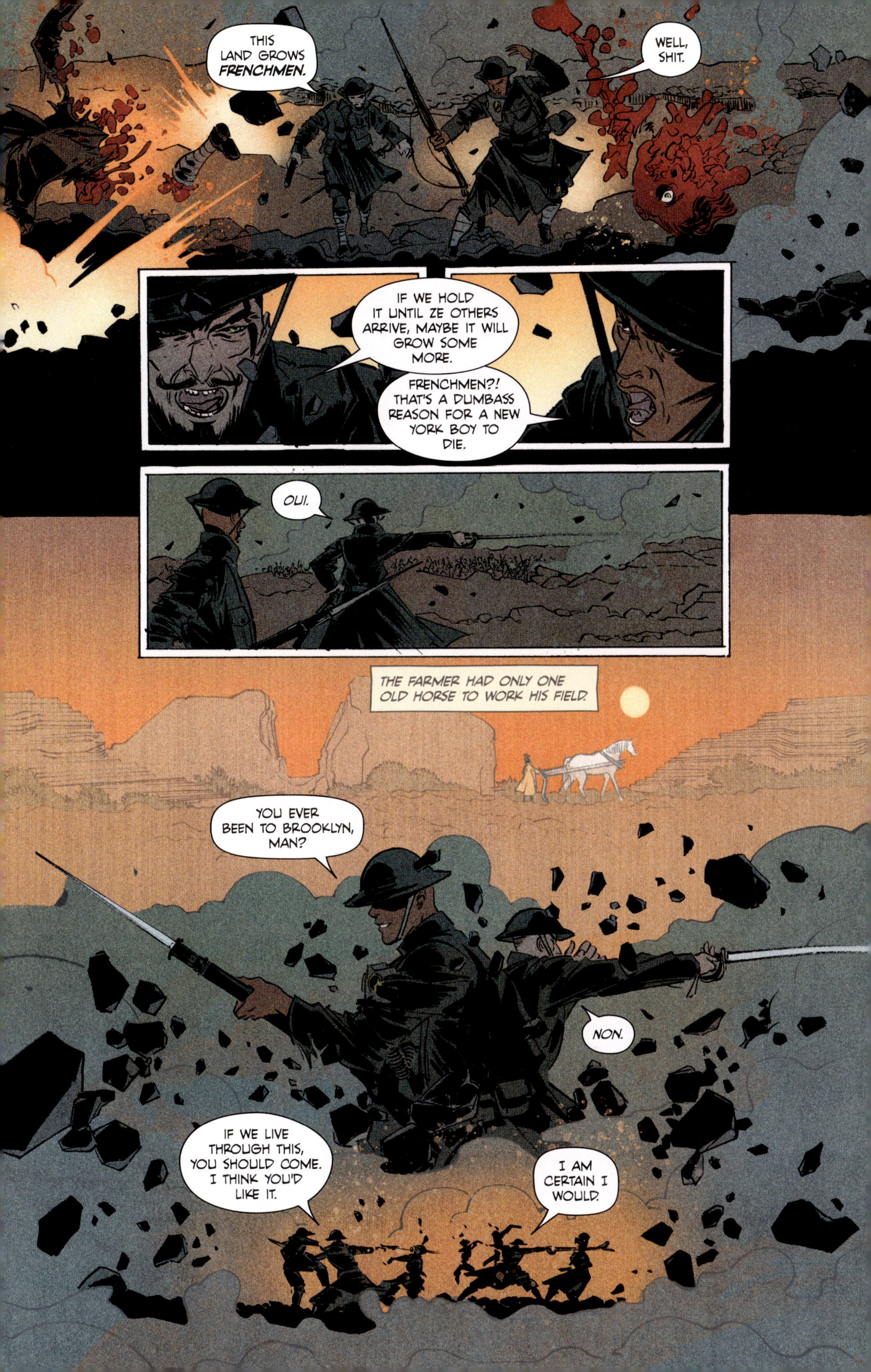
THIS LAND GROWS FRENCHMEN.
WELL, SHIT.
IF WE HOLD IT UNTIL ZE OTHERS ARRIVE, MAYBE IT WILL GROW SOME MORE.
FRENCHMEN?! THAT'S A DUMBASS REASON FOR A NEW YORK BOY TO DIE.
OUI.
THE FARMER HAD ONLY ONE OLD HORSE TO WORK HIS FIELD.
YOU EVER BEEN TO BROOKLYN, MAN?
NON.
IF WE LIVE THROUGH THIS, YOU SHOULD COME. I THINK YOU'D LIKE IT.
I AM CERTAIN I WOULD.

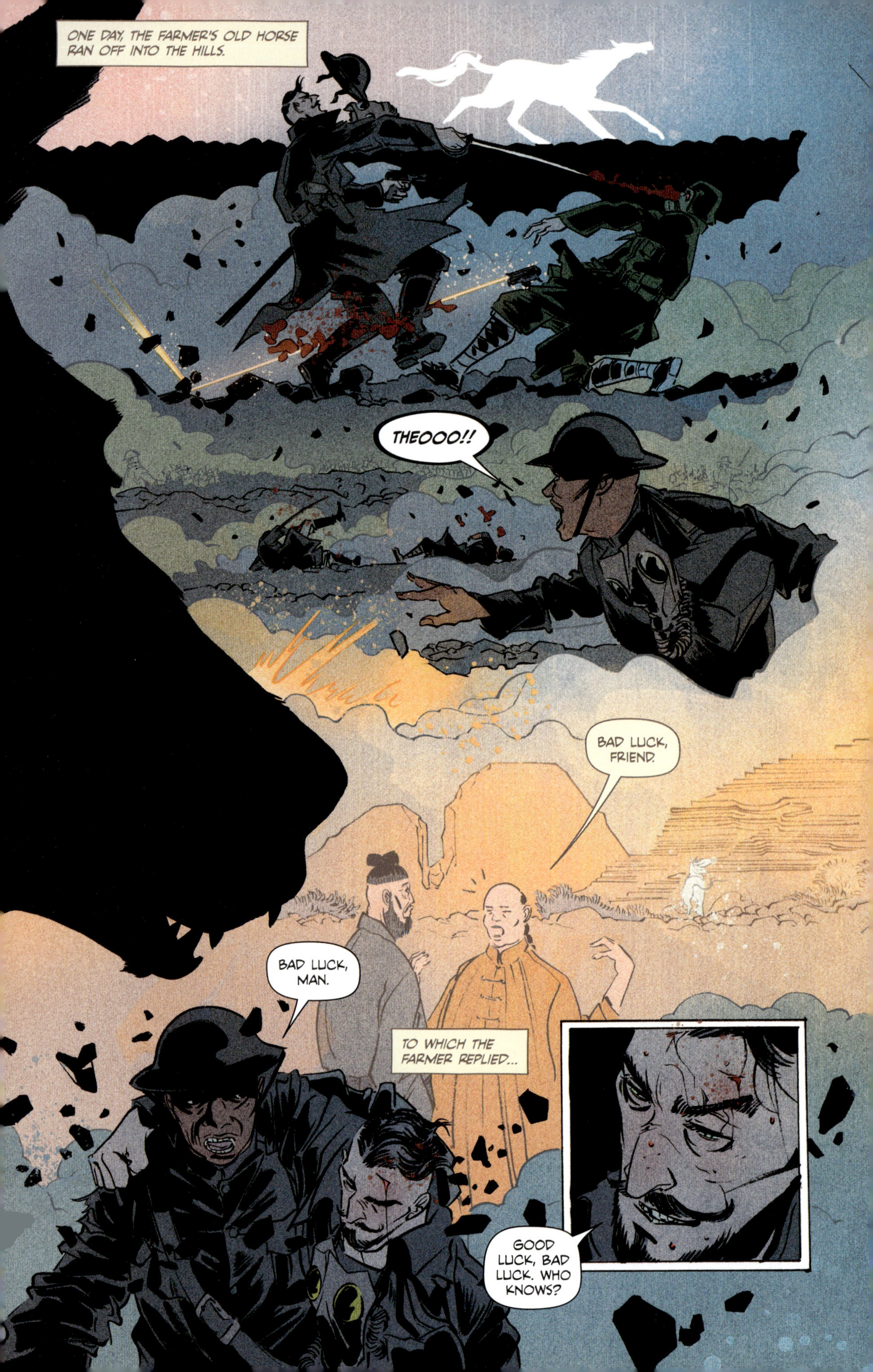
ONE DAY, THE FARMER'S OLD HORSE RAN OFF INTO THE HILLS.
THEOOO!!
BAD LUCK, FRIEND.
BAD LUCK, MAN.
TO WHICH THE FARMER REPLIED...
GOOD LUCK, BAD LUCK. WHO KNOWS?

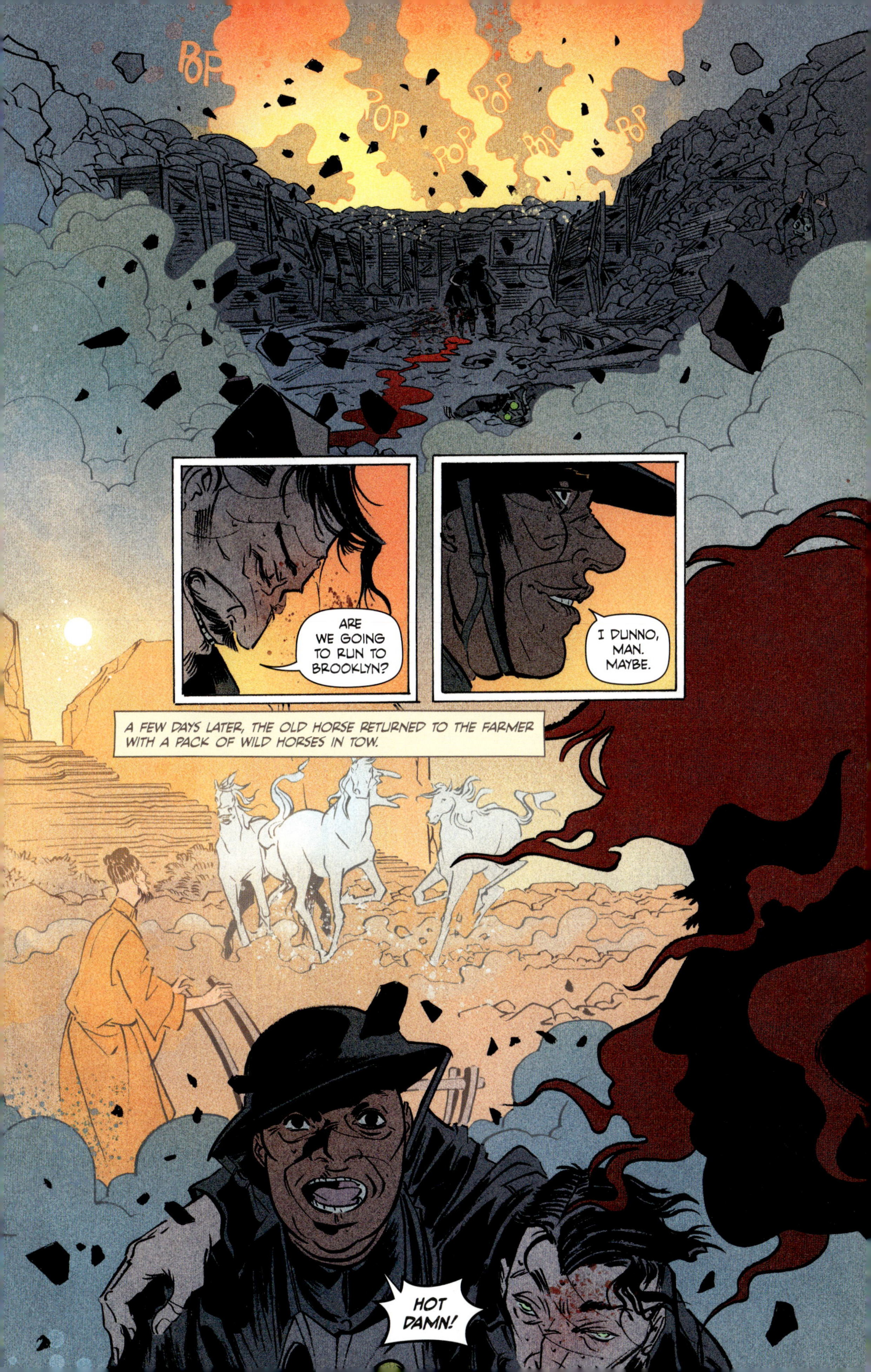
POP
POP
POP
POP
POP
POP
ARE WE GOING TO RUN TO BROOKLYN?
I DUNNO, MAN. MAYBE.
A FEW DAYS LATER, THE OLD HORSE RETURNED TO THE FARMER WITH A PACK OF WILD HORSES IN TOW.
HOT DAMN!

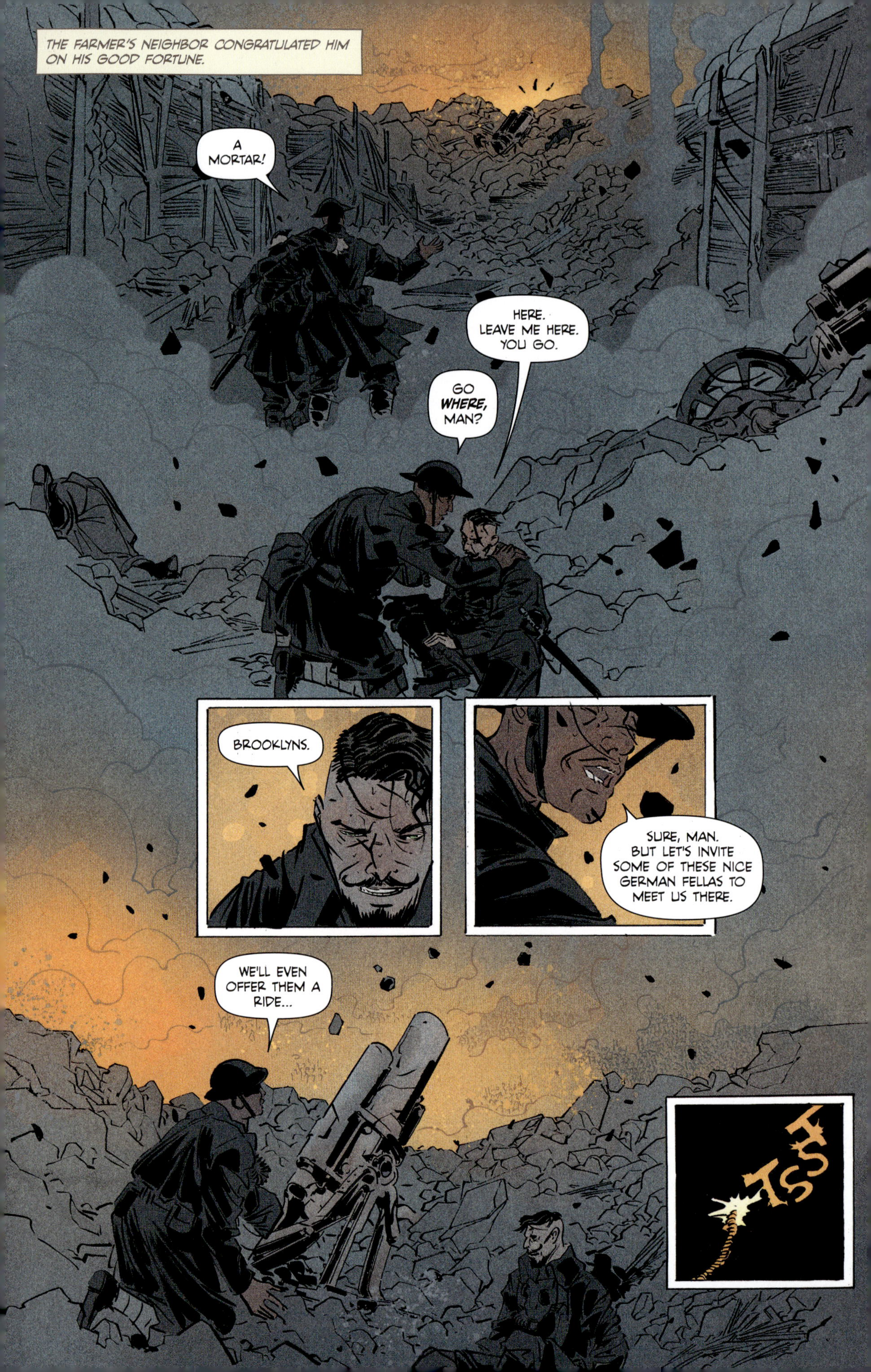
THE FARMER'S NEIGHBOR CONGRATULATED HIM ON HIS GOOD FORTUNE.
A MORTAR!
HERE. LEAVE ME HERE. YOU GO.
GO WHERE, MAN?
BROOKLYNS.
SURE, MAN. BUT LET'S INVITE SOME OF THESE NICE GERMAN FELLAS TO MEET US THERE.
WE'LL EVEN OFFER THEM A RIDE...
TSSH

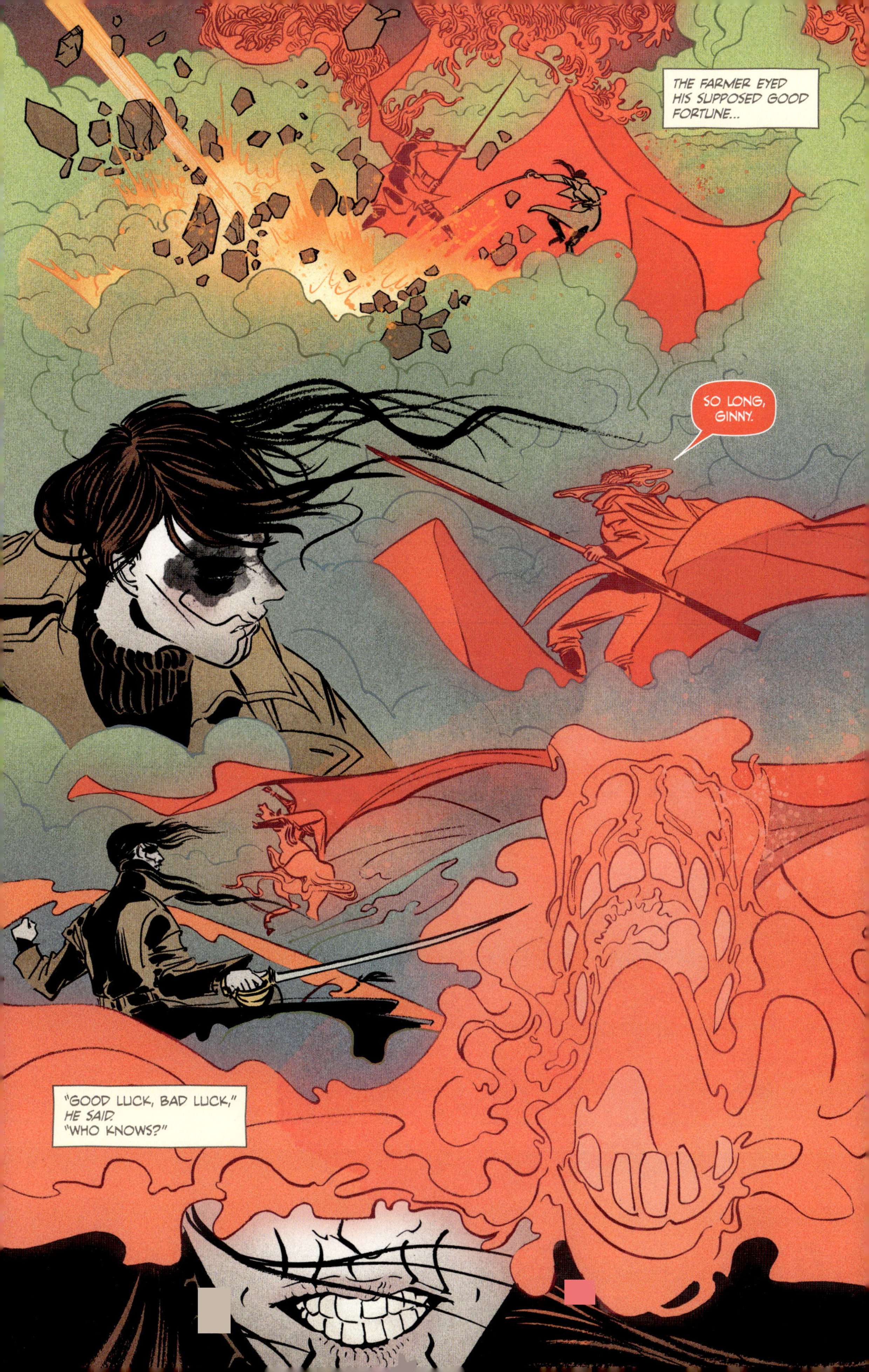
THE FARMER EYED HIS SUPPOSED GOOD FORTUNE...
SO LONG, GINNY.
"GOOD LUCK, BAD LUCK," HE SAID. "WHO KNOWS?"

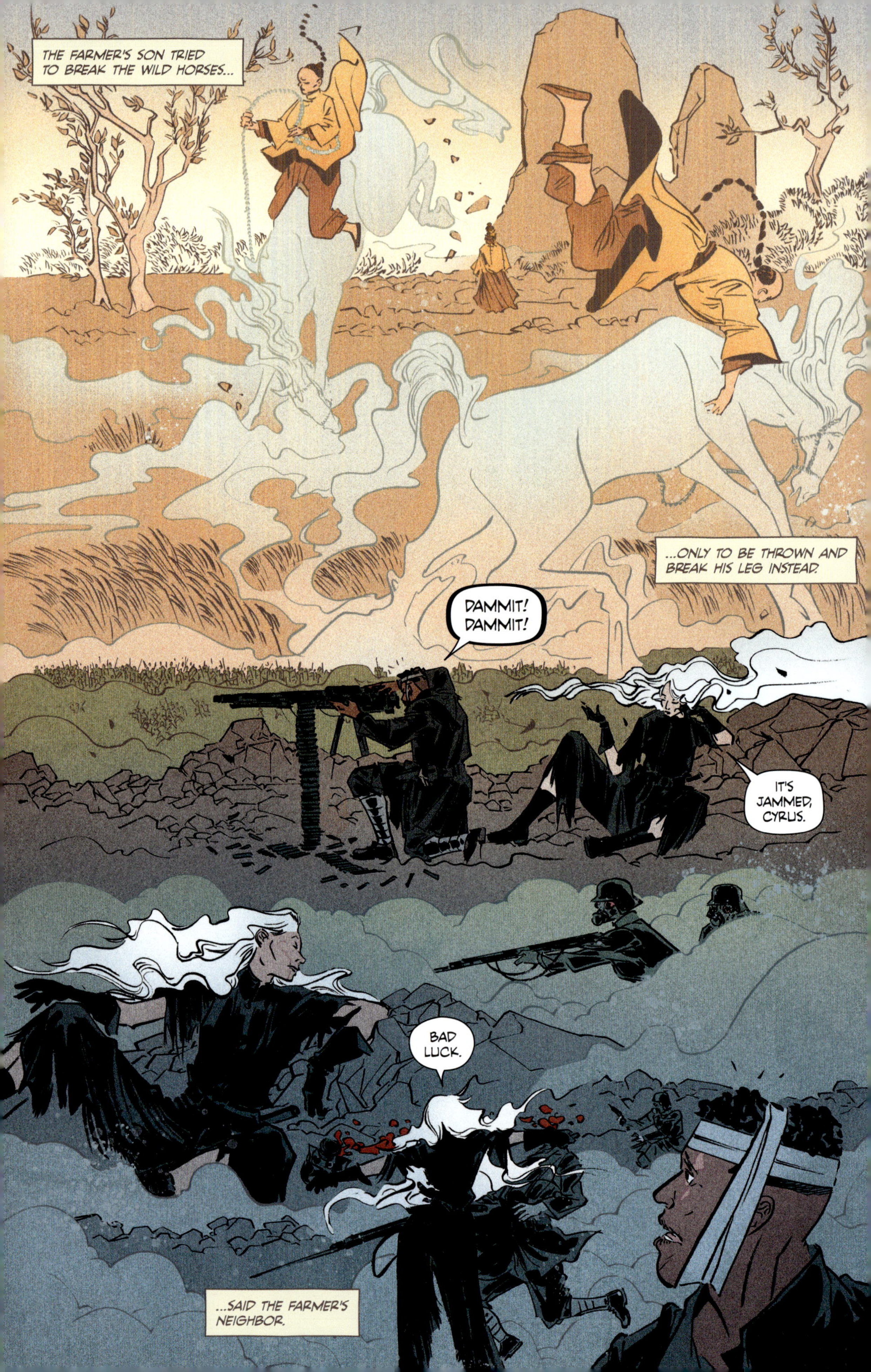
THE FARMER'S SON TRIED TO BREAK THE WILD HORSES...
...ONLY TO BE THROWN AND BREAK HIS LEG INSTEAD.
DAMMIT! DAMMIT!
IT'S JAMMED, CYRUS.
BAD LUCK.
...SAID THE FARMER'S NEIGHBOR.

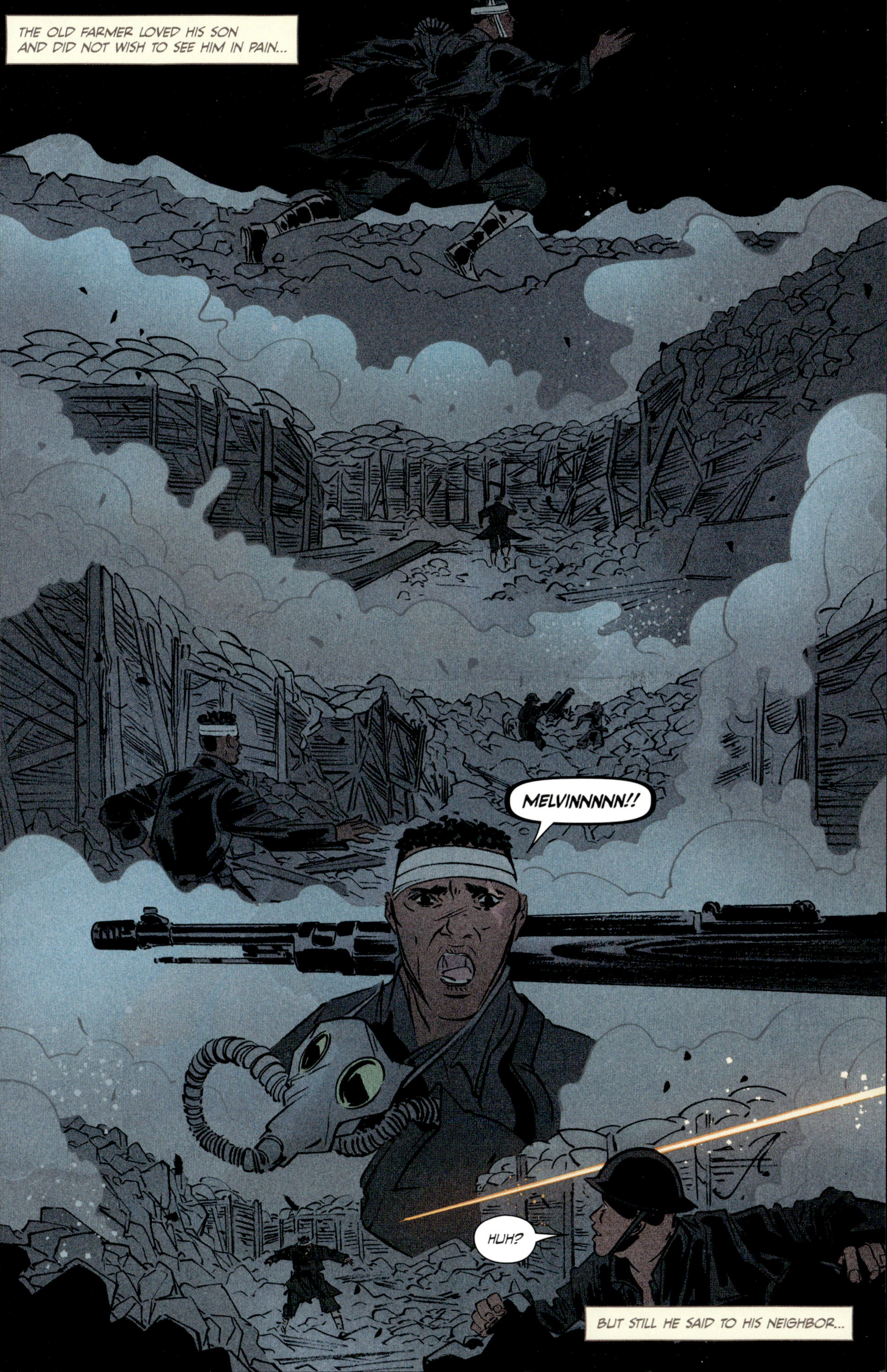
THE OLD FARMER LOVED HIS SON AND DID NOT WISH TO SEE HIM IN PAIN...
MELVINNNNN!!
HUH?
BUT STILL HE SAID TO HIS NEIGHBOR...

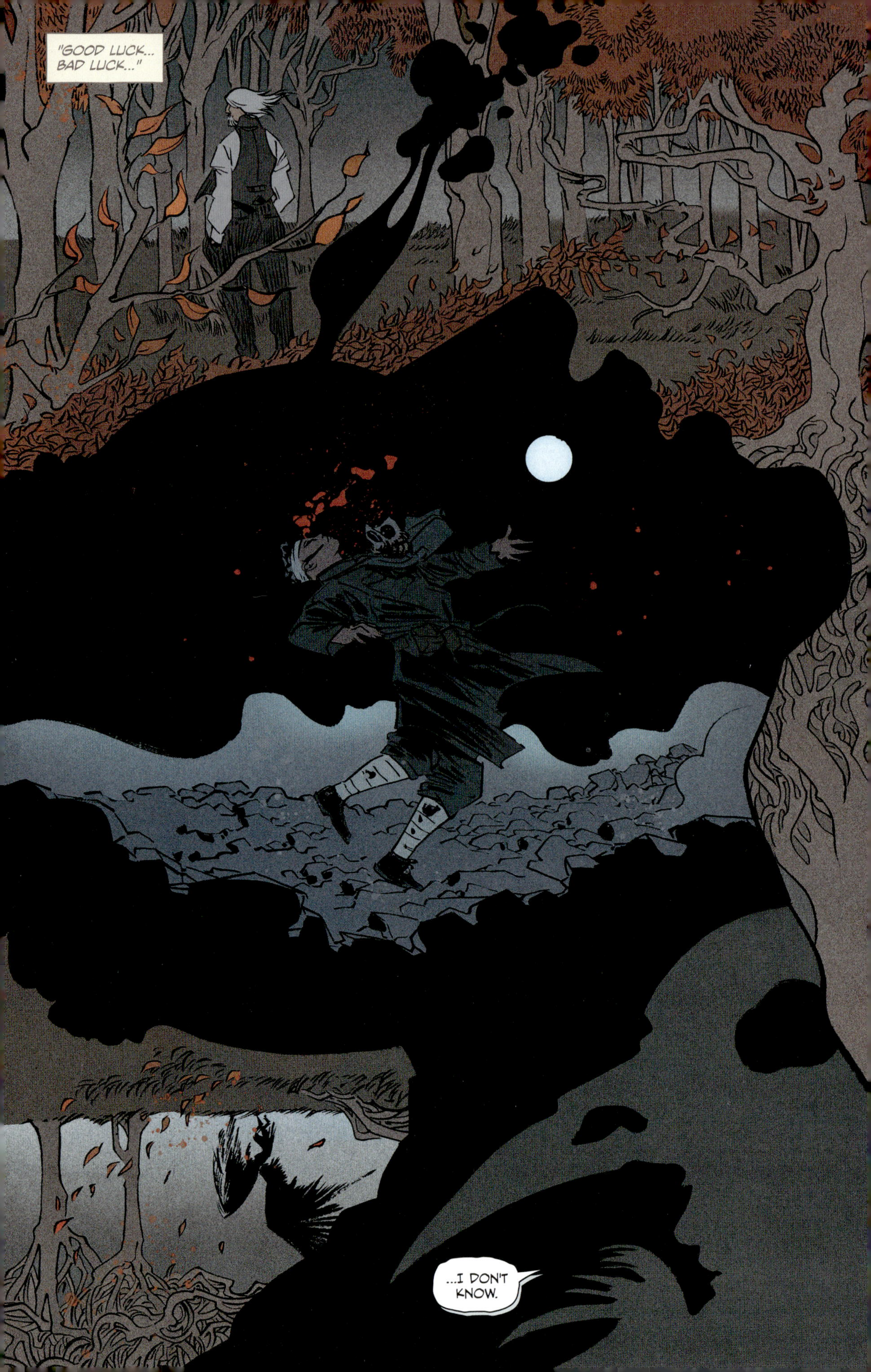
"GOOD LUCK...
BAD LUCK..."
...I DON'T KNOW.

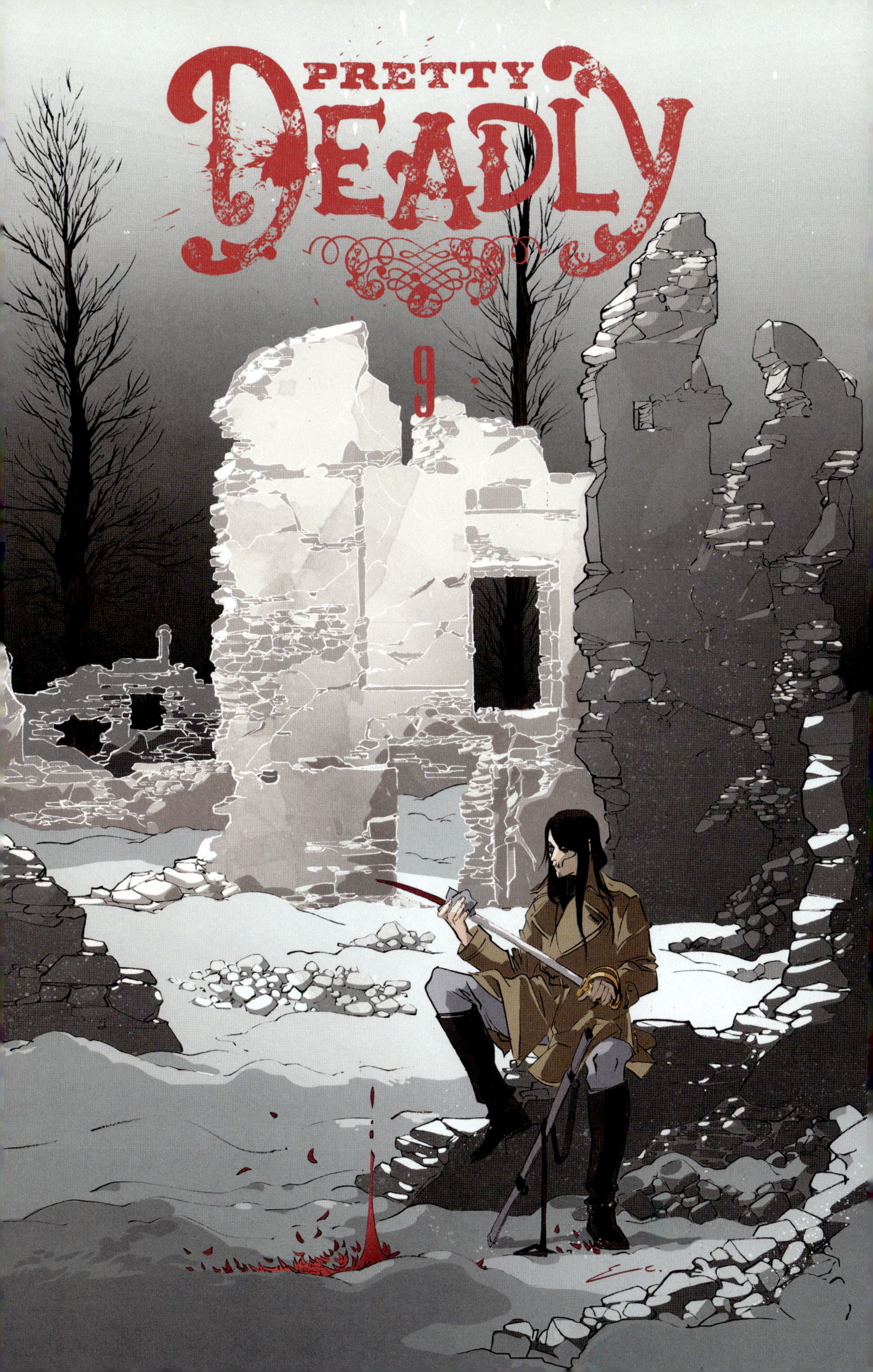

PRETTY
DEADLY
9

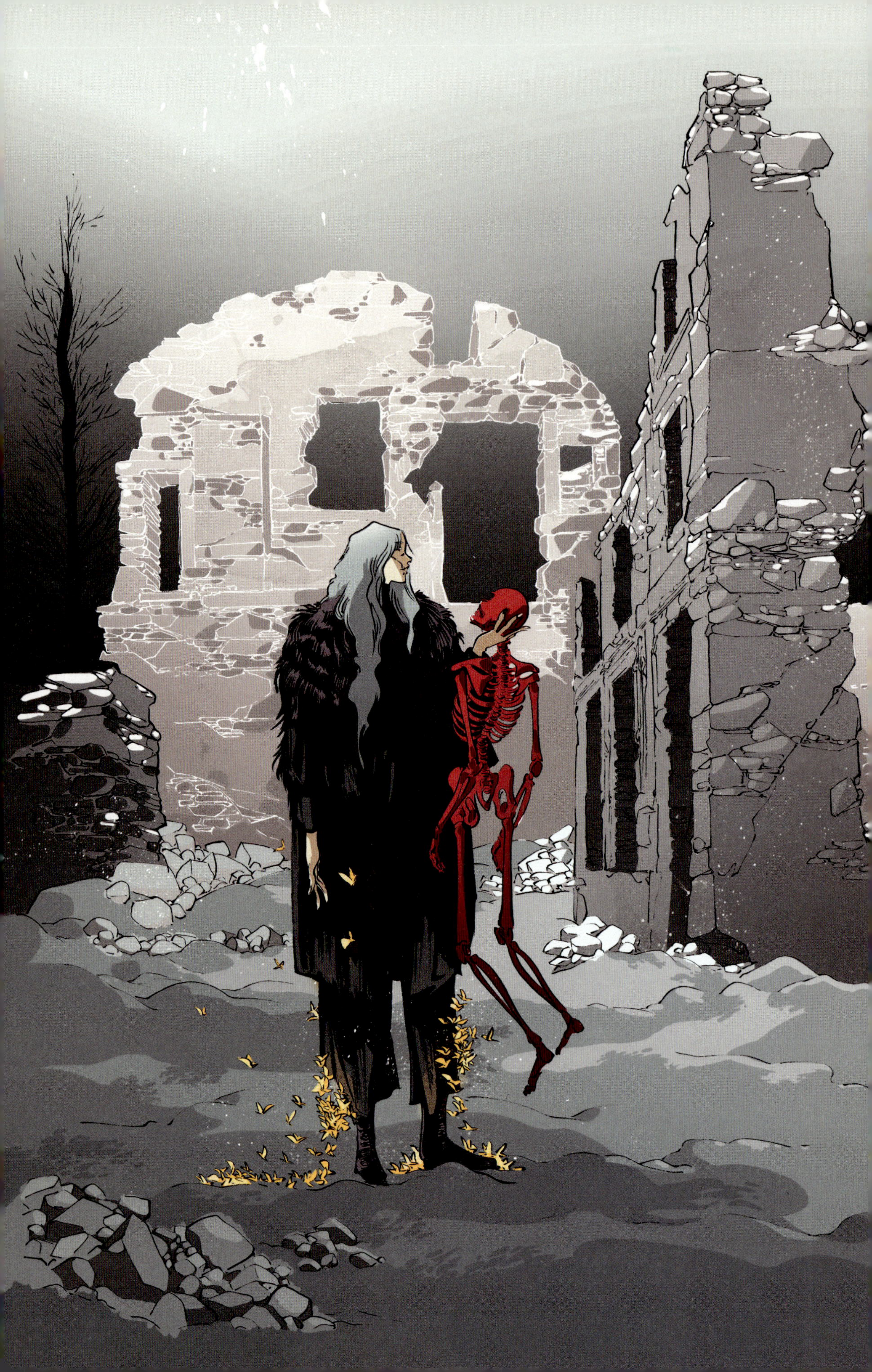

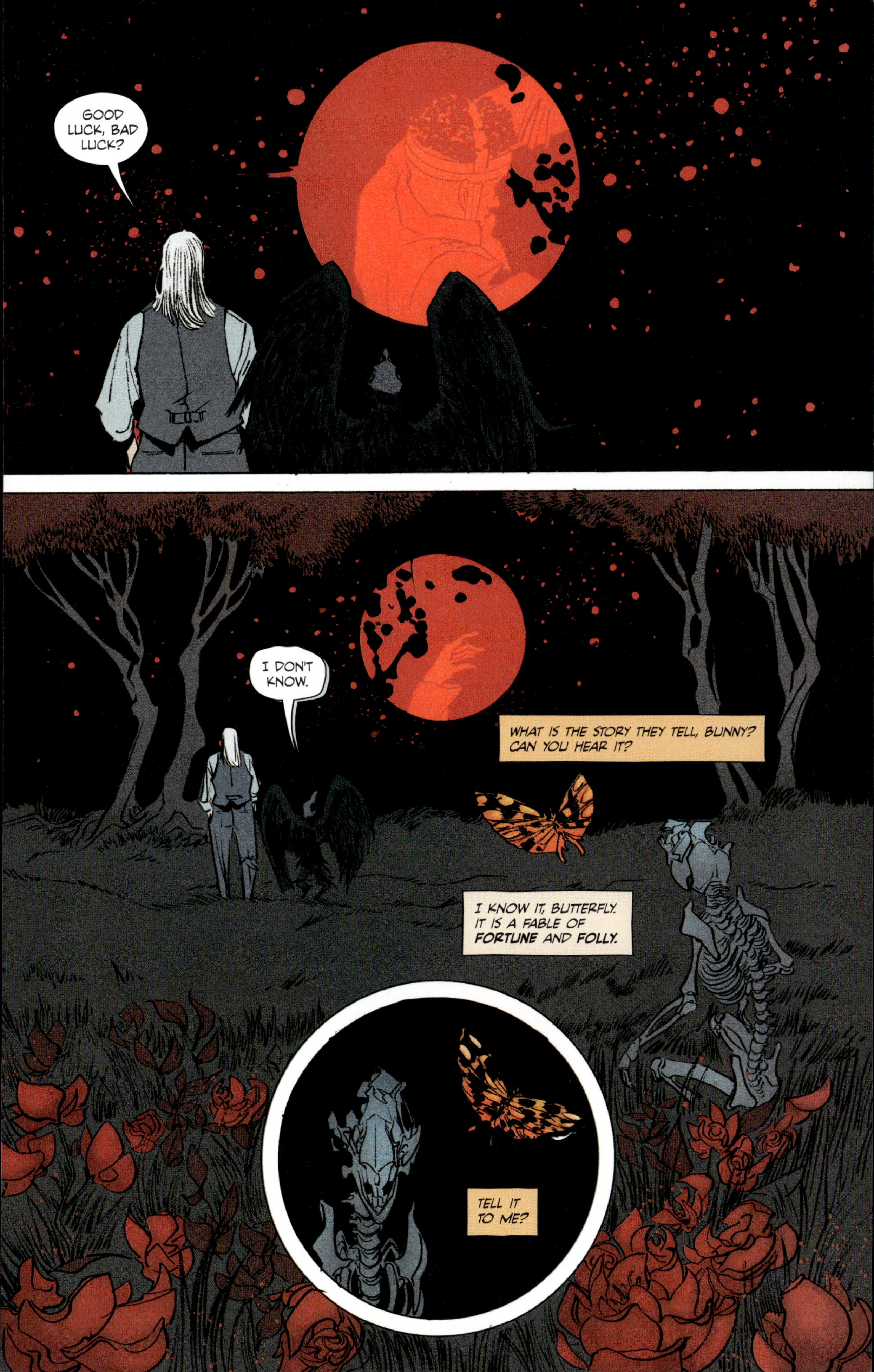
GOOD LUCK, BAD LUCK?
I DON'T KNOW.
WHAT IS THE STORY THEY TELL, BUNNY? CAN YOU HEAR IT?
I KNOW IT, BUTTERFLY. IT IS A FABLE OF **FORTUNE** AND **FOLLY.**
TELL IT TO ME?

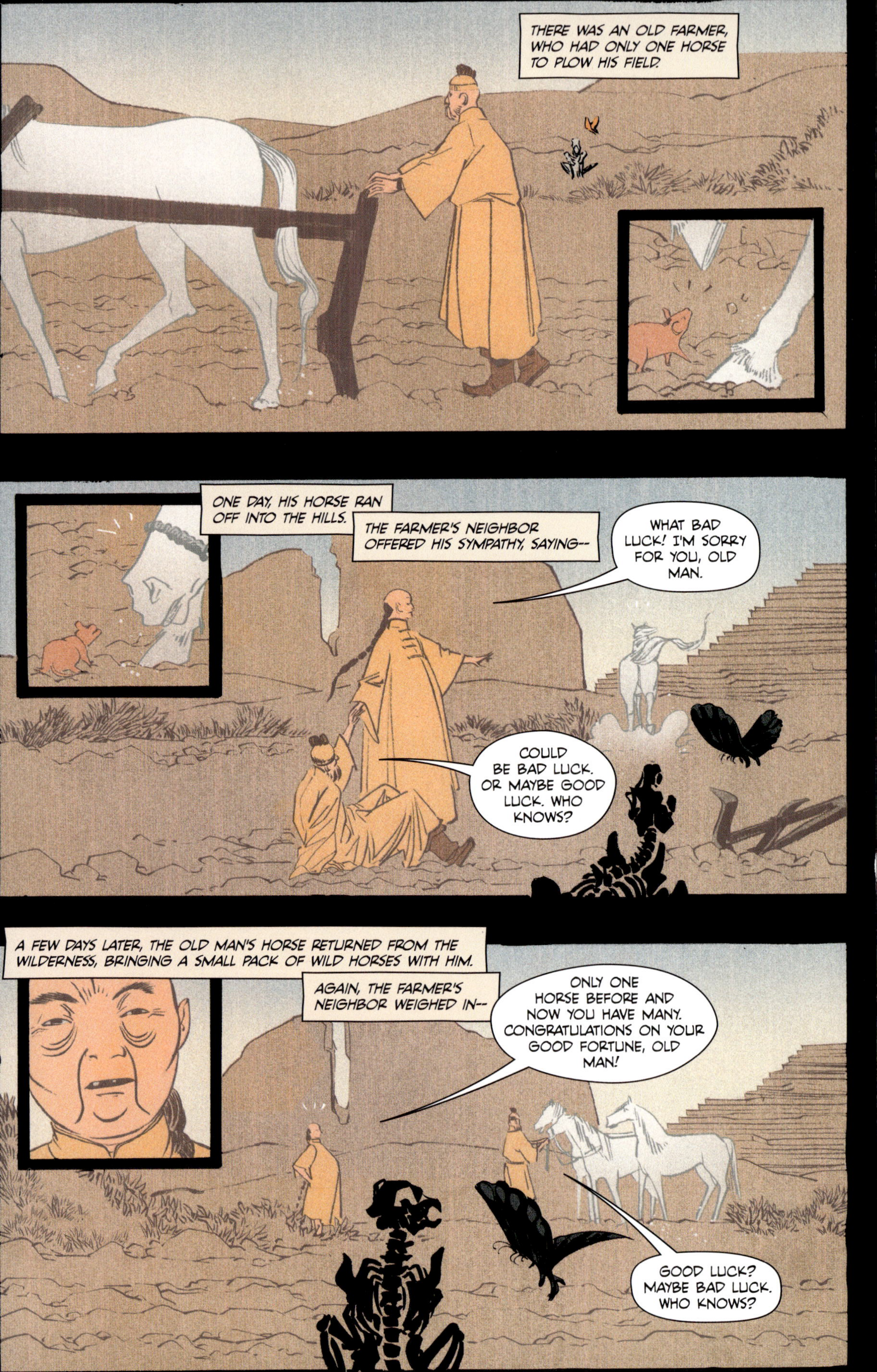
THERE WAS AN OLD FARMER, WHO HAD ONLY ONE HORSE TO PLOW HIS FIELD.
ONE DAY, HIS HORSE RAN OFF INTO THE HILLS.
THE FARMER'S NEIGHBOR OFFERED HIS SYMPATHY, SAYING--
WHAT BAD LUCK! I'M SORRY FOR YOU, OLD MAN.
COULD BE BAD LUCK. OR MAYBE GOOD LUCK. WHO KNOWS?
A FEW DAYS LATER, THE OLD MAN'S HORSE RETURNED FROM THE WILDERNESS, BRINGING A SMALL PACK OF WILD HORSES WITH HIM.
AGAIN, THE FARMER'S NEIGHBOR WEIGHED IN--
ONLY ONE HORSE BEFORE AND NOW YOU HAVE MANY. CONGRATULATIONS ON YOUR GOOD FORTUNE, OLD MAN!
GOOD LUCK? MAYBE BAD LUCK. WHO KNOWS?

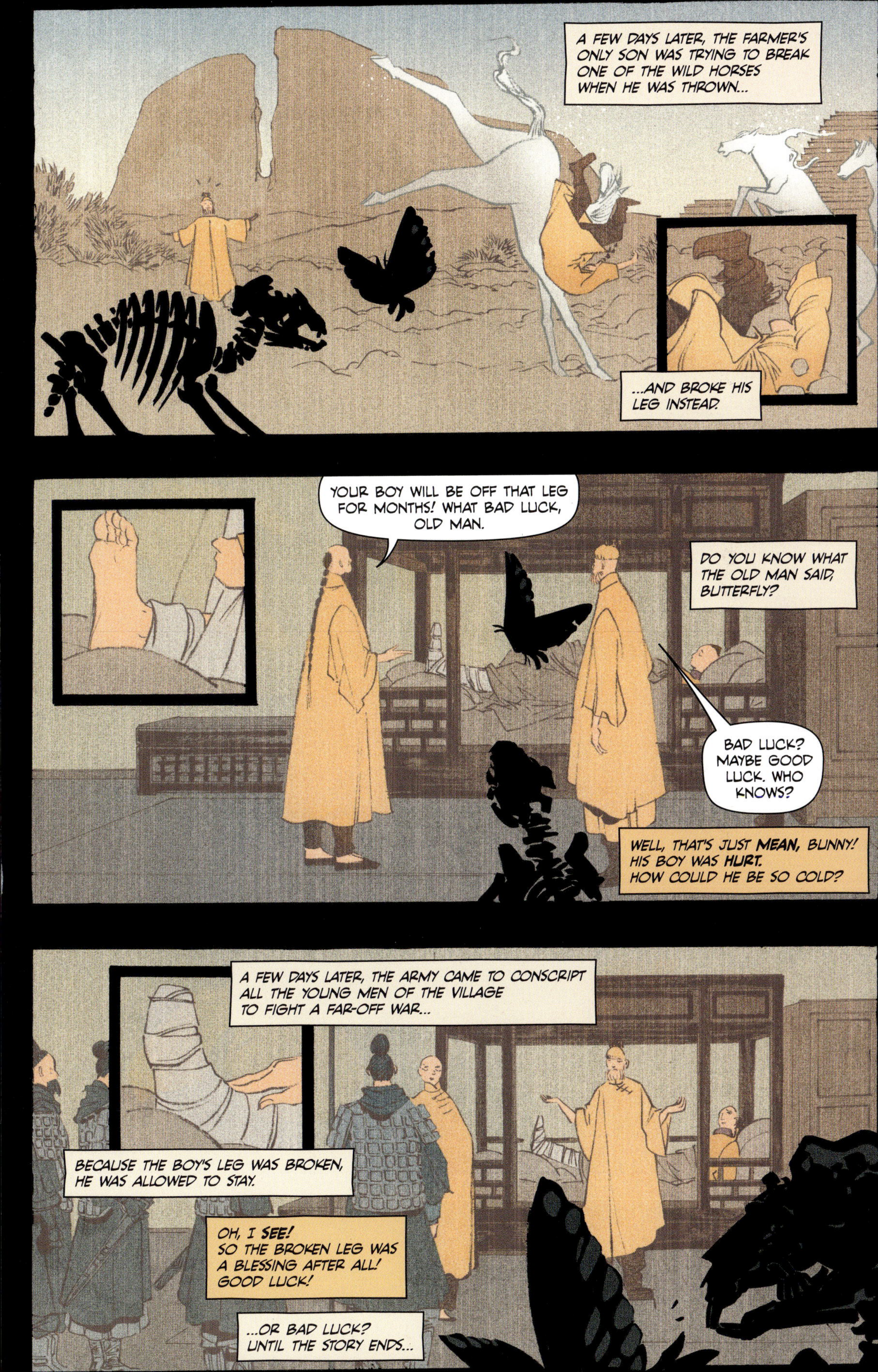

A FEW DAYS LATER, THE FARMER'S ONLY SON WAS TRYING TO BREAK ONE OF THE WILD HORSES WHEN HE WAS THROWN...
...AND BROKE HIS LEG INSTEAD.
YOUR BOY WILL BE OFF THAT LEG FOR MONTHS! WHAT BAD LUCK, OLD MAN.
DO YOU KNOW WHAT THE OLD MAN SAID, BUTTERFLY?
BAD LUCK? MAYBE GOOD LUCK. WHO KNOWS?
WELL, THAT'S JUST MEAN, BUNNY! HIS BOY WAS HURT. HOW COULD HE BE SO COLD?
A FEW DAYS LATER, THE ARMY CAME TO CONSCRIPT ALL THE YOUNG MEN OF THE VILLAGE TO FIGHT A FAR-OFF WAR...
BECAUSE THE BOY'S LEG WAS BROKEN, HE WAS ALLOWED TO STAY.
OH, I SEE! SO THE BROKEN LEG WAS A BLESSING AFTER ALL! GOOD LUCK!
...OR BAD LUCK? UNTIL THE STORY ENDS...

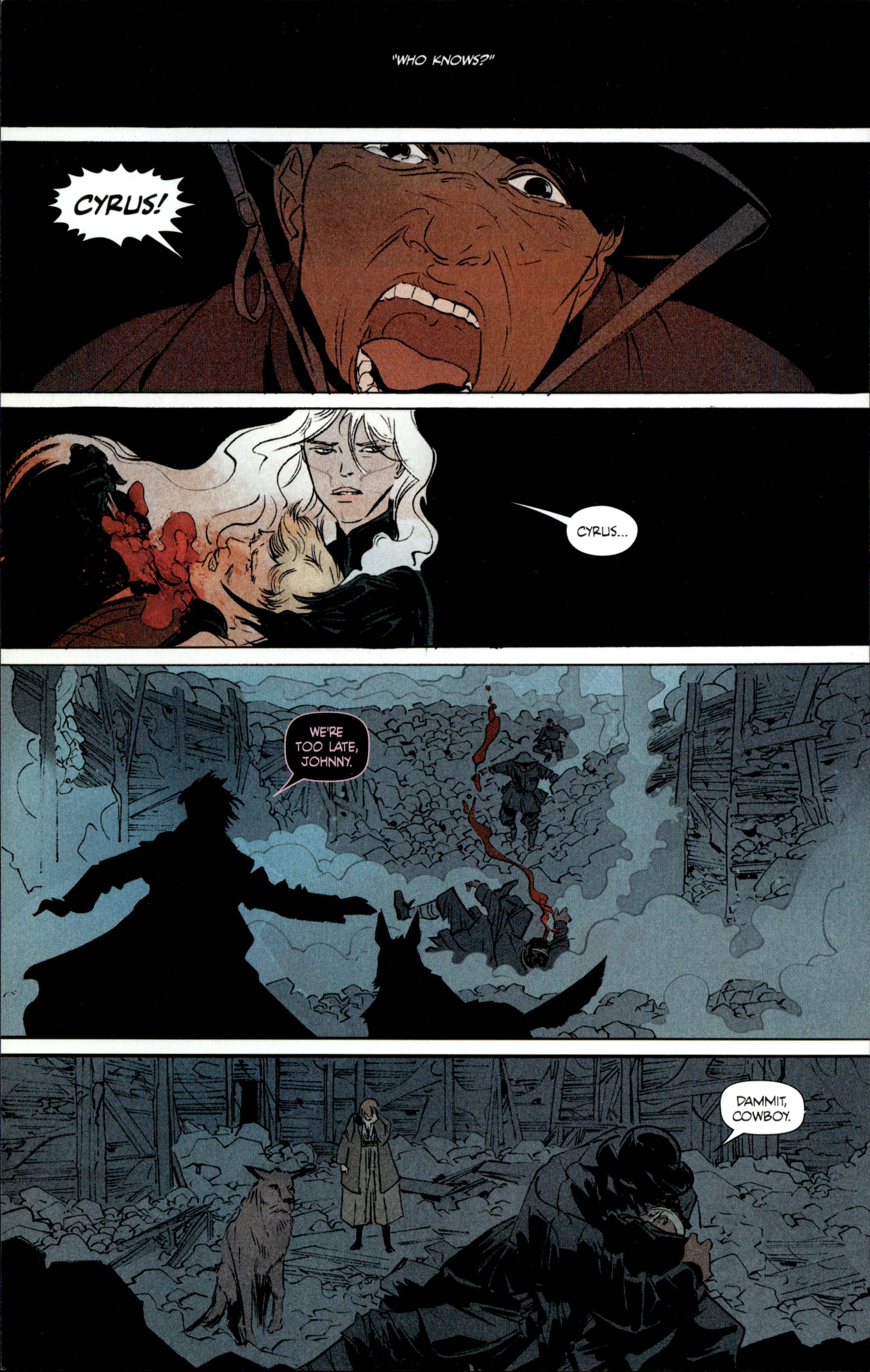
"WHO KNOWS?"
CYRUS!
CYRUS...
WE'RE TOO LATE, JOHNNY.
DAMMIT, COWBOY.

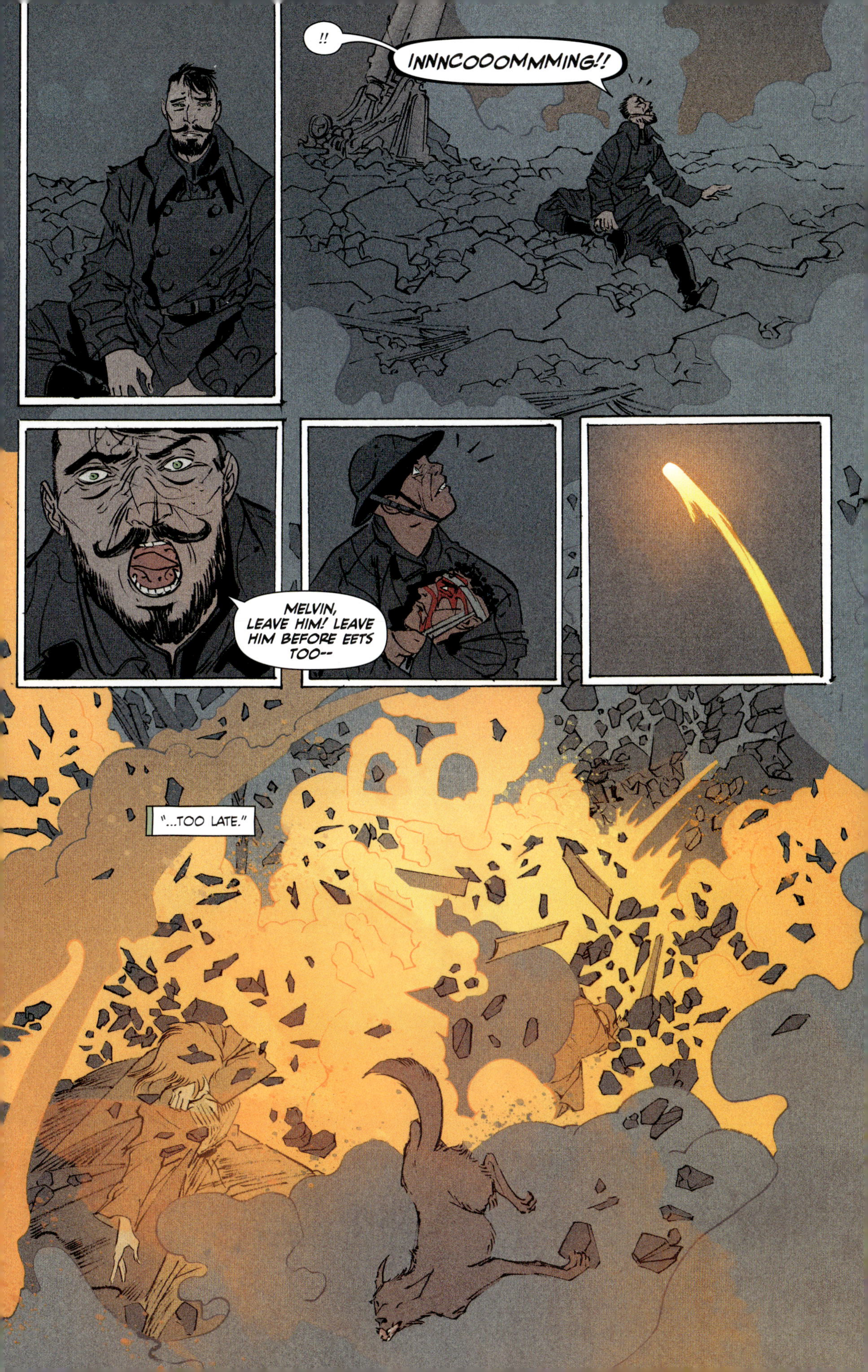
!!
INNNCOOOMMMING!!
MELVIN, LEAVE HIM! LEAVE HIM BEFORE EETS TOO--
"...TOO LATE."

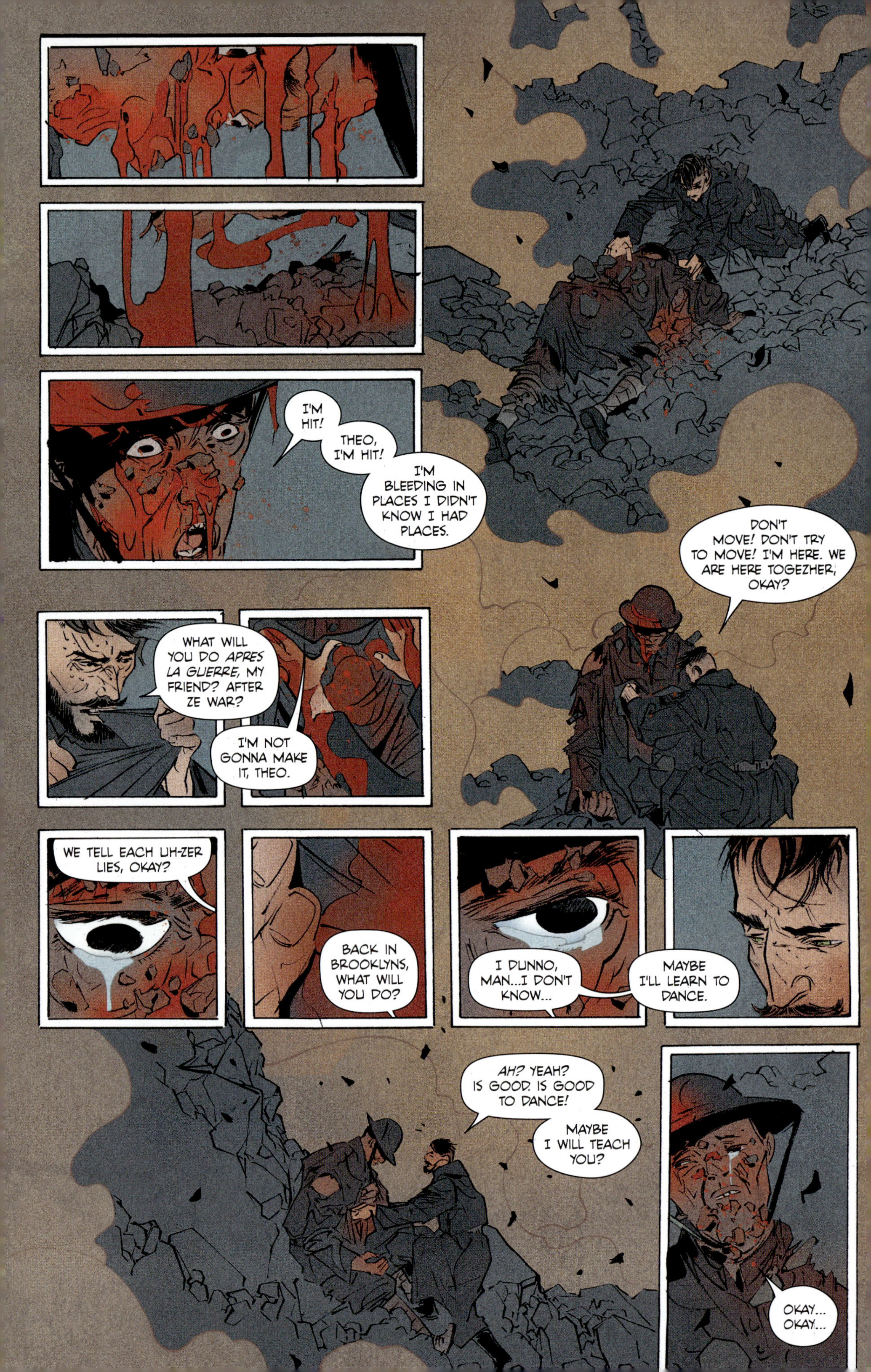
I'M HIT!
THEO, I'M HIT!
I'M BLEEDING IN PLACES I DIDN'T KNOW I HAD PLACES.
DON'T MOVE! DON'T TRY TO MOVE! I'M HERE. WE ARE HERE TOGEZHER, OKAY?
WHAT WILL YOU DO *APRES LA GUERRE*, MY FRIEND? AFTER ZE WAR?
I'M NOT GONNA MAKE IT, THEO.
WE TELL EACH UH-ZER LIES, OKAY?
BACK IN BROOKLYNS, WHAT WILL YOU DO?
I DUNNO, MAN...I DON'T KNOW...
MAYBE I'LL LEARN TO DANCE.
AH? YEAH? IS GOOD. IS GOOD TO DANCE!
MAYBE I WILL TEACH YOU?
OKAY... OKAY...

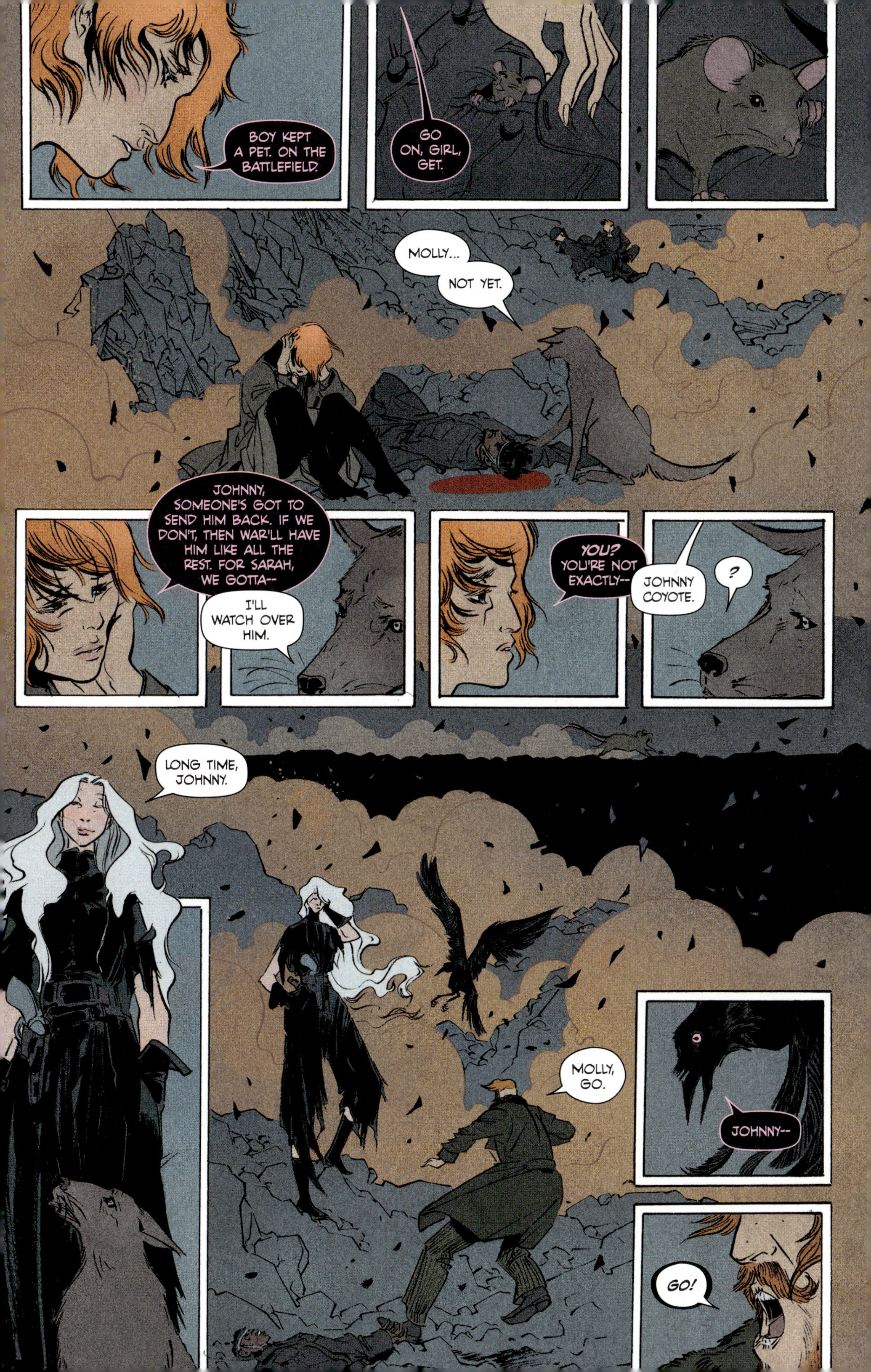
BOY KEPT A PET. ON THE BATTLEFIELD.
GO ON, GIRL, GET.
MOLLY...
NOT YET.
JOHNNY, SOMEONE'S GOT TO SEND HIM BACK. IF WE DON'T, THEN WAR'LL HAVE HIM LIKE ALL THE REST. FOR SARAH, WE GOTTA--
I'LL WATCH OVER HIM.
YOU? YOU'RE NOT EXACTLY--
JOHNNY COYOTE.
?
LONG TIME, JOHNNY.
MOLLY, GO.
JOHNNY--
GO!

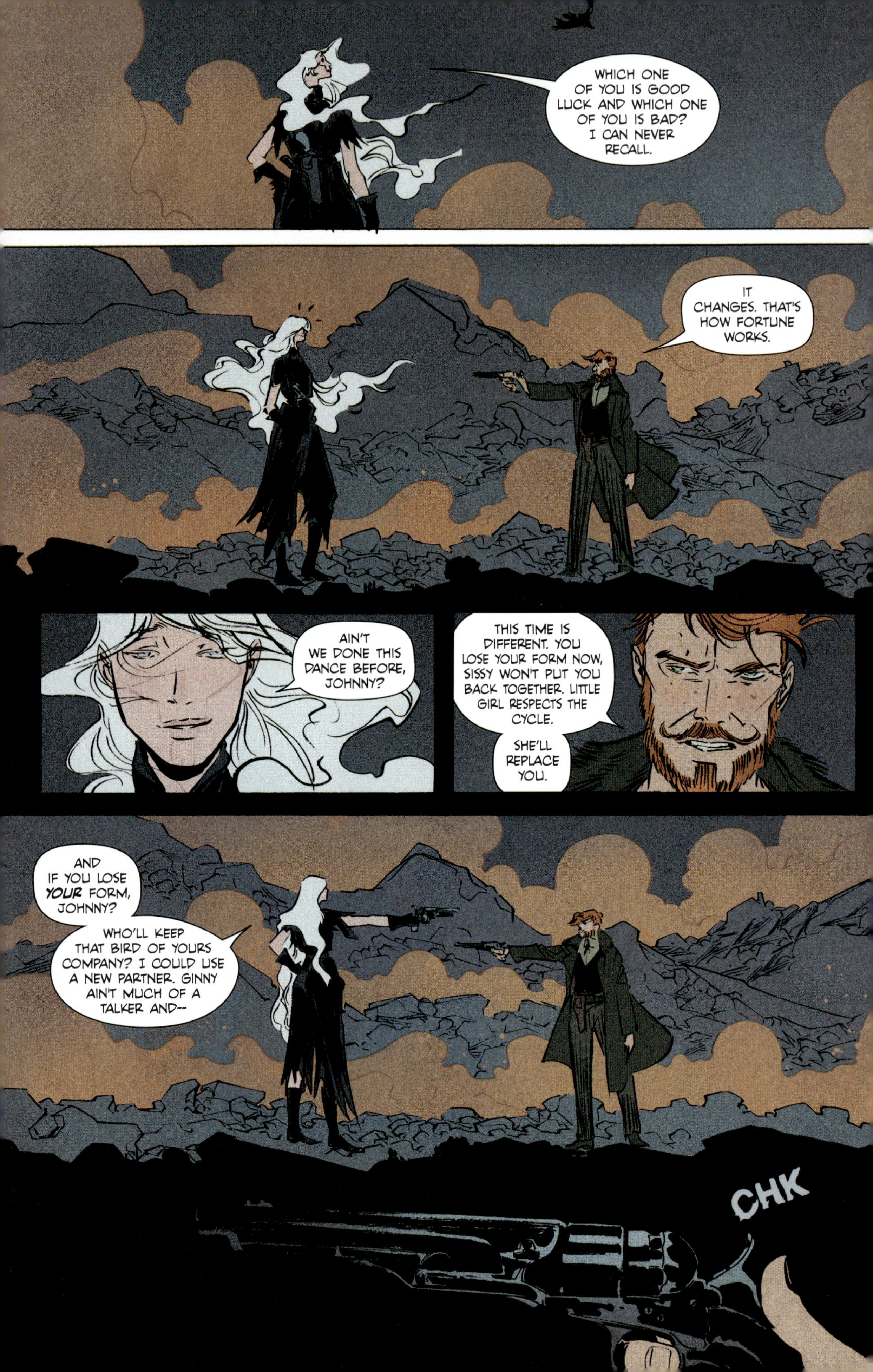
WHICH ONE OF YOU IS GOOD LUCK AND WHICH ONE OF YOU IS BAD? I CAN NEVER RECALL.
IT CHANGES. THAT'S HOW FORTUNE WORKS.
AIN'T WE DONE THIS DANCE BEFORE, JOHNNY?
THIS TIME IS DIFFERENT. YOU LOSE YOUR FORM NOW, SISSY WON'T PUT YOU BACK TOGETHER. LITTLE GIRL RESPECTS THE CYCLE.
SHE'LL REPLACE YOU.
AND IF YOU LOSE *YOUR* FORM, JOHNNY?
WHO'LL KEEP THAT BIRD OF YOURS COMPANY? I COULD USE A NEW PARTNER. GINNY AIN'T MUCH OF A TALKER AND--
CHK

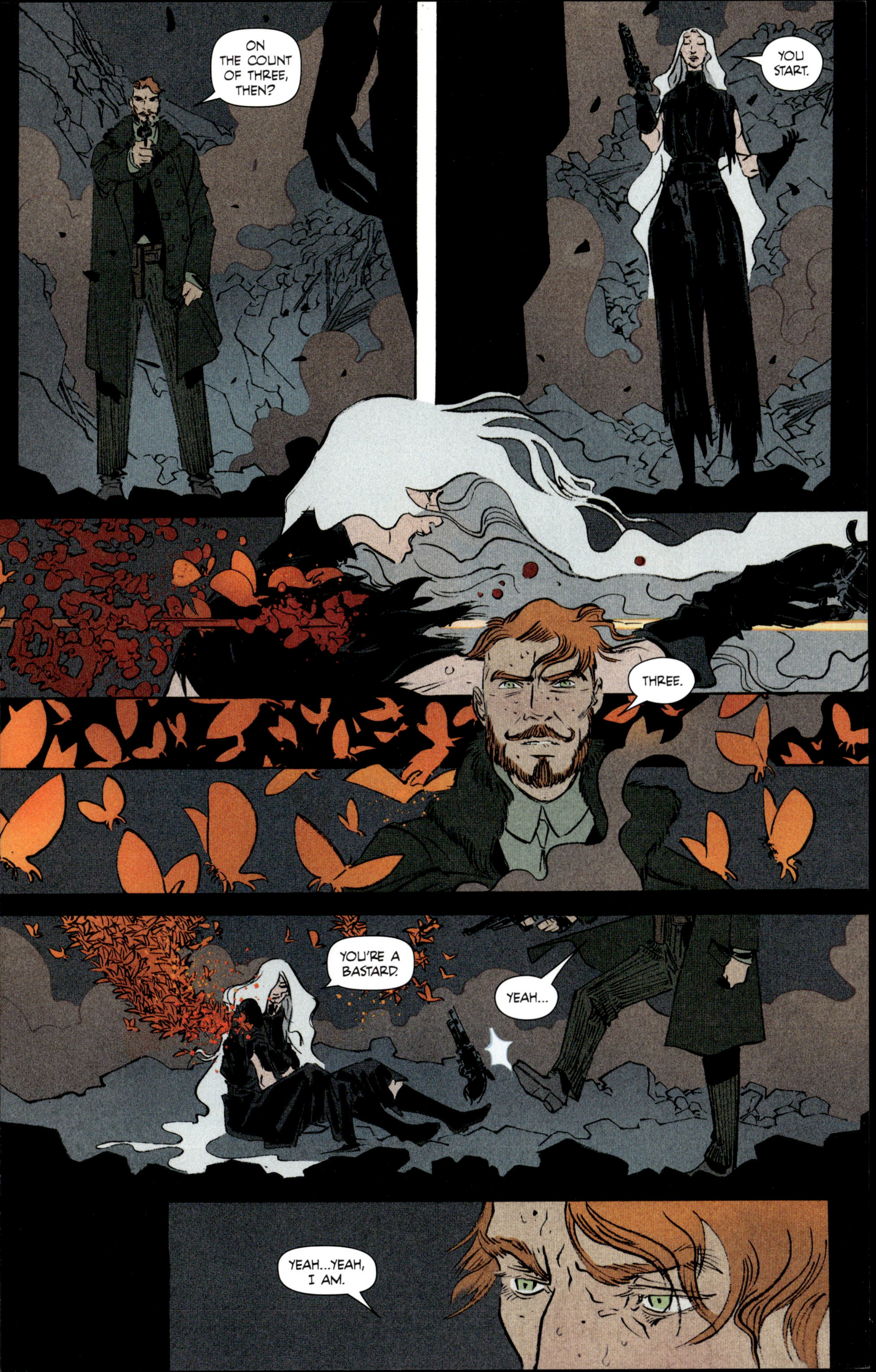
ON THE COUNT OF THREE, THEN?
YOU START.
THREE.
YOU'RE A BASTARD.
YEAH...
YEAH...YEAH, I AM.

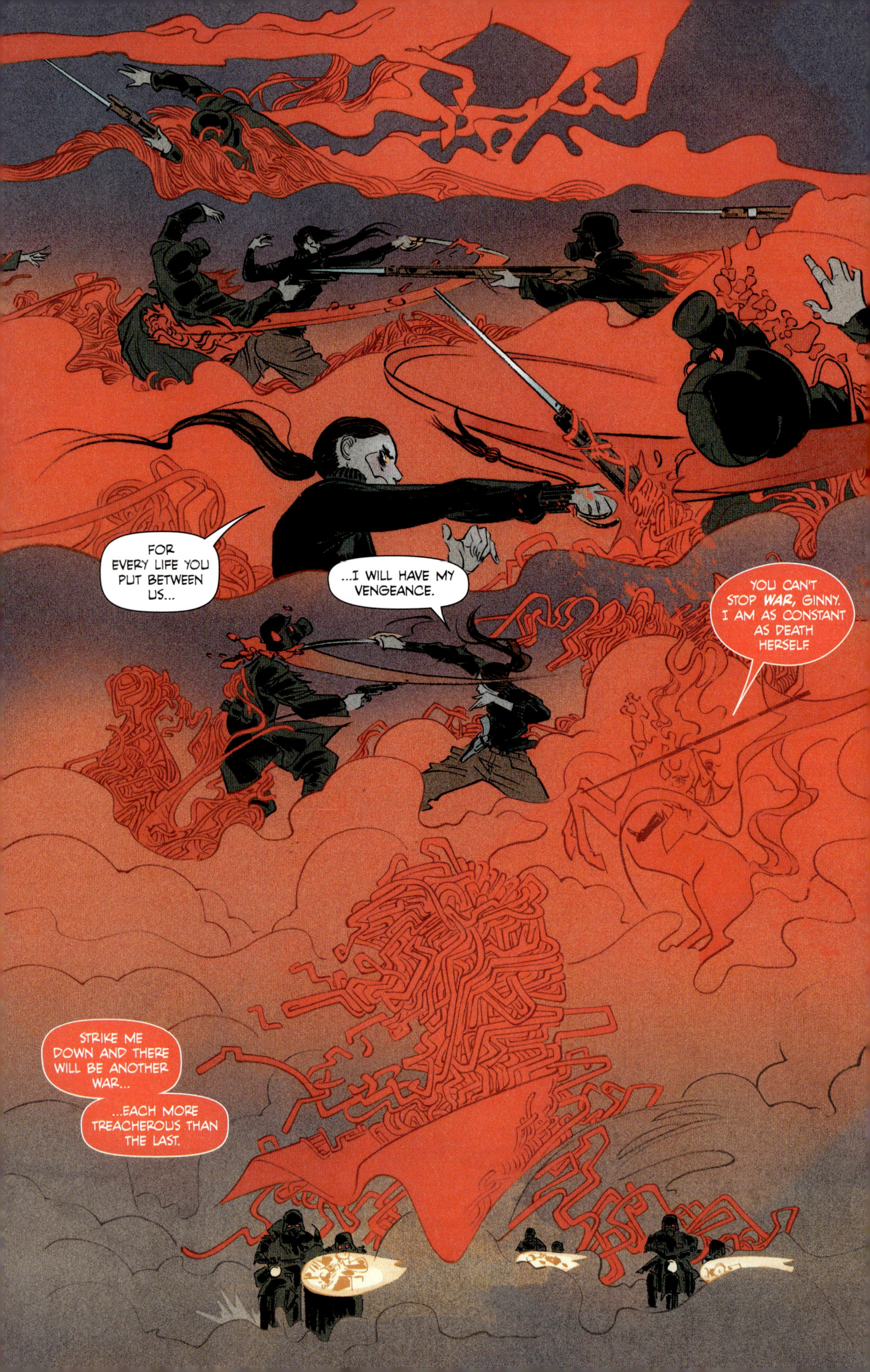
FOR EVERY LIFE YOU PUT BETWEEN US...
...I WILL HAVE MY VENGEANCE.
YOU CAN'T STOP WAR, GINNY. I AM AS CONSTANT AS DEATH HERSELF.
STRIKE ME DOWN AND THERE WILL BE ANOTHER WAR...
...EACH MORE TREACHEROUS THAN THE LAST.

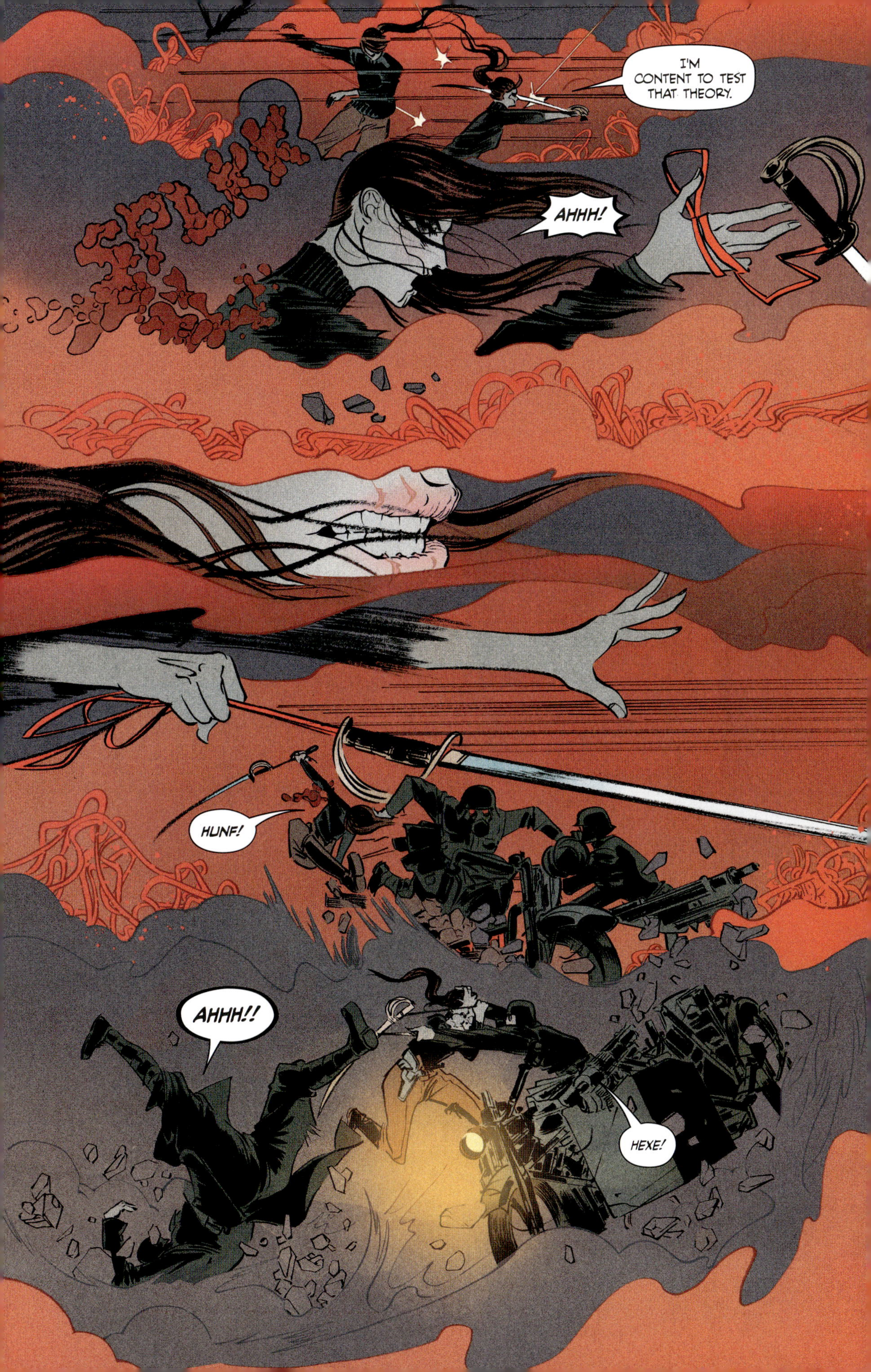
I'M CONTENT TO TEST THAT THEORY.
SPLKK
AHHH!
HUNF!
AHHH!!
HEXE!

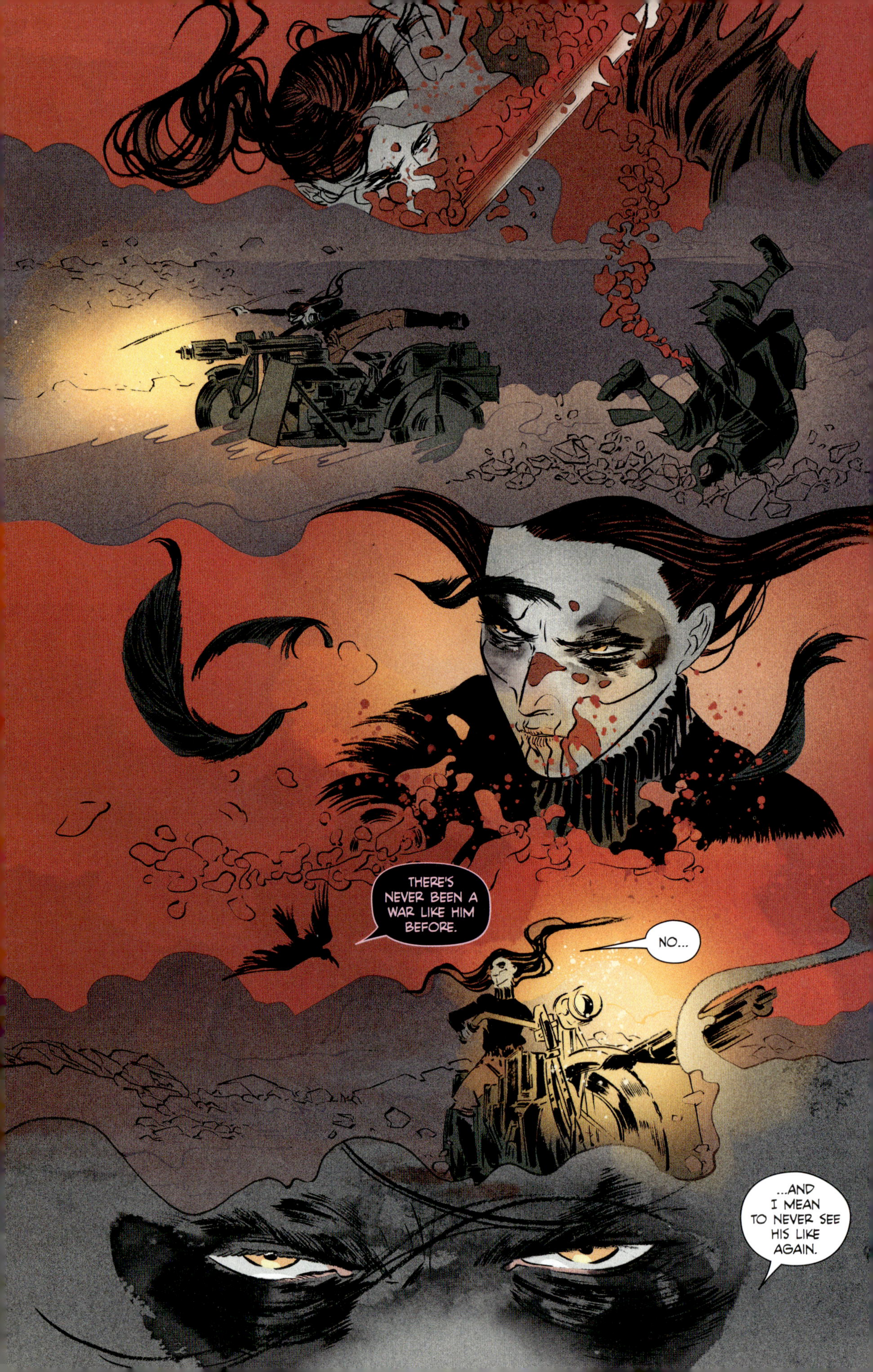
THERE'S NEVER BEEN A WAR LIKE HIM BEFORE.
NO...
...AND I MEAN TO NEVER SEE HIS LIKE AGAIN.

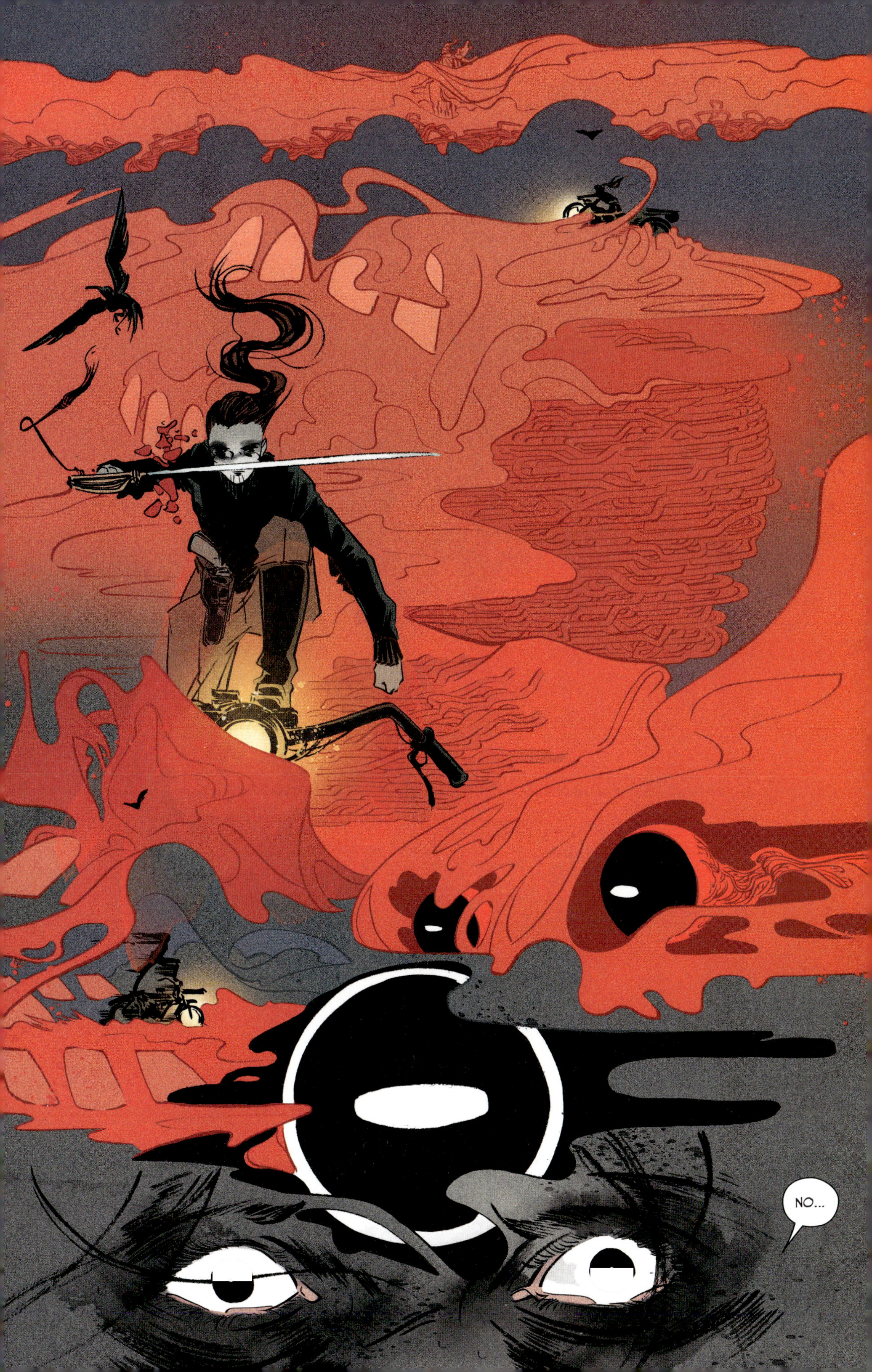
NO...

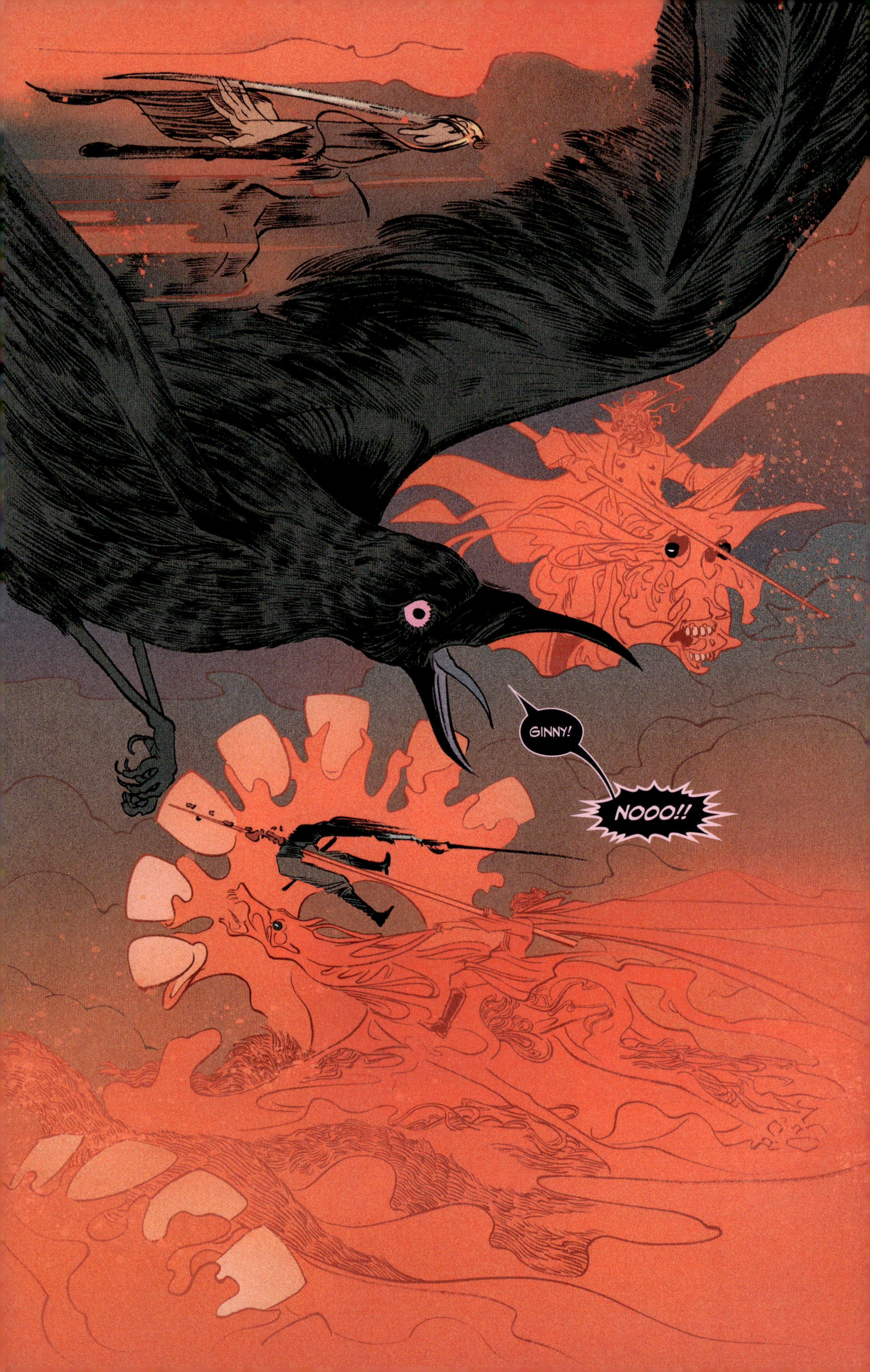
GINNY!
NOOO!!

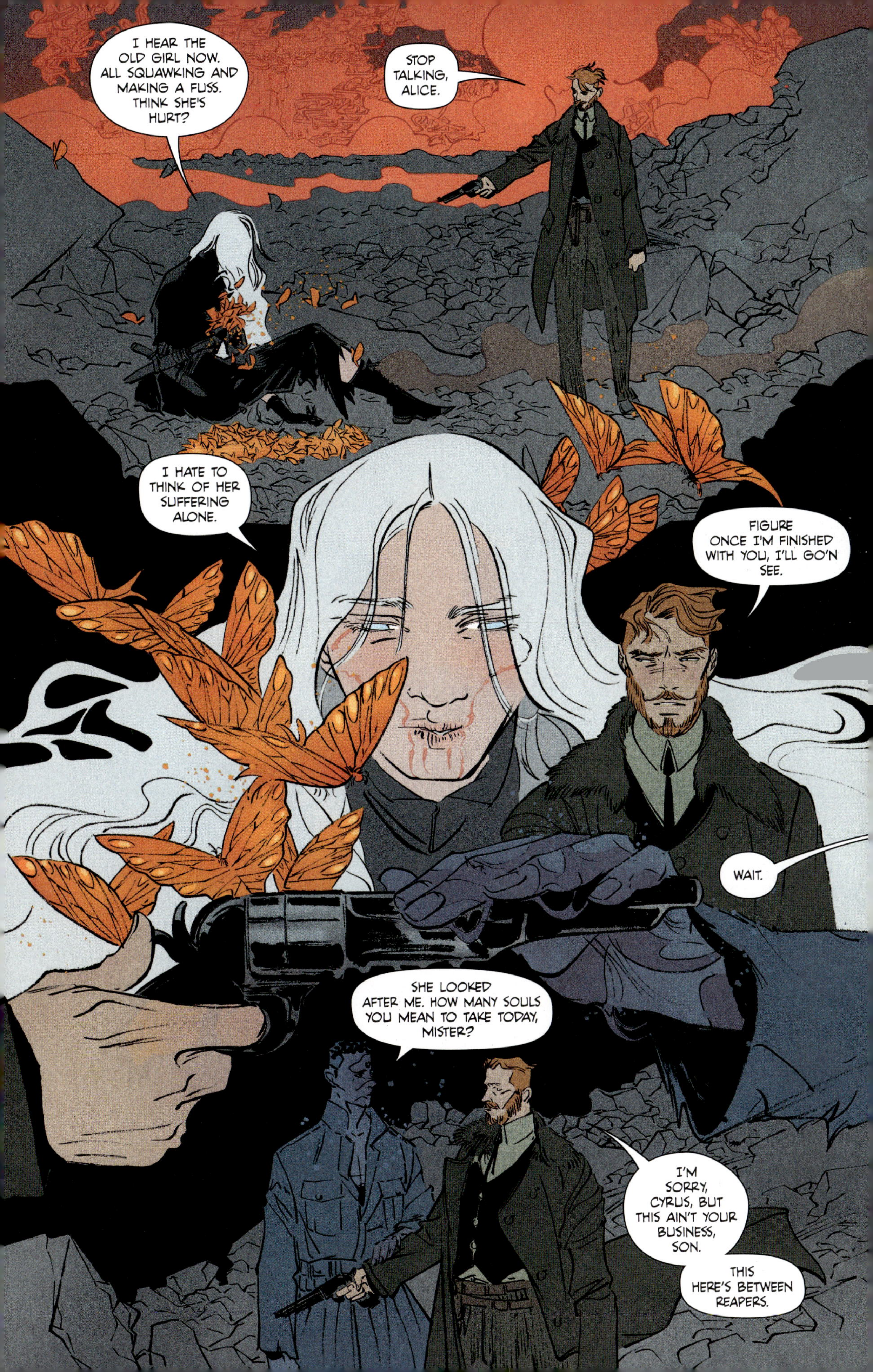
I HEAR THE OLD GIRL NOW. ALL SQUAWKING AND MAKING A FUSS. THINK SHE'S HURT?
STOP TALKING, ALICE.
I HATE TO THINK OF HER SUFFERING ALONE.
FIGURE ONCE I'M FINISHED WITH YOU, I'LL GO'N SEE.
WAIT.
SHE LOOKED AFTER ME. HOW MANY SOULS YOU MEAN TO TAKE TODAY, MISTER?
I'M SORRY, CYRUS, BUT THIS AIN'T YOUR BUSINESS, SON.
THIS HERE'S BETWEEN REAPERS.

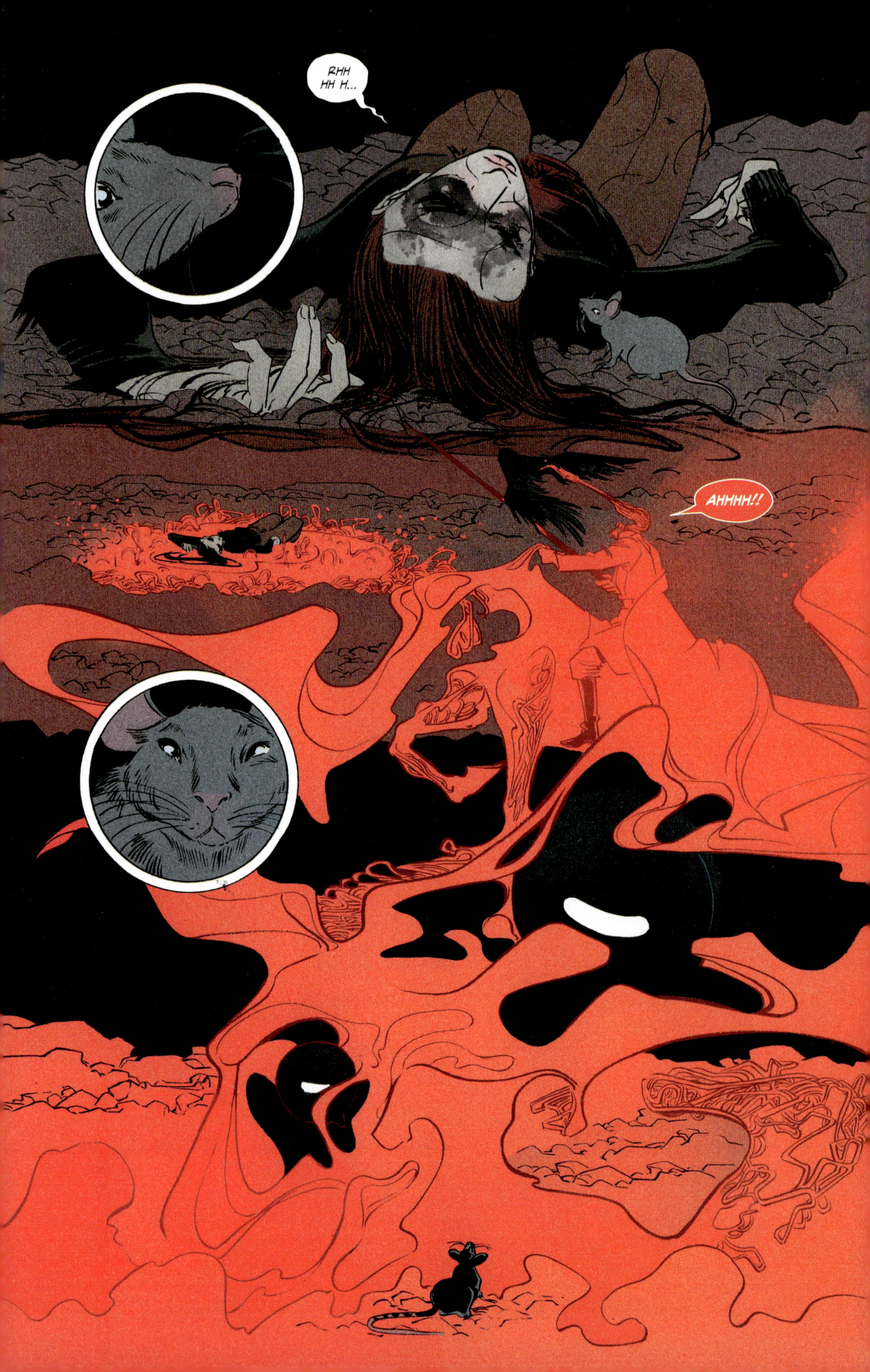
RHH HH H...
AHHHH!!

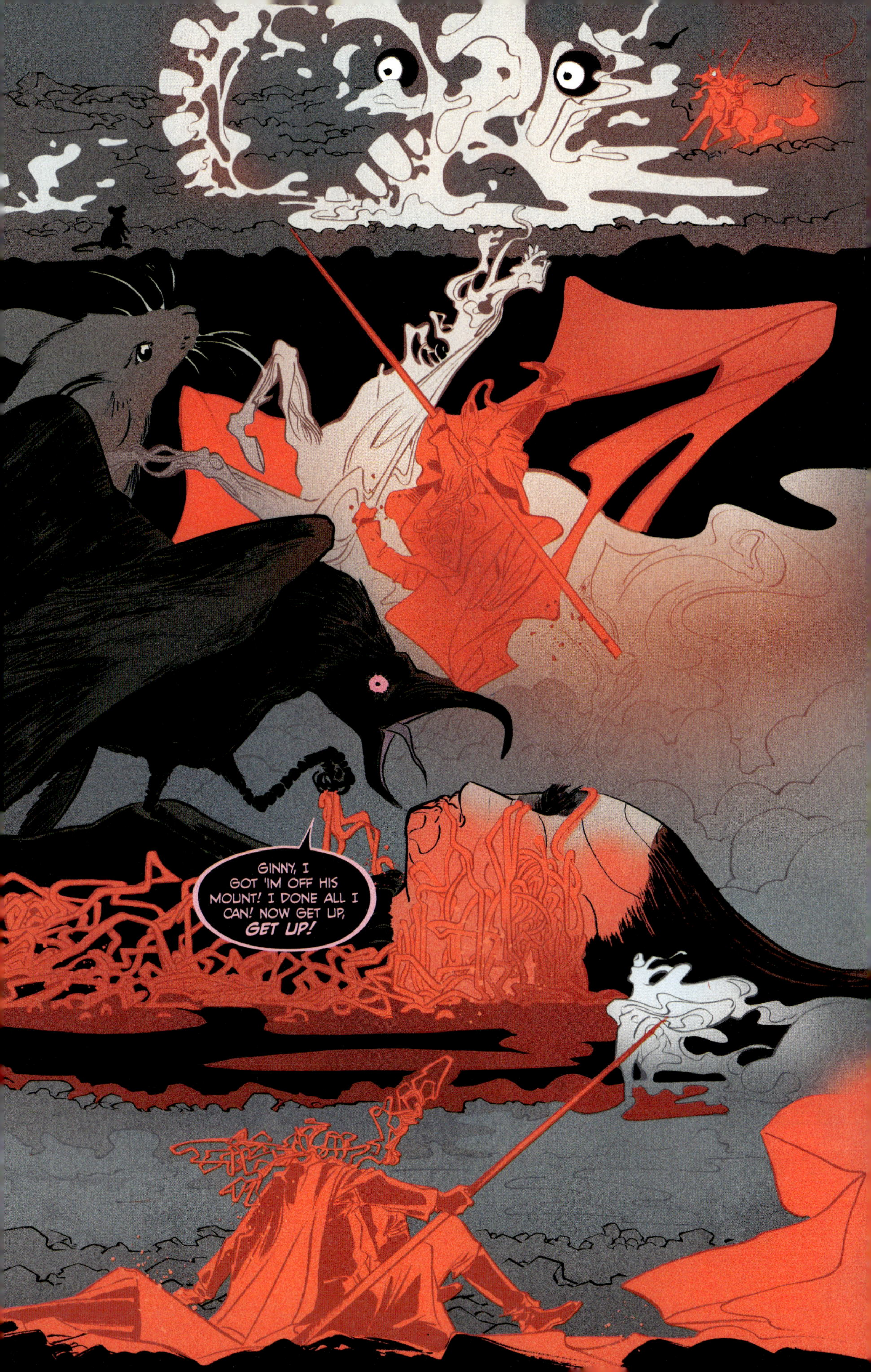
GINNY, I GOT 'IM OFF HIS MOUNT! I DONE ALL I CAN! NOW GET UP, **GET UP!**

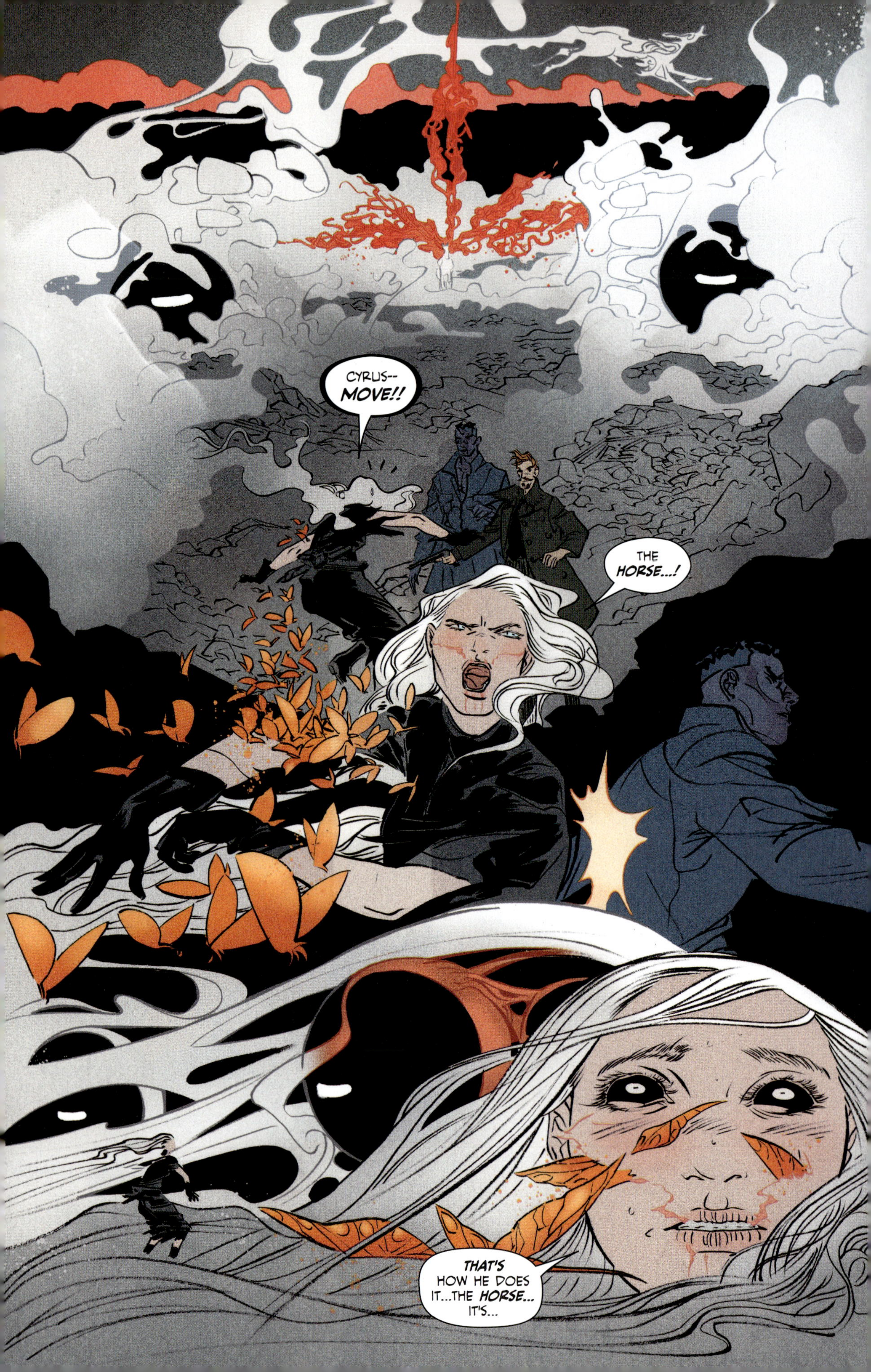
CYRUS-- MOVE!!
THE HORSE...!
THAT'S HOW HE DOES IT...THE HORSE... IT'S...

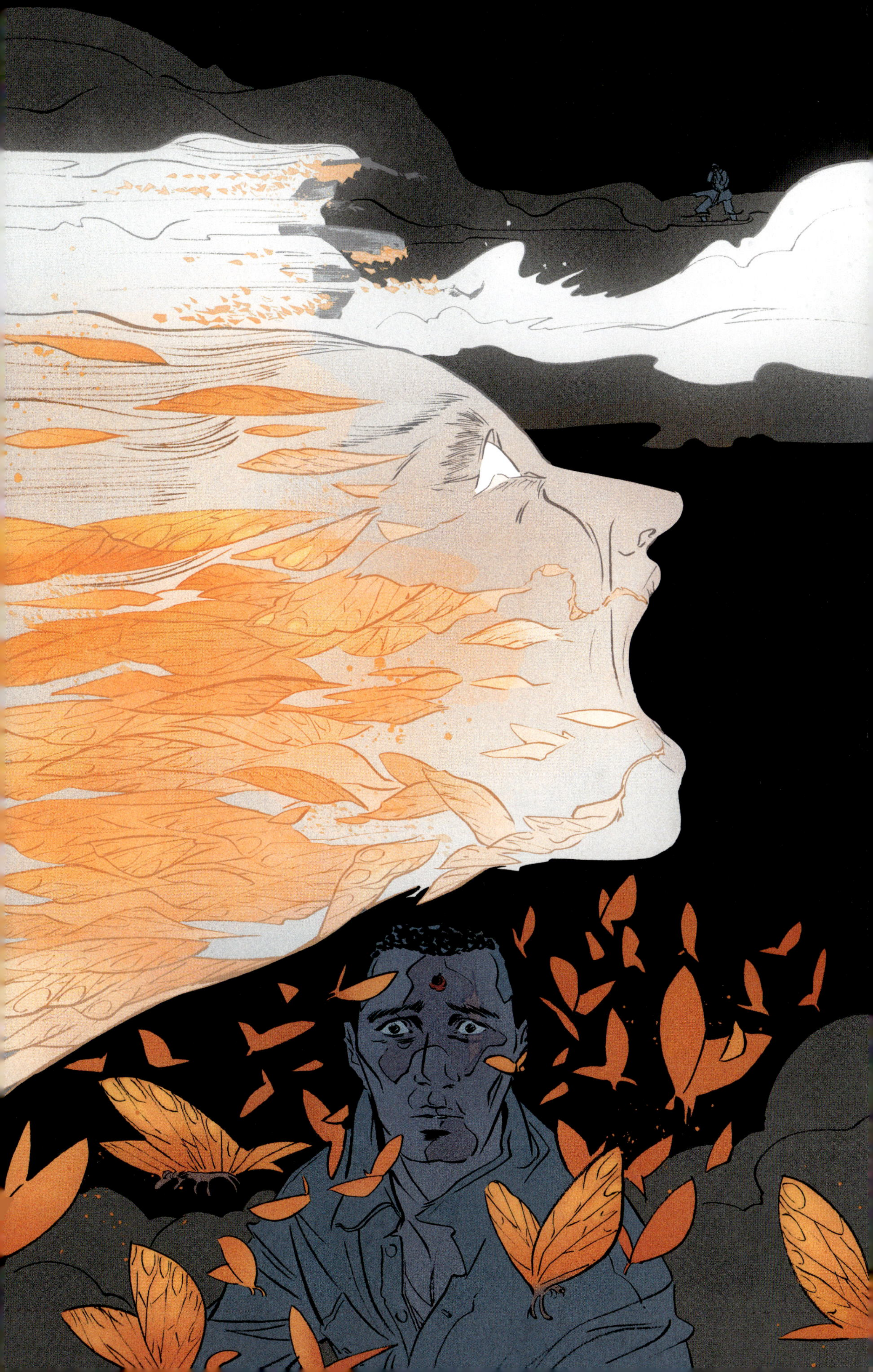

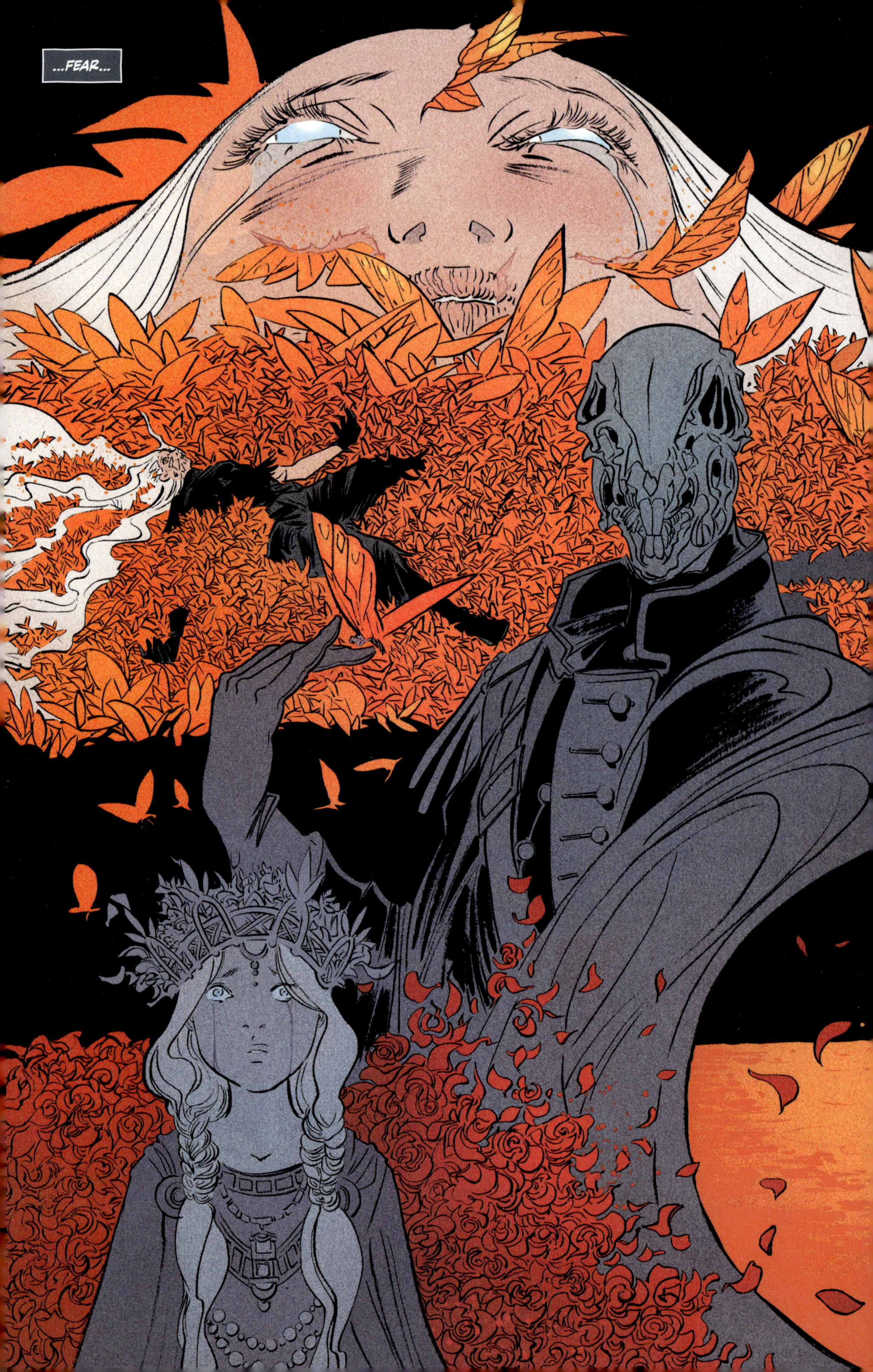
...FEAR...

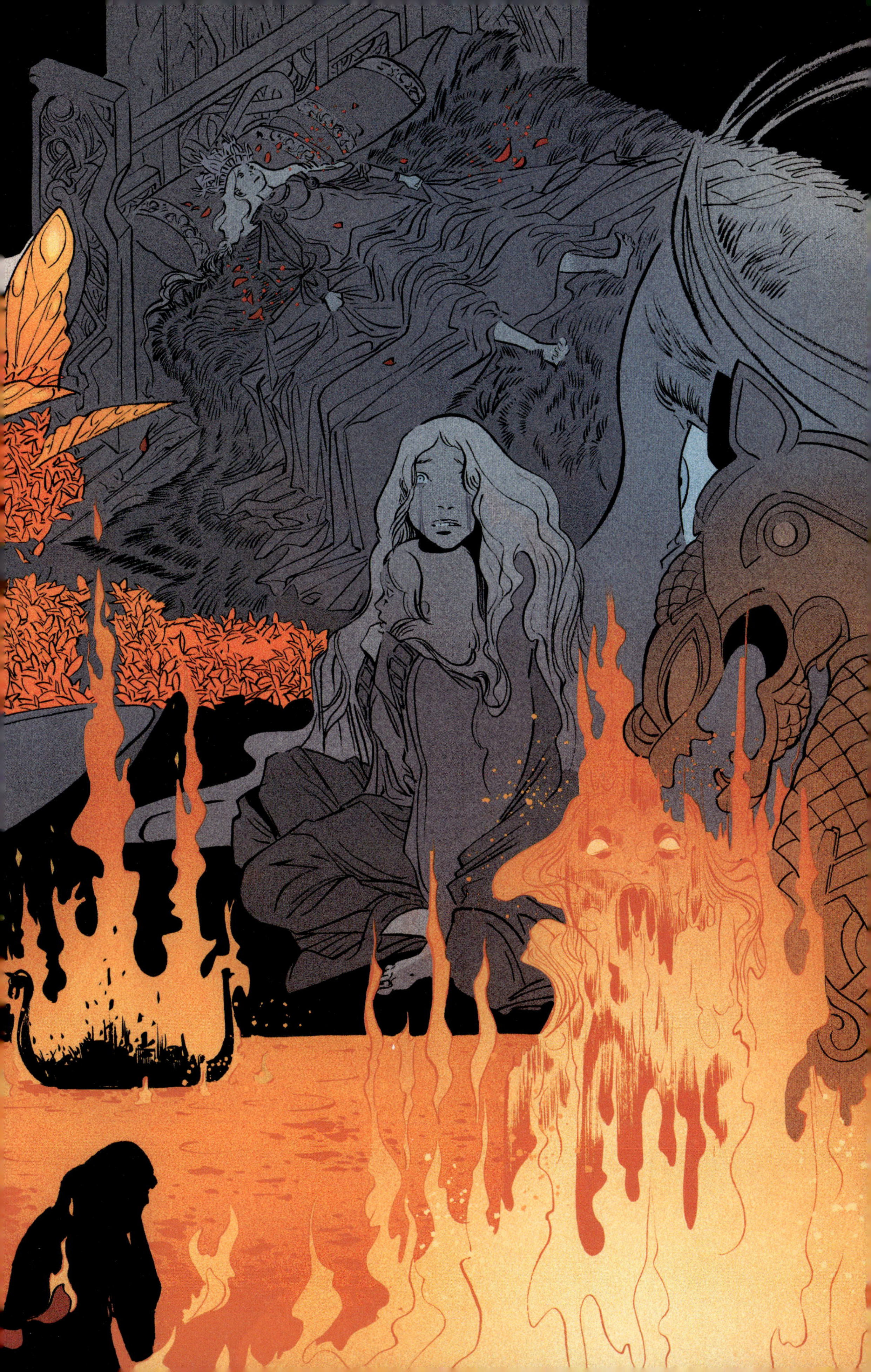

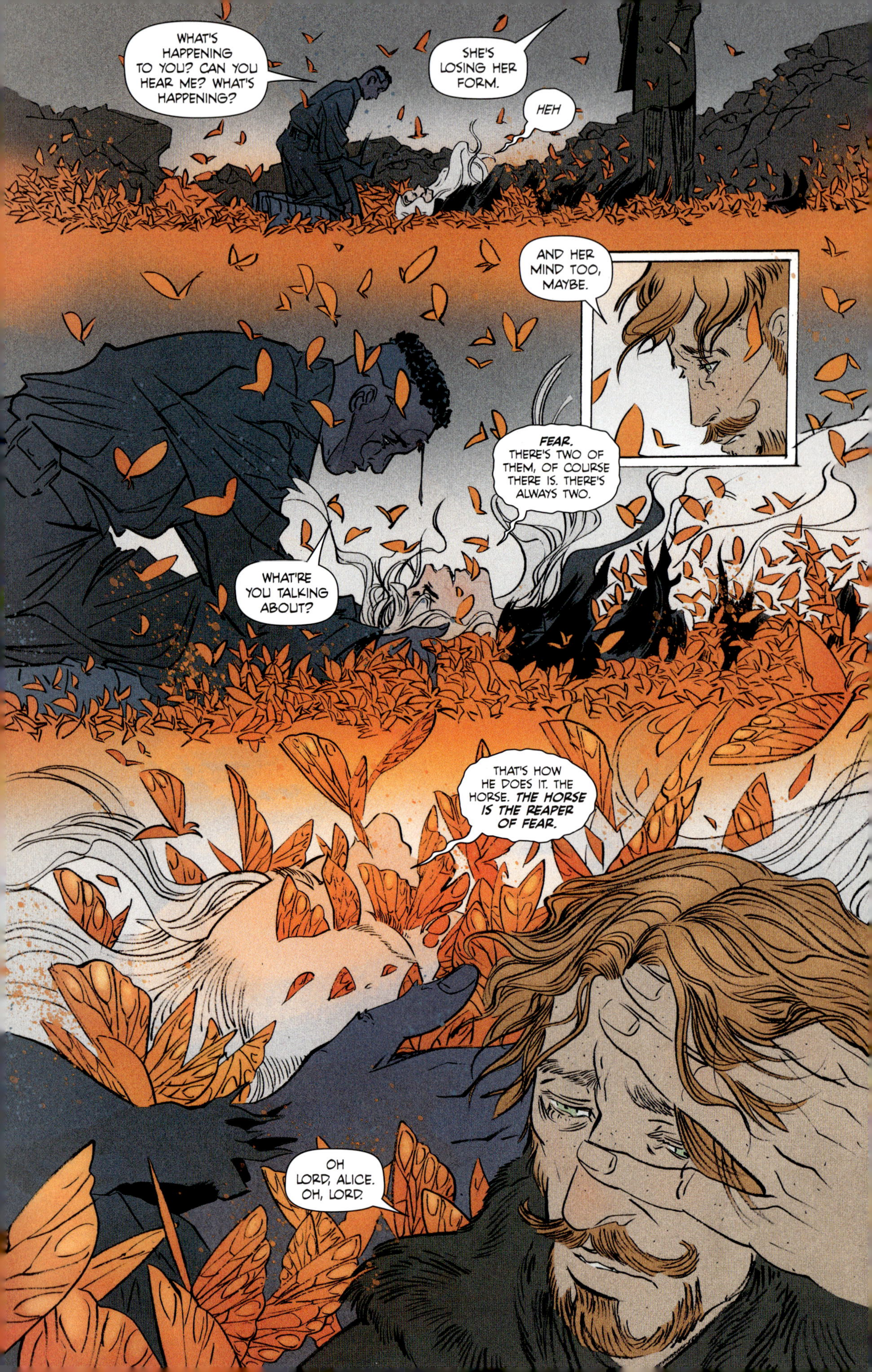
WHAT'S HAPPENING TO YOU? CAN YOU HEAR ME? WHAT'S HAPPENING?
SHE'S LOSING HER FORM.
HEH
AND HER MIND TOO, MAYBE.
FEAR. THERE'S TWO OF THEM, OF COURSE THERE IS. THERE'S ALWAYS TWO.
WHAT'RE YOU TALKING ABOUT?
THAT'S HOW HE DOES IT. THE HORSE. THE HORSE IS THE REAPER OF FEAR.
OH LORD, ALICE. OH, LORD.

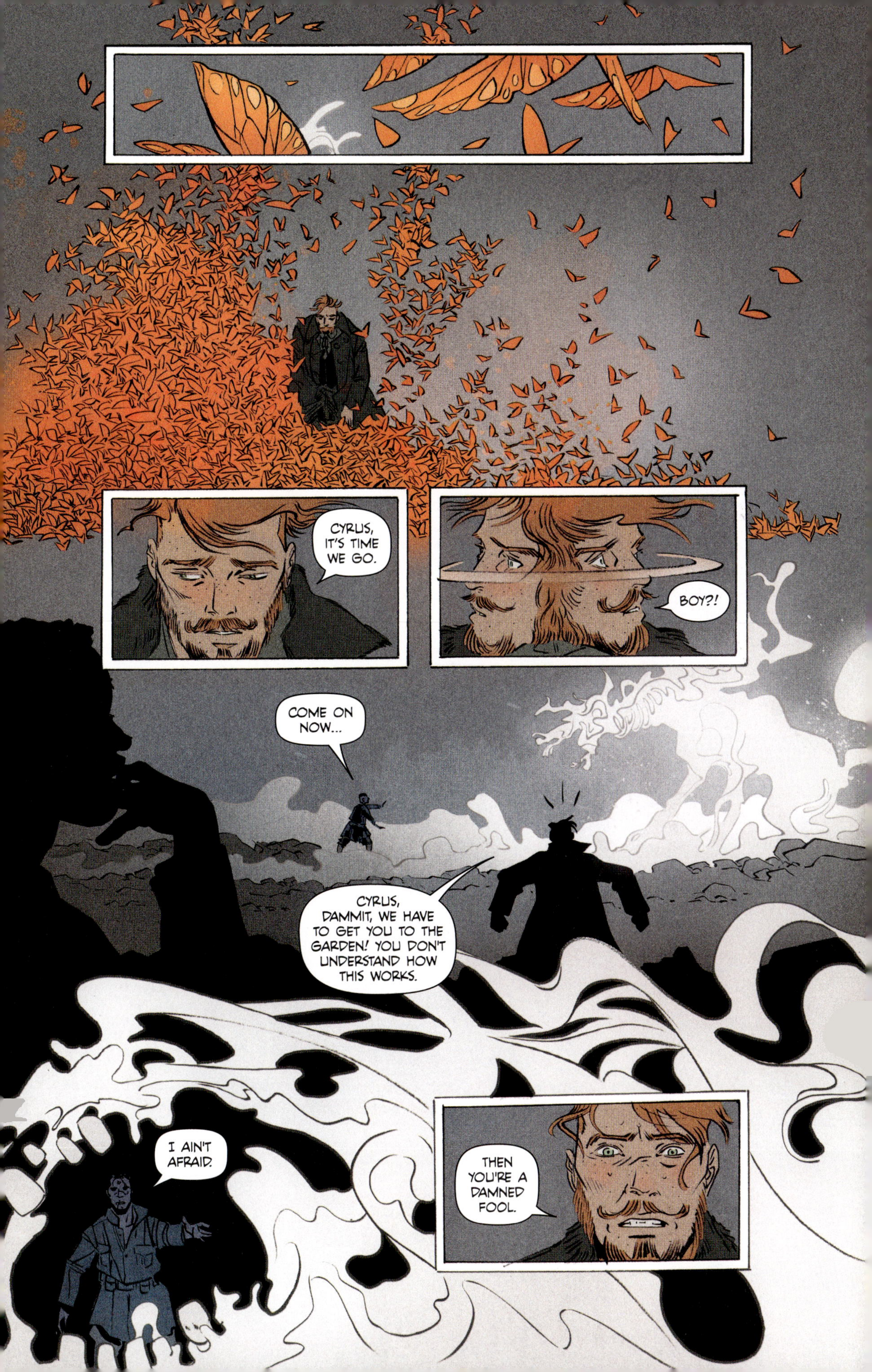
CYRUS, IT'S TIME WE GO.
BOY?!
COME ON NOW...
CYRUS, DAMMIT, WE HAVE TO GET YOU TO THE GARDEN! YOU DON'T UNDERSTAND HOW THIS WORKS.
I AIN'T AFRAID.
THEN YOU'RE A DAMNED FOOL.

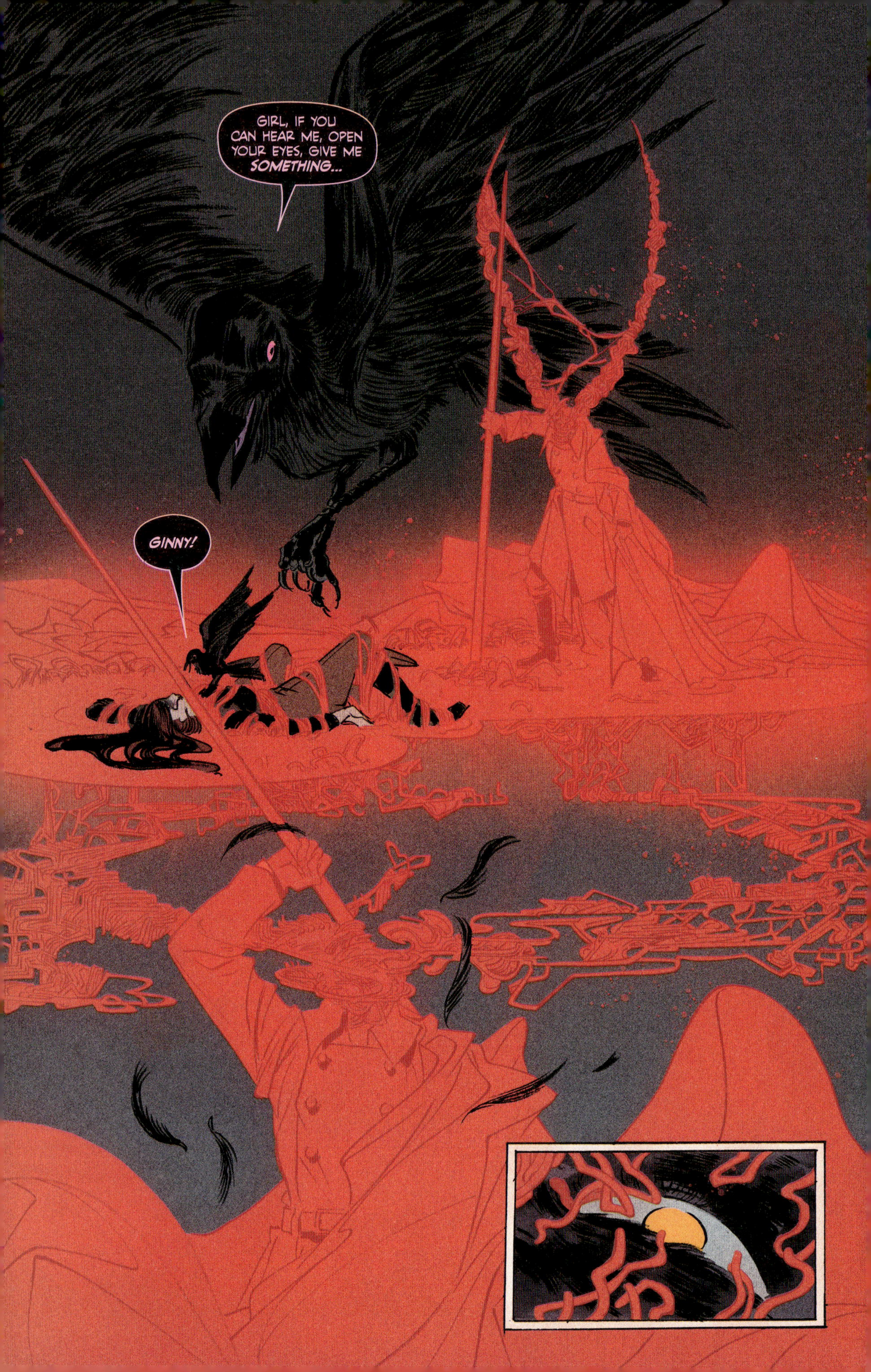
GIRL, IF YOU CAN HEAR ME, OPEN YOUR EYES, GIVE ME SOMETHING...
GINNY!

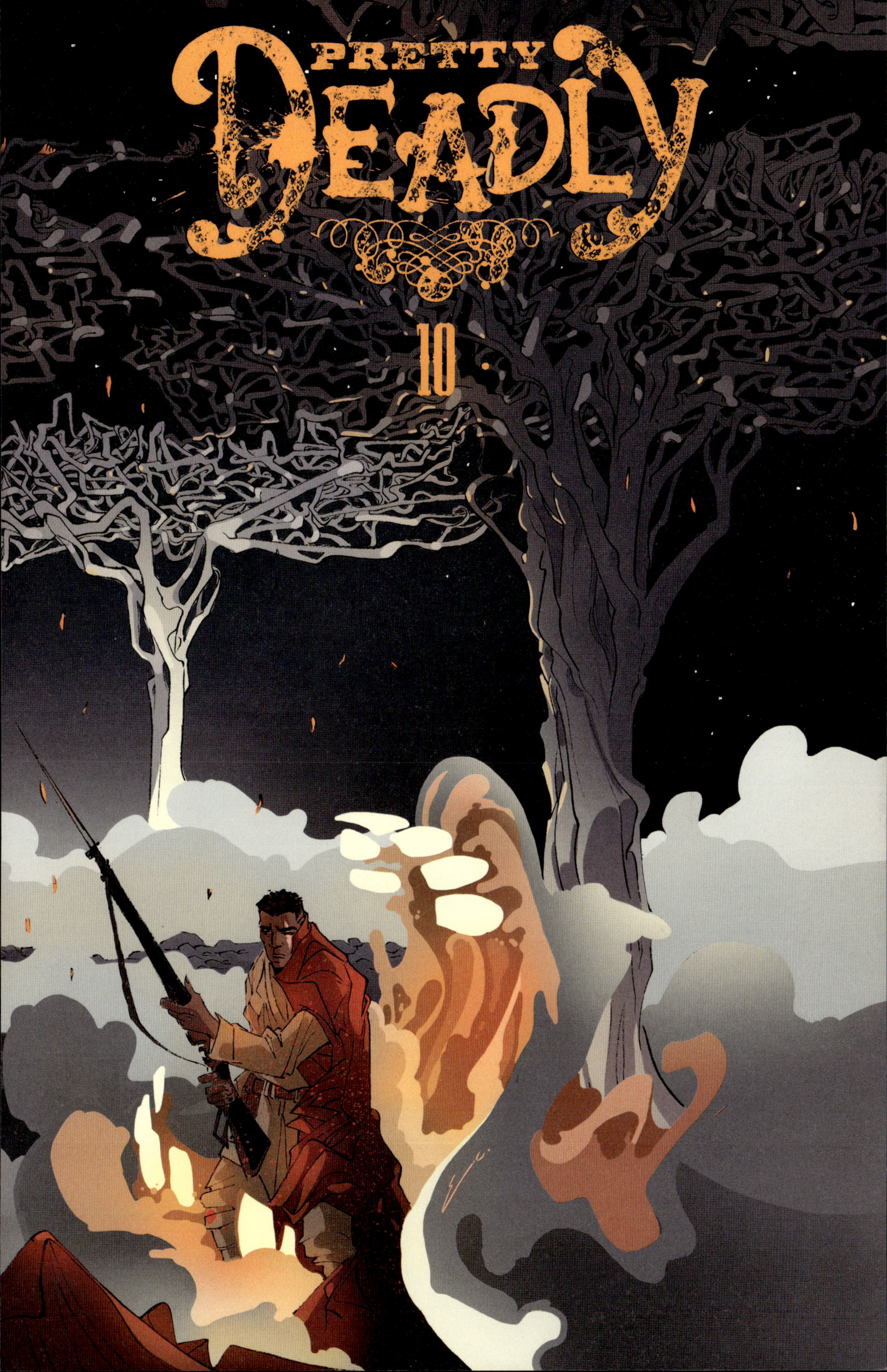
PRETTY
DEADLY
10

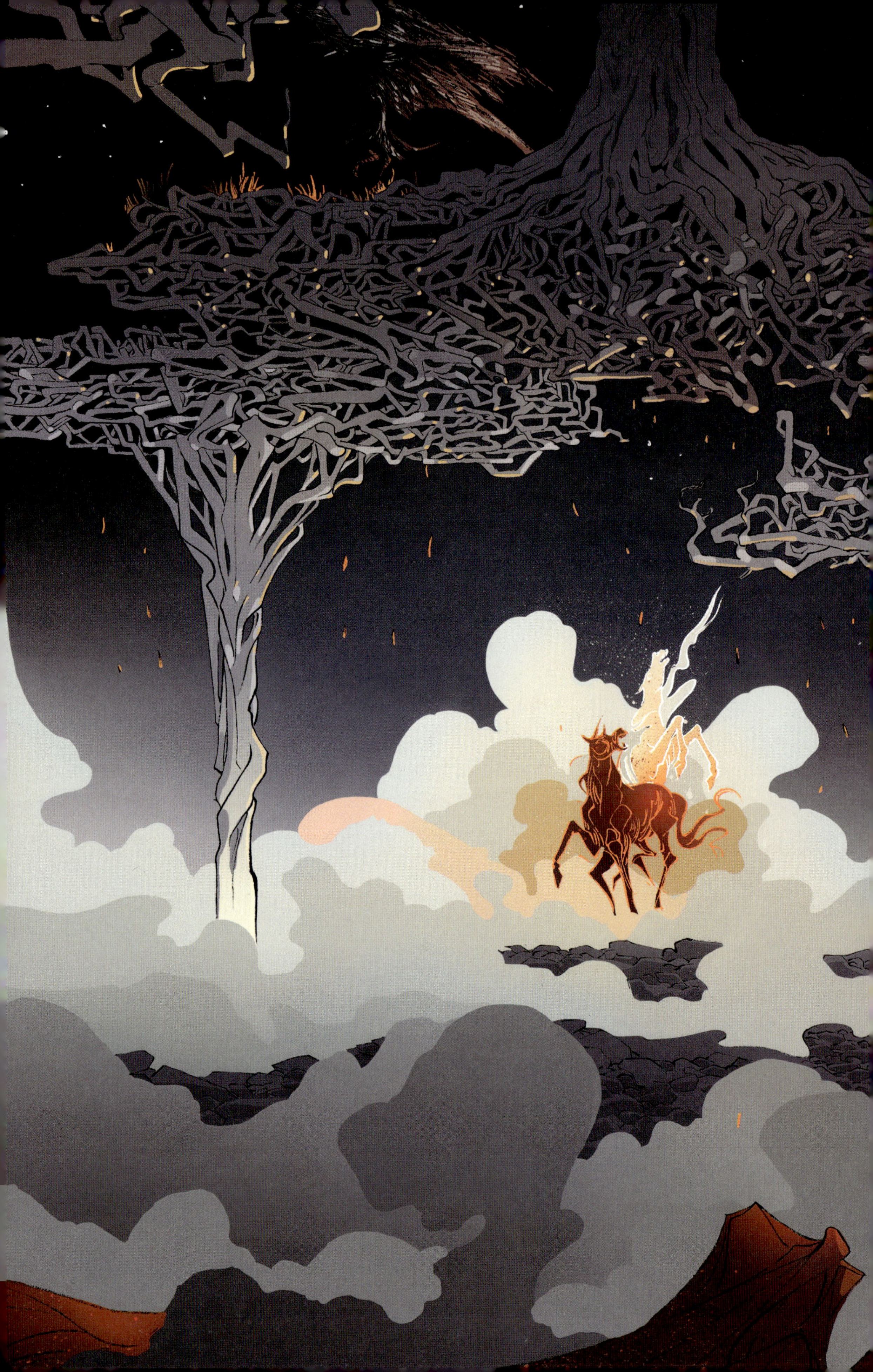

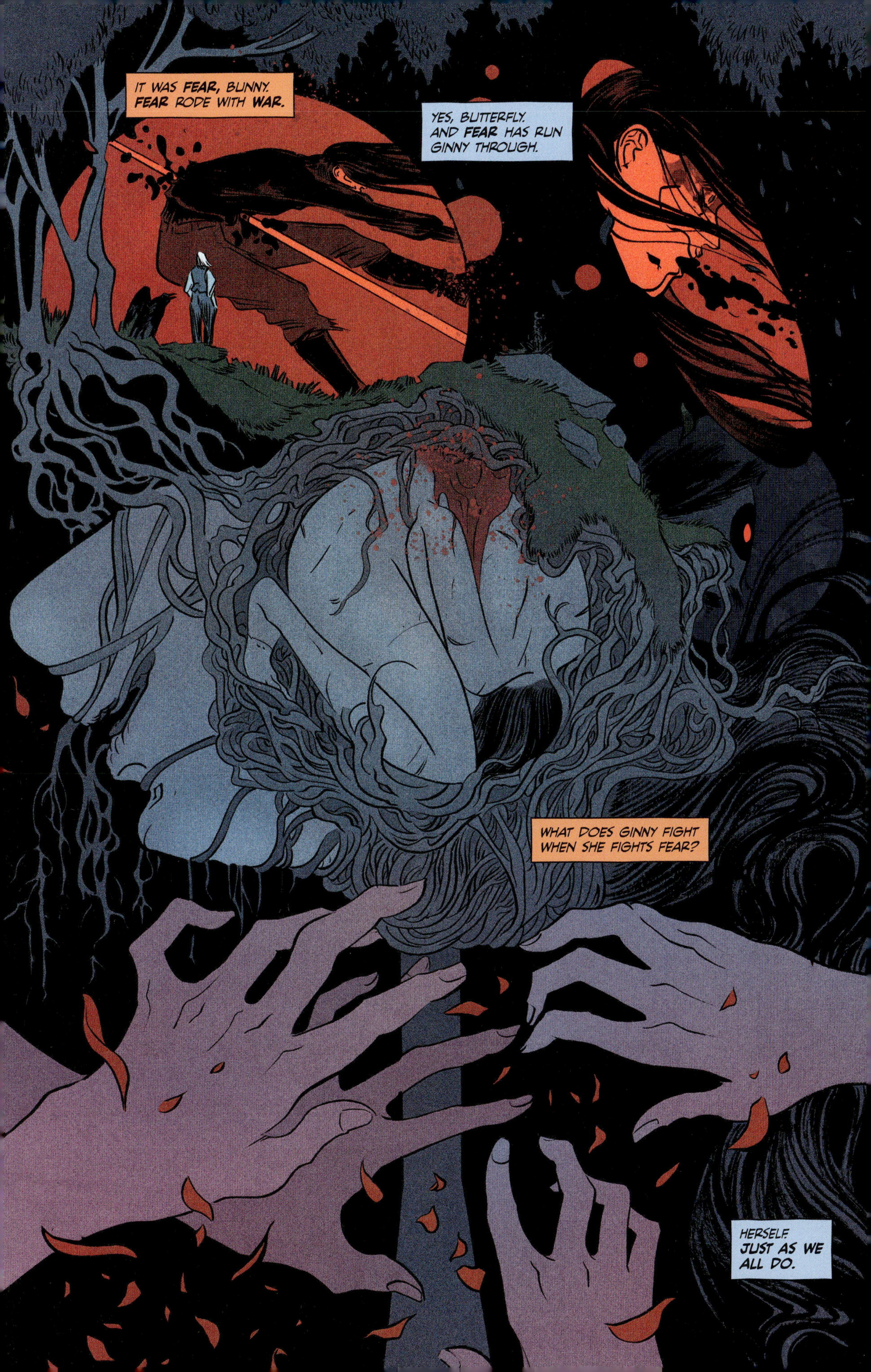
IT WAS FEAR, BUNNY. FEAR RODE WITH WAR.
YES, BUTTERFLY. AND FEAR HAS RUN GINNY THROUGH.
WHAT DOES GINNY FIGHT WHEN SHE FIGHTS FEAR?
HERSELF. JUST AS WE ALL DO.

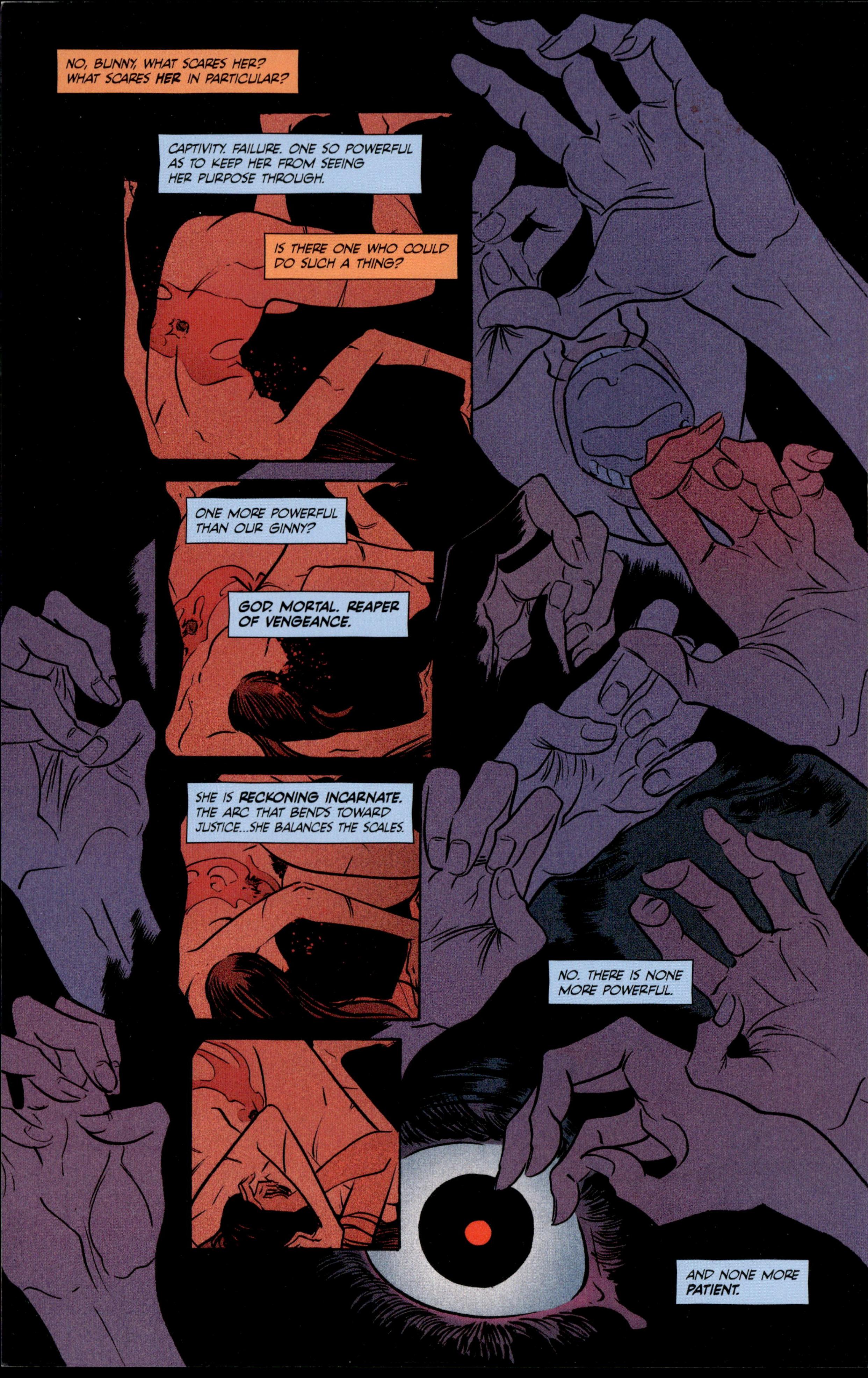
NO, BUNNY, WHAT SCARES HER? WHAT SCARES **HER** IN PARTICULAR?
CAPTIVITY. FAILURE. ONE SO POWERFUL AS TO KEEP HER FROM SEEING HER PURPOSE THROUGH.
IS THERE ONE WHO COULD DO SUCH A THING?
ONE MORE POWERFUL THAN OUR GINNY?
GOD. MORTAL. REAPER OF VENGEANCE.
SHE IS **RECKONING INCARNATE.** THE ARC THAT BENDS TOWARD JUSTICE...SHE BALANCES THE SCALES.
NO. THERE IS NONE MORE POWERFUL.
AND NONE MORE **PATIENT.**

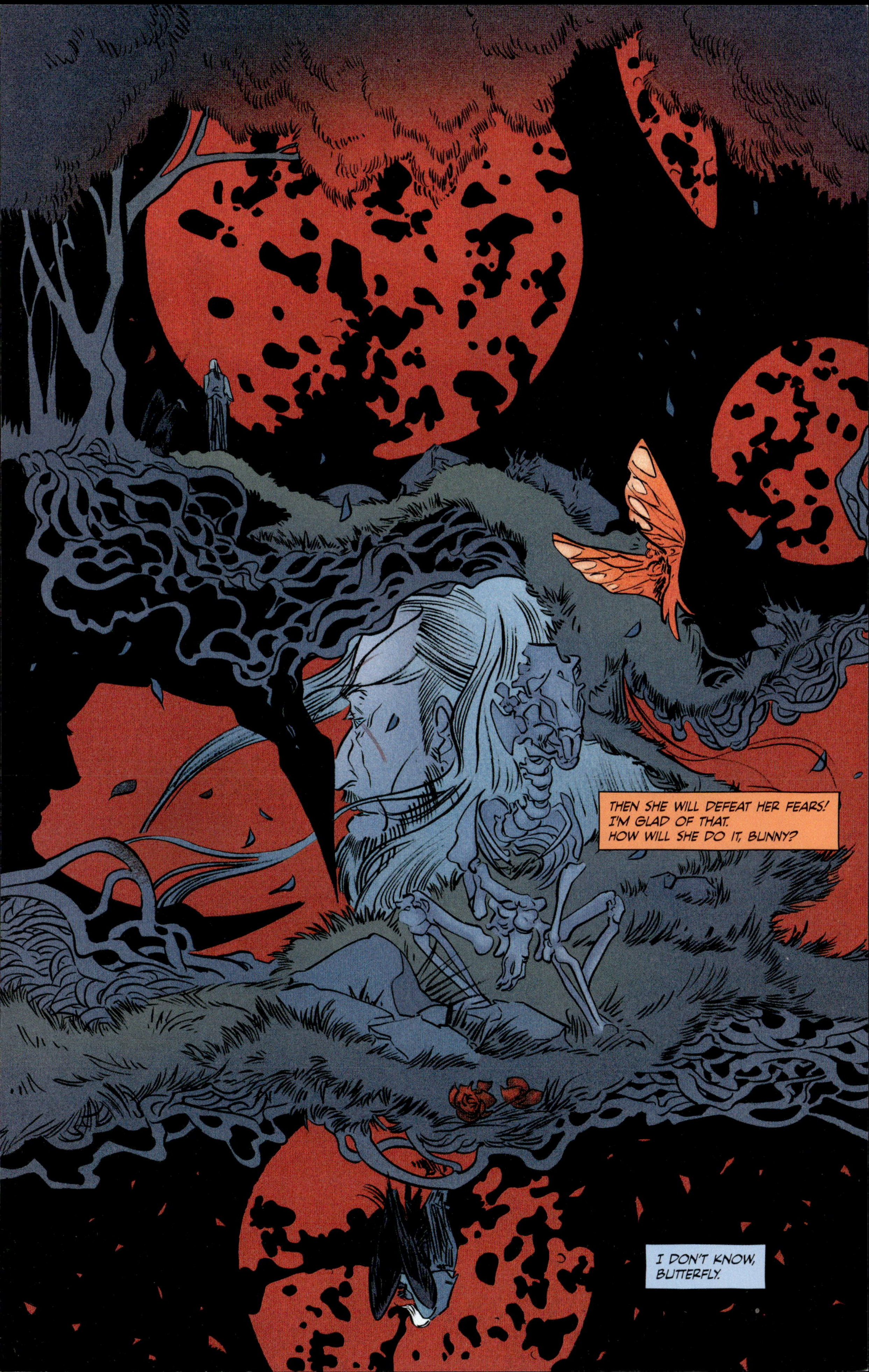
THEN SHE WILL DEFEAT HER FEARS! I'M GLAD OF THAT. HOW WILL SHE DO IT, BUNNY?
I DON'T KNOW, BUTTERFLY.

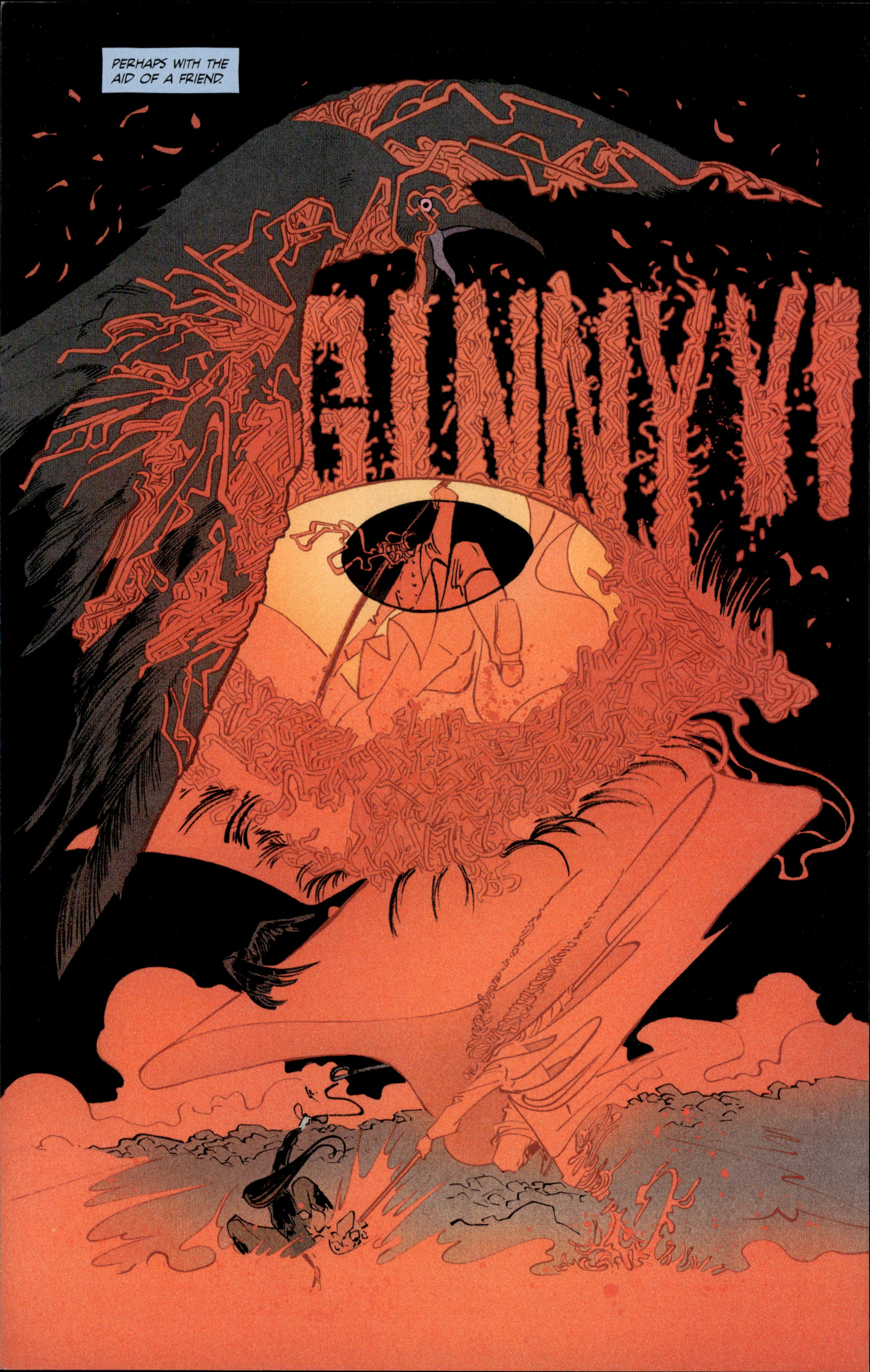
PERHAPS WITH THE AID OF A FRIEND.

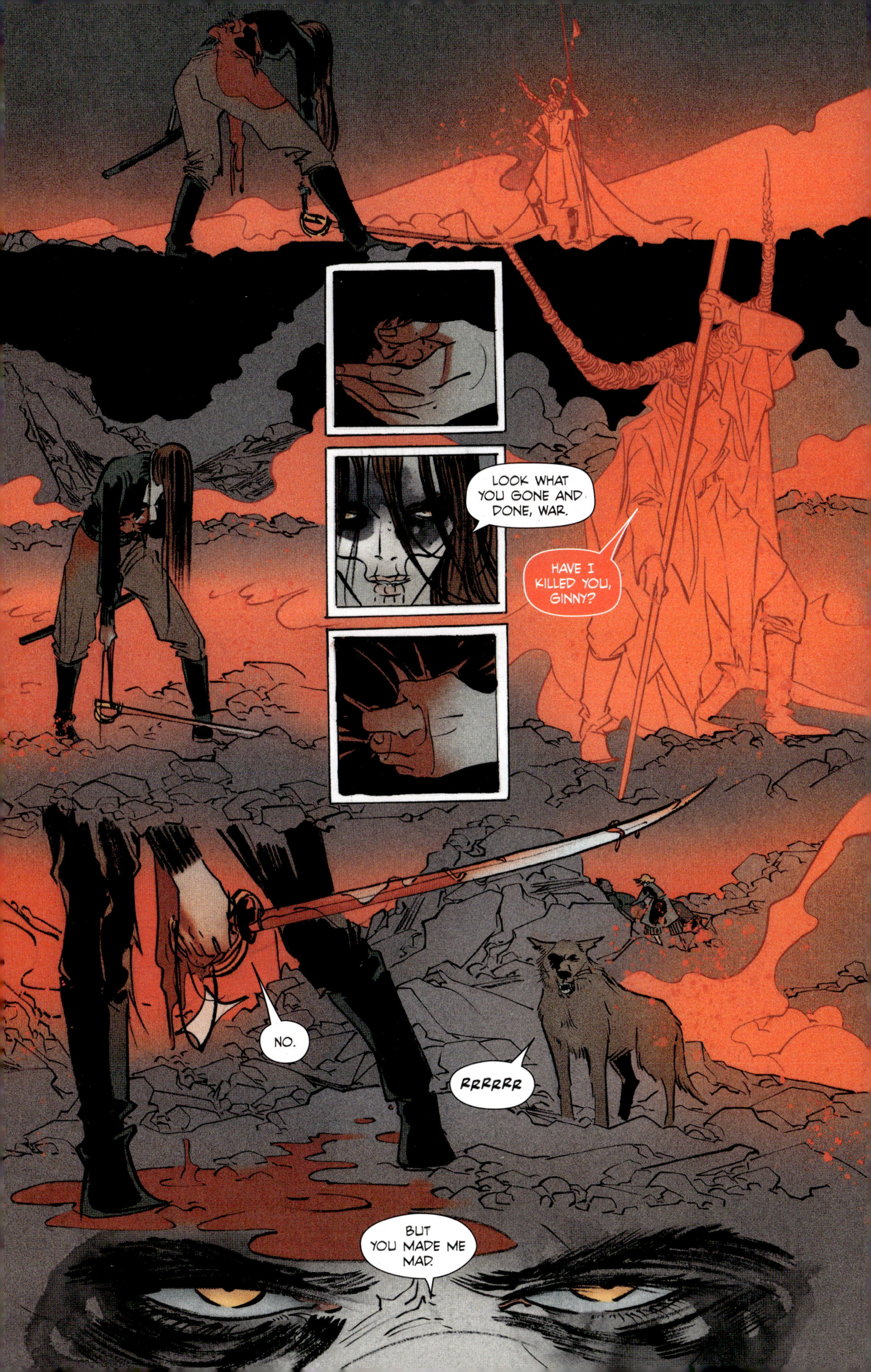
LOOK WHAT YOU GONE AND DONE, WAR.
HAVE I KILLED YOU, GINNY?
NO.
RRRRRR
BUT YOU MADE ME MAD.

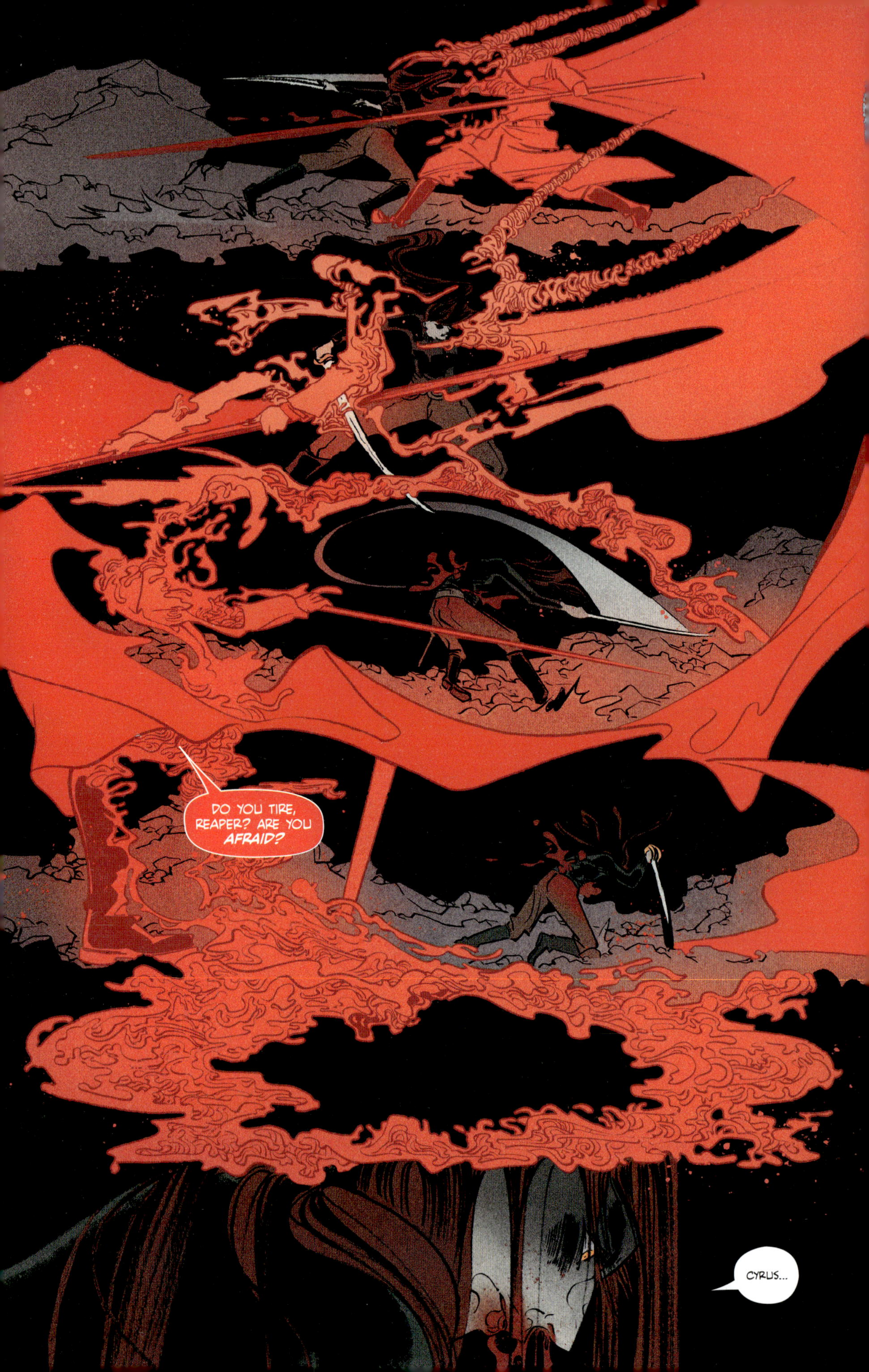
DO YOU TIRE, REAPER? ARE YOU *AFRAID?*
CYRUS...

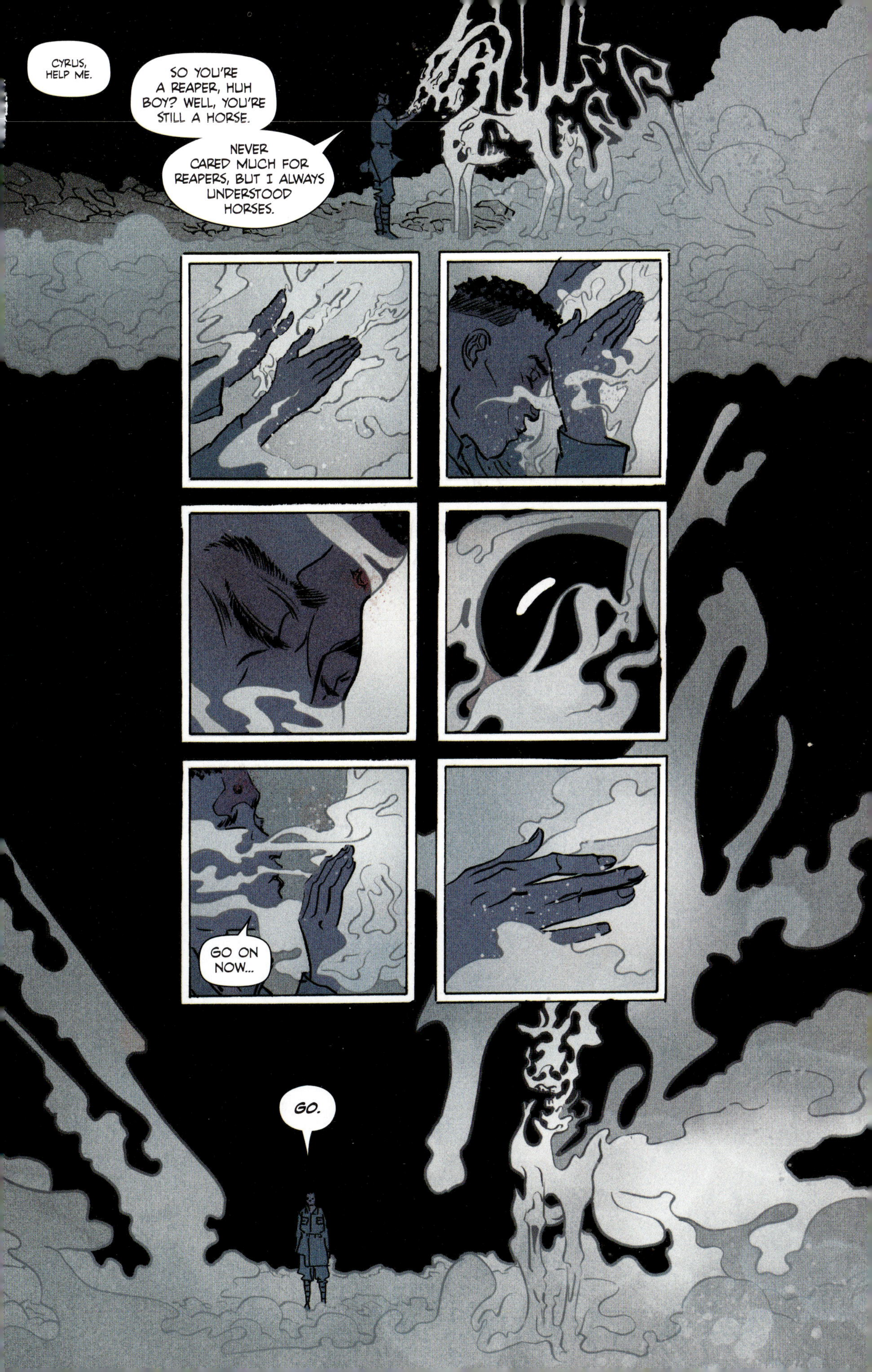
CYRUS, HELP ME.
SO YOU'RE A REAPER, HUH BOY? WELL, YOU'RE STILL A HORSE.
NEVER CARED MUCH FOR REAPERS, BUT I ALWAYS UNDERSTOOD HORSES.
GO ON NOW...
GO.

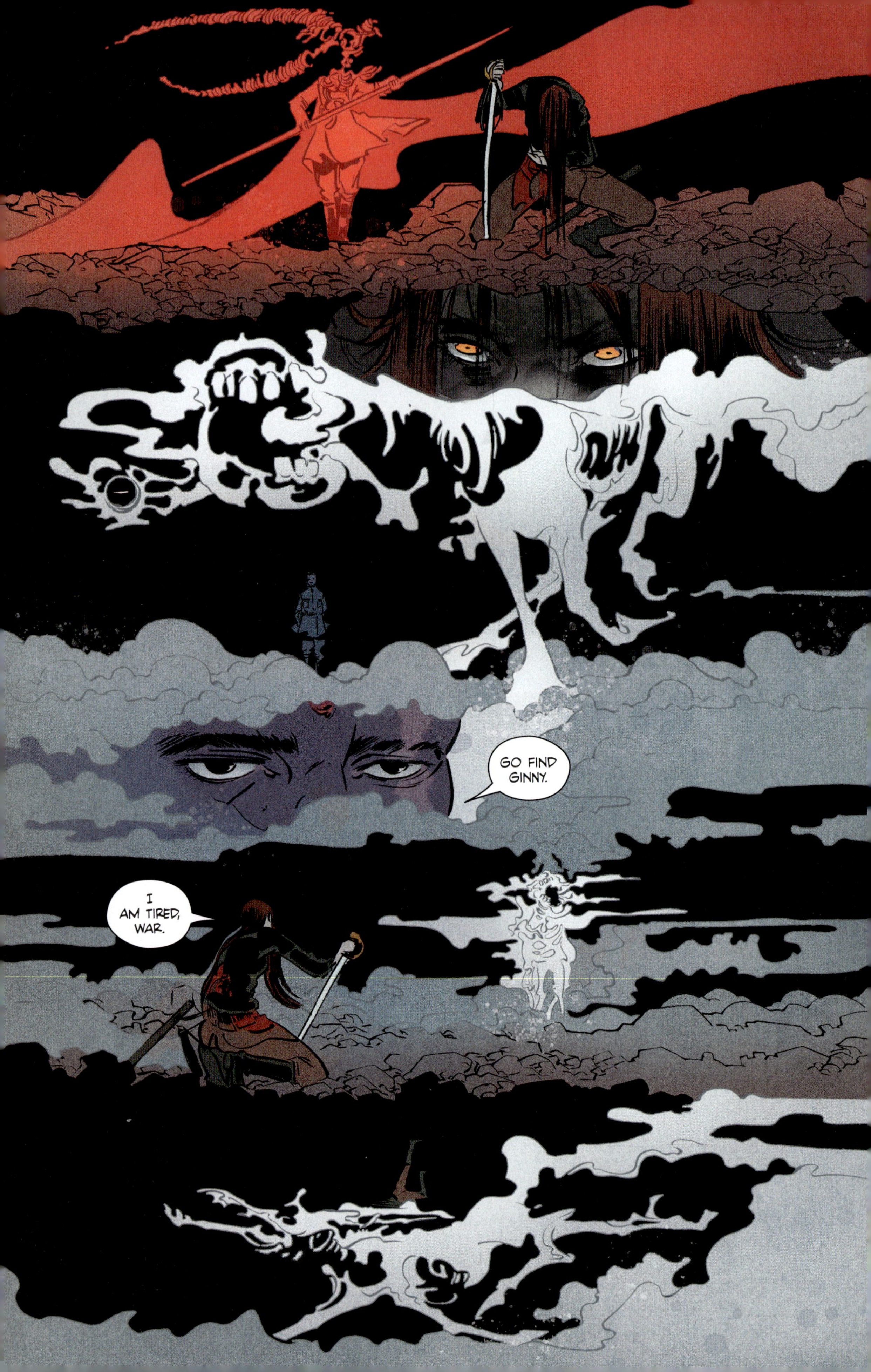
GO FIND GINNY.
I AM TIRED, WAR.

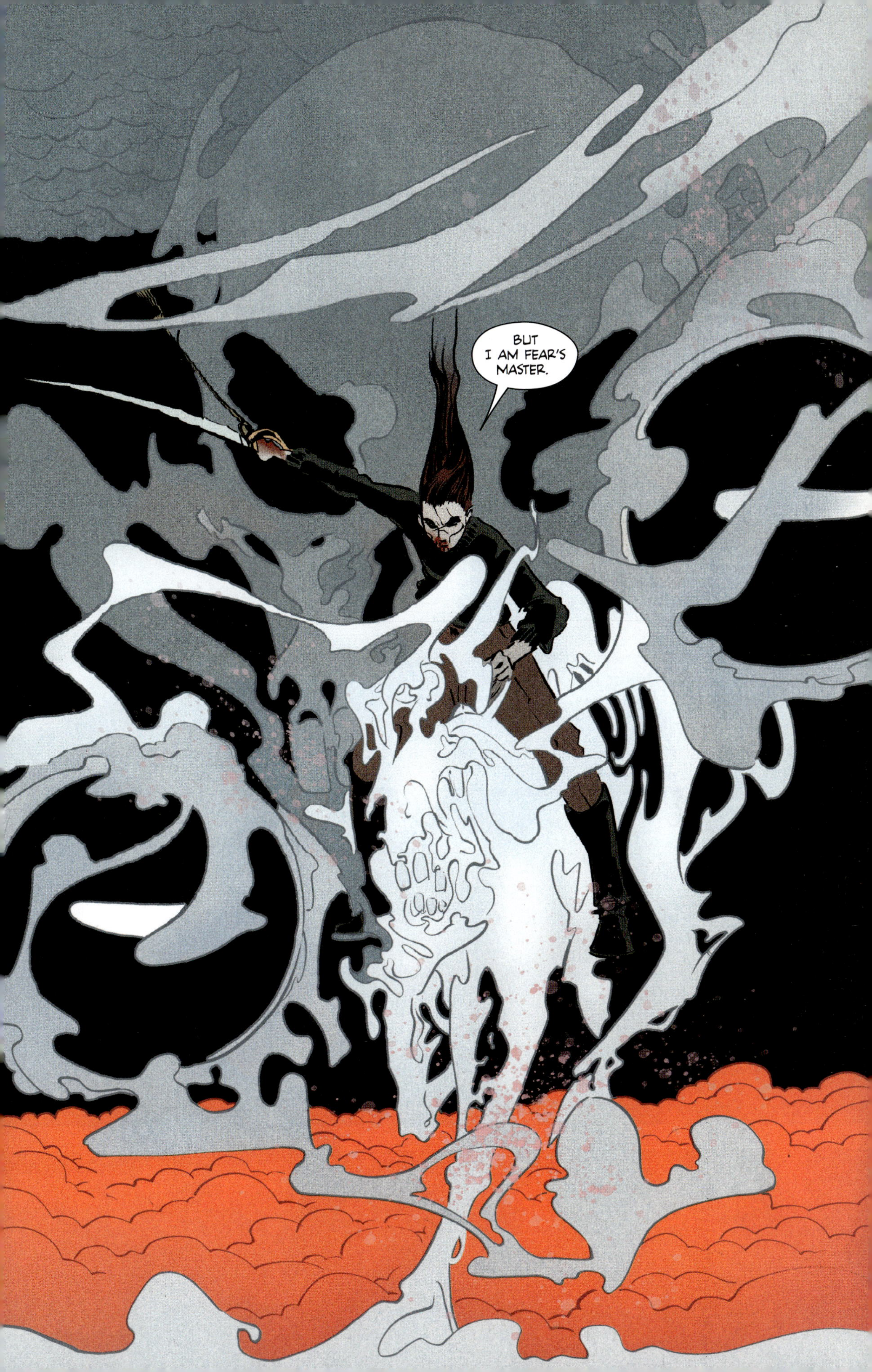
BUT I AM FEAR'S MASTER.

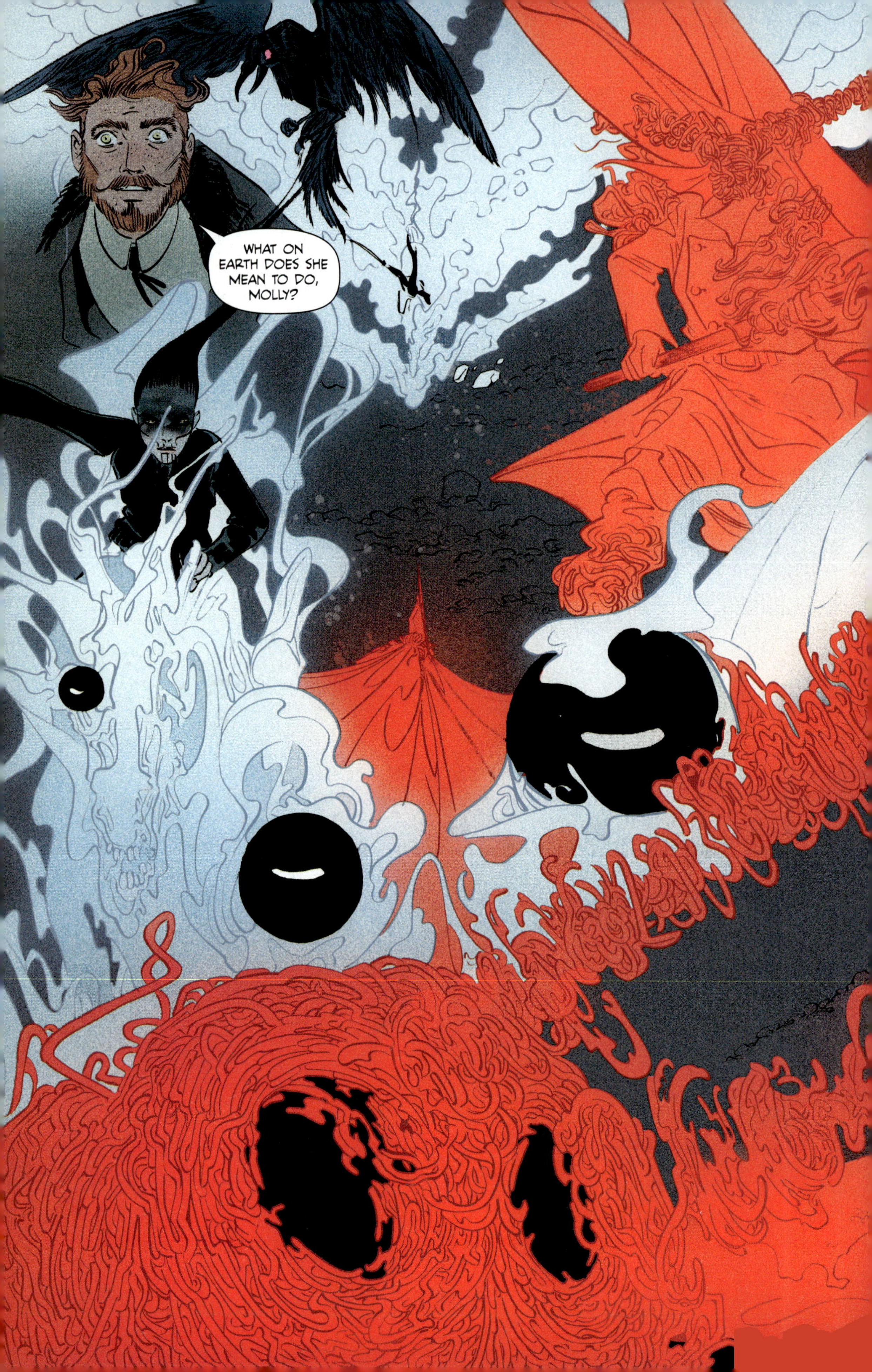
WHAT ON EARTH DOES SHE MEAN TO DO, MOLLY?

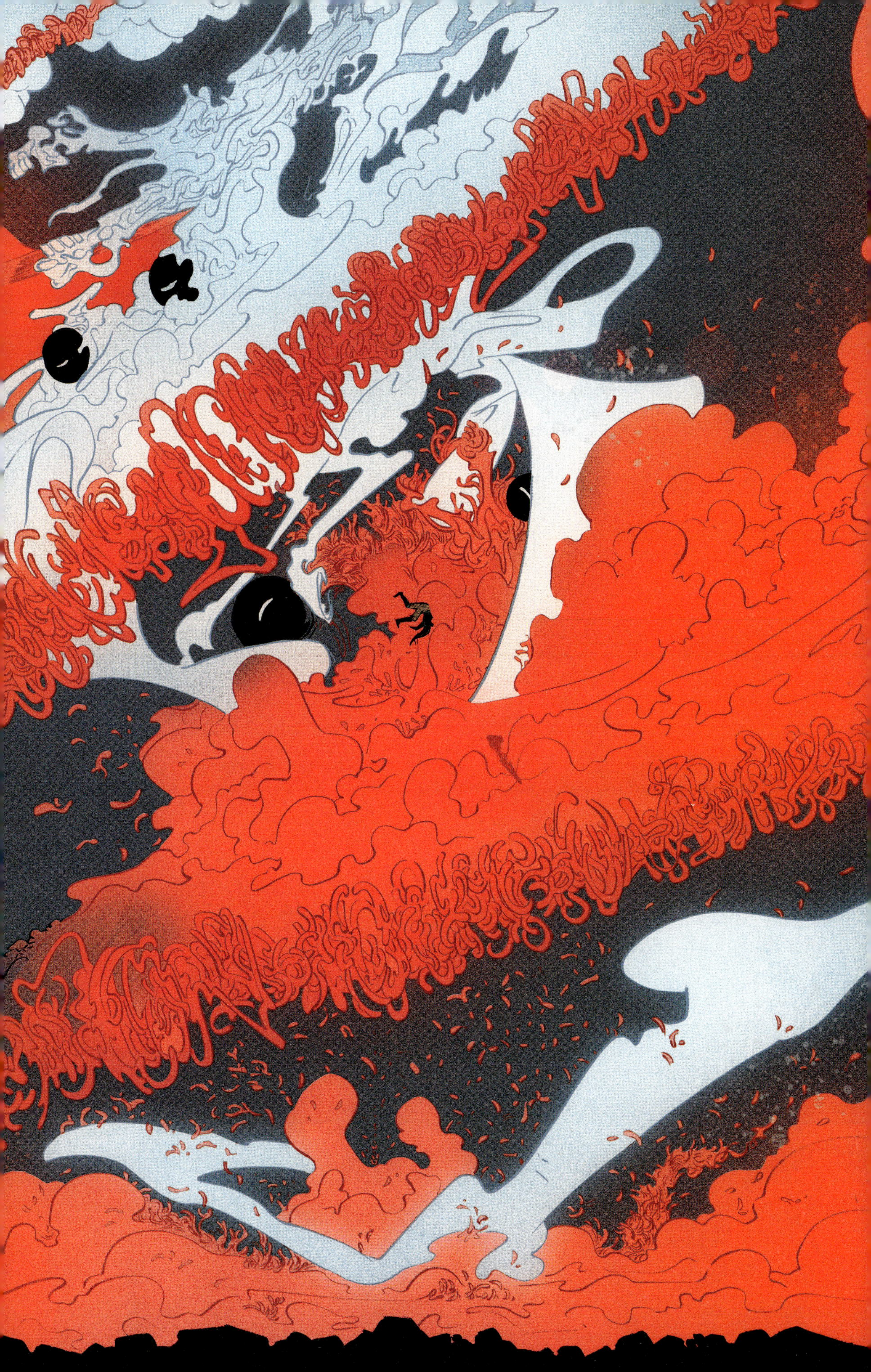

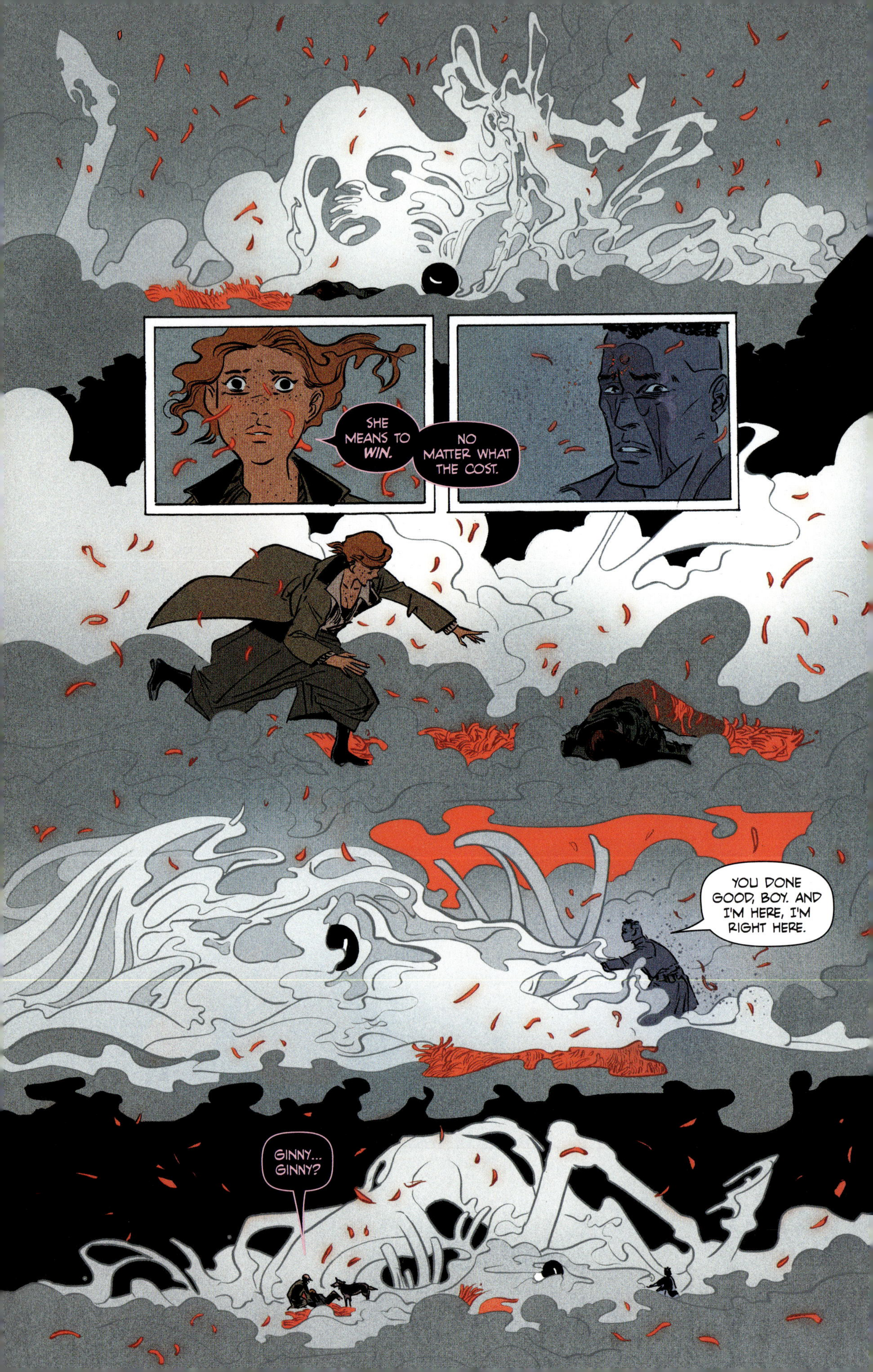
SHE MEANS TO WIN.
NO MATTER WHAT THE COST.
YOU DONE GOOD, BOY. AND I'M HERE, I'M RIGHT HERE.
GINNY... GINNY?

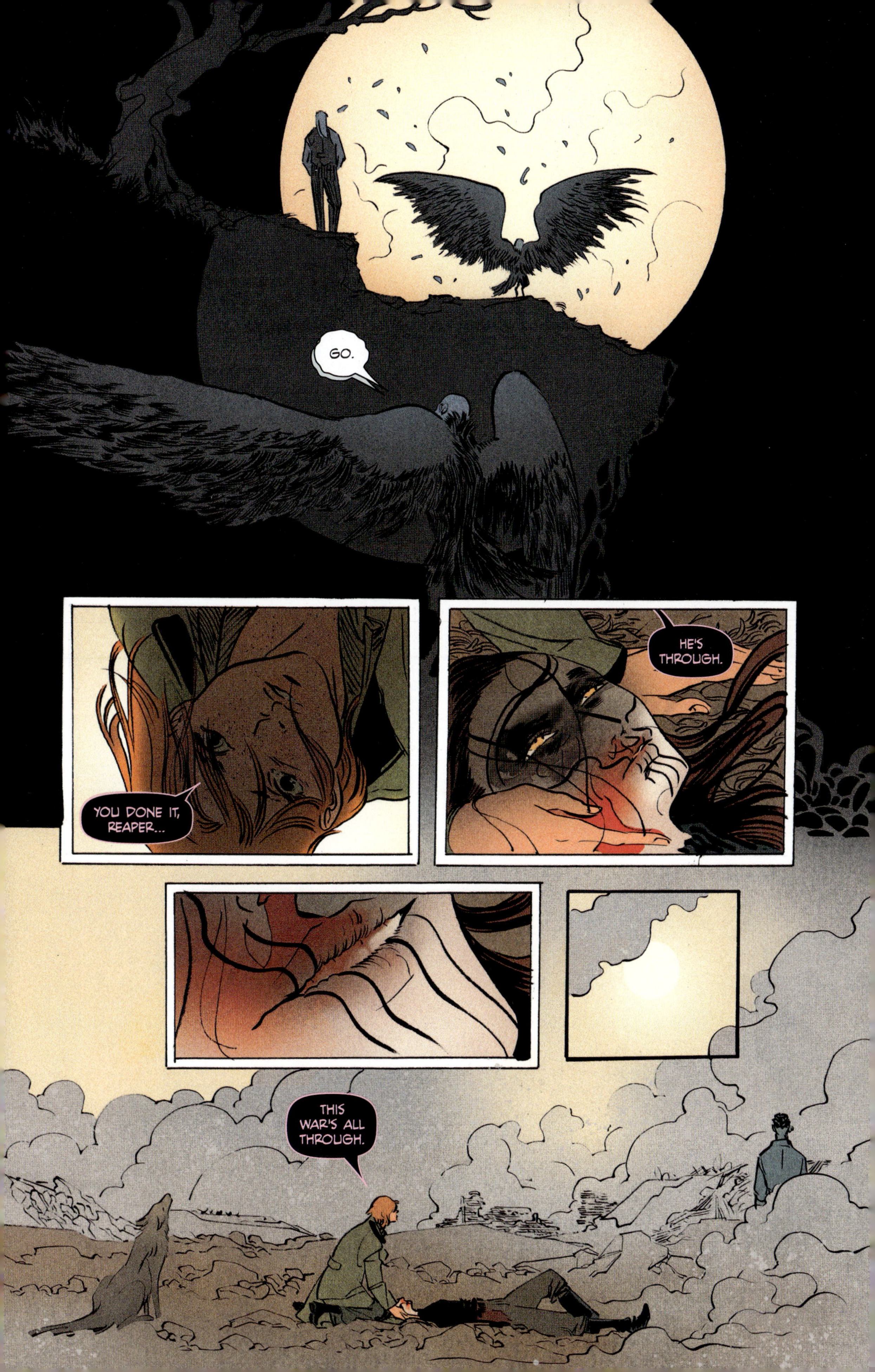
GO.
YOU DONE IT, REAPER...
HE'S THROUGH.
THIS WAR'S ALL THROUGH.

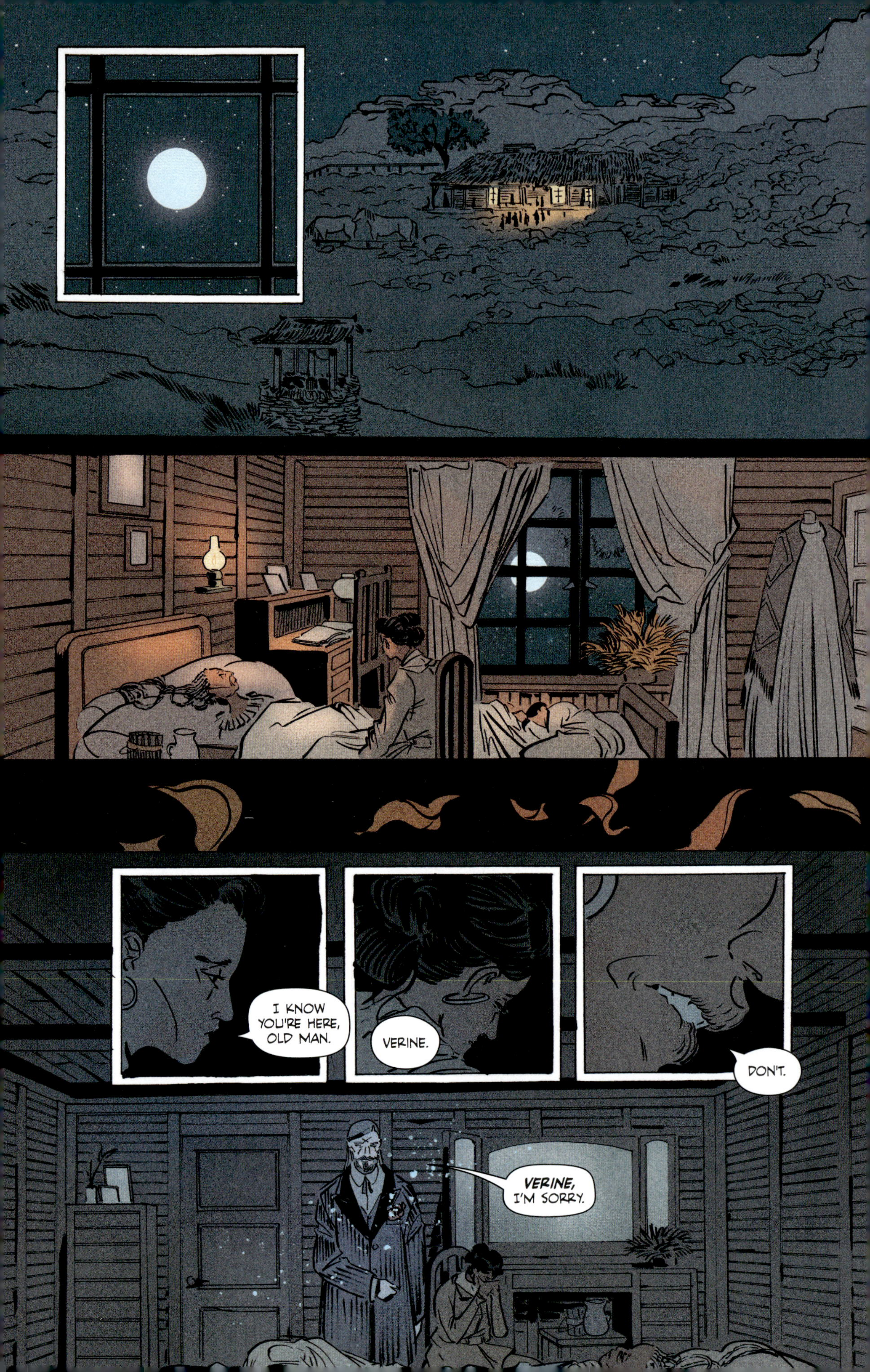
I KNOW YOU'RE HERE, OLD MAN.
VERINE.
DON'T.
VERINE, I'M SORRY.

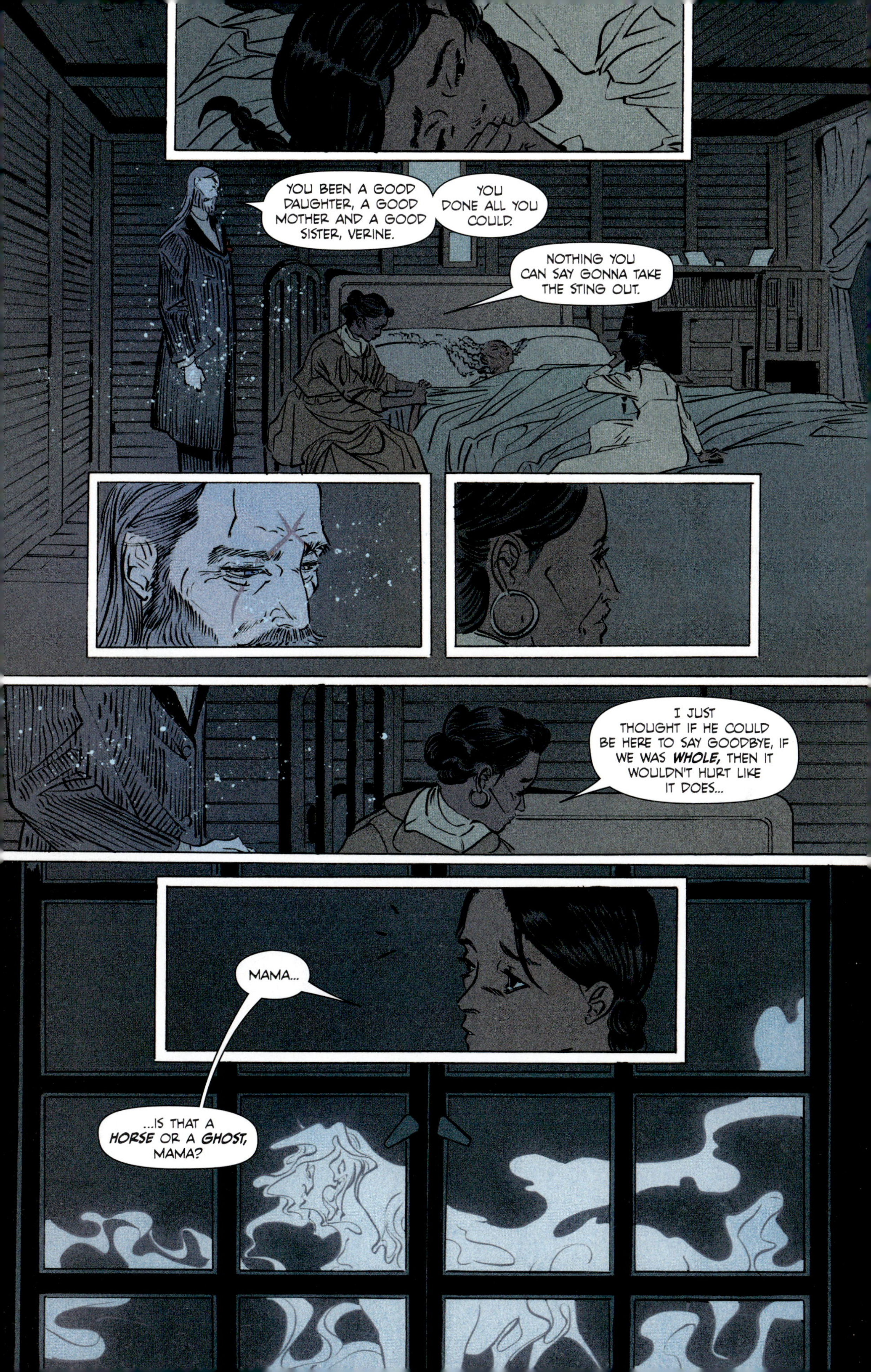
YOU BEEN A GOOD DAUGHTER, A GOOD MOTHER AND A GOOD SISTER, VERINE.
YOU DONE ALL YOU COULD.
NOTHING YOU CAN SAY GONNA TAKE THE STING OUT.
I JUST THOUGHT IF HE COULD BE HERE TO SAY GOODBYE, IF WE WAS ***WHOLE,*** THEN IT WOULDN'T HURT LIKE IT DOES...
MAMA...
...IS THAT A ***HORSE*** OR A ***GHOST,*** MAMA?

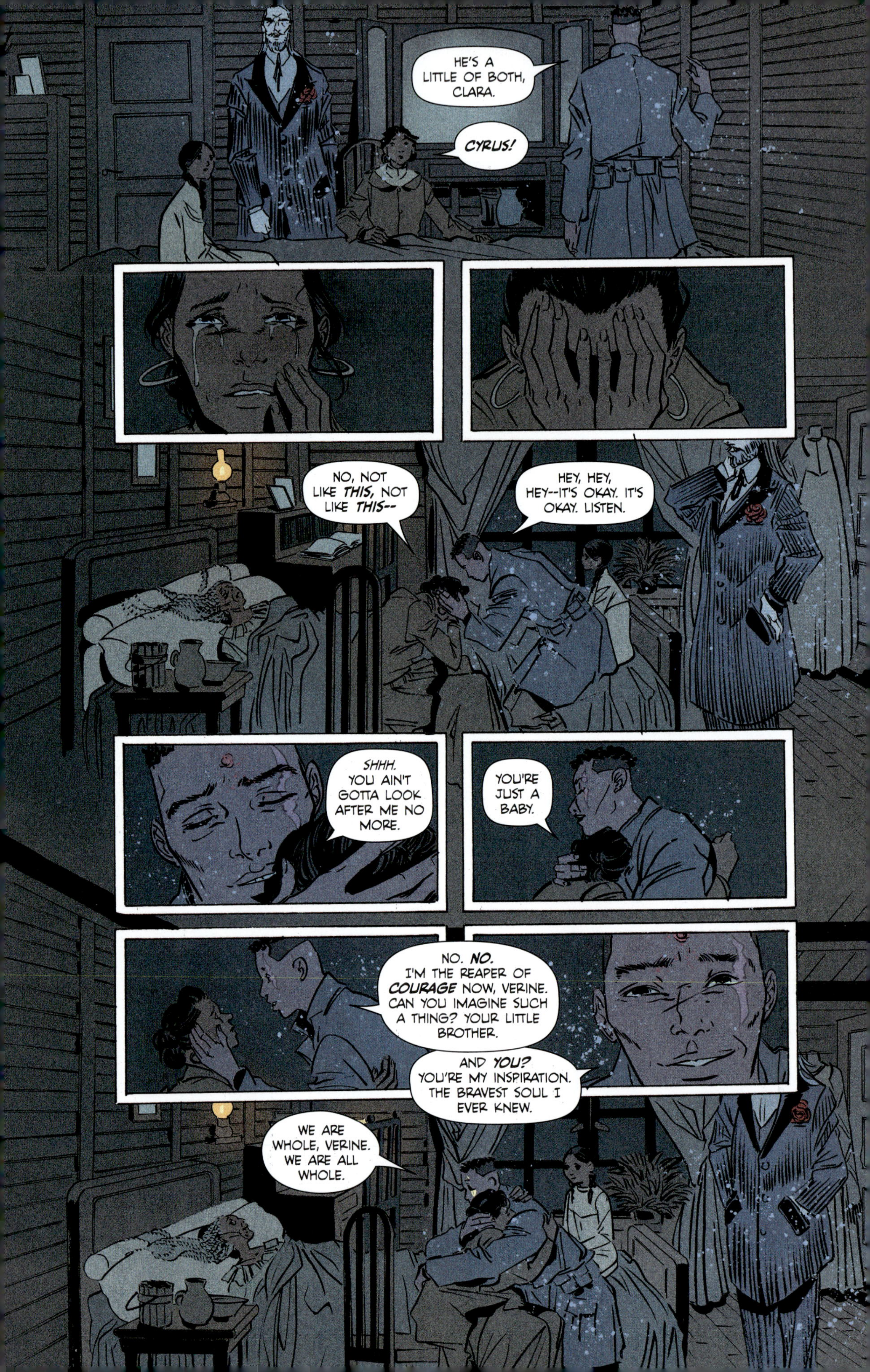
HE'S A LITTLE OF BOTH, CLARA.
CYRUS!
NO, NOT LIKE THIS, NOT LIKE THIS--
HEY, HEY, HEY--IT'S OKAY. IT'S OKAY. LISTEN.
SHHH. YOU AIN'T GOTTA LOOK AFTER ME NO MORE.
YOU'RE JUST A BABY.
NO. NO. I'M THE REAPER OF COURAGE NOW, VERINE. CAN YOU IMAGINE SUCH A THING? YOUR LITTLE BROTHER.
AND YOU? YOU'RE MY INSPIRATION. THE BRAVEST SOUL I EVER KNEW.
WE ARE WHOLE, VERINE. WE ARE ALL WHOLE.

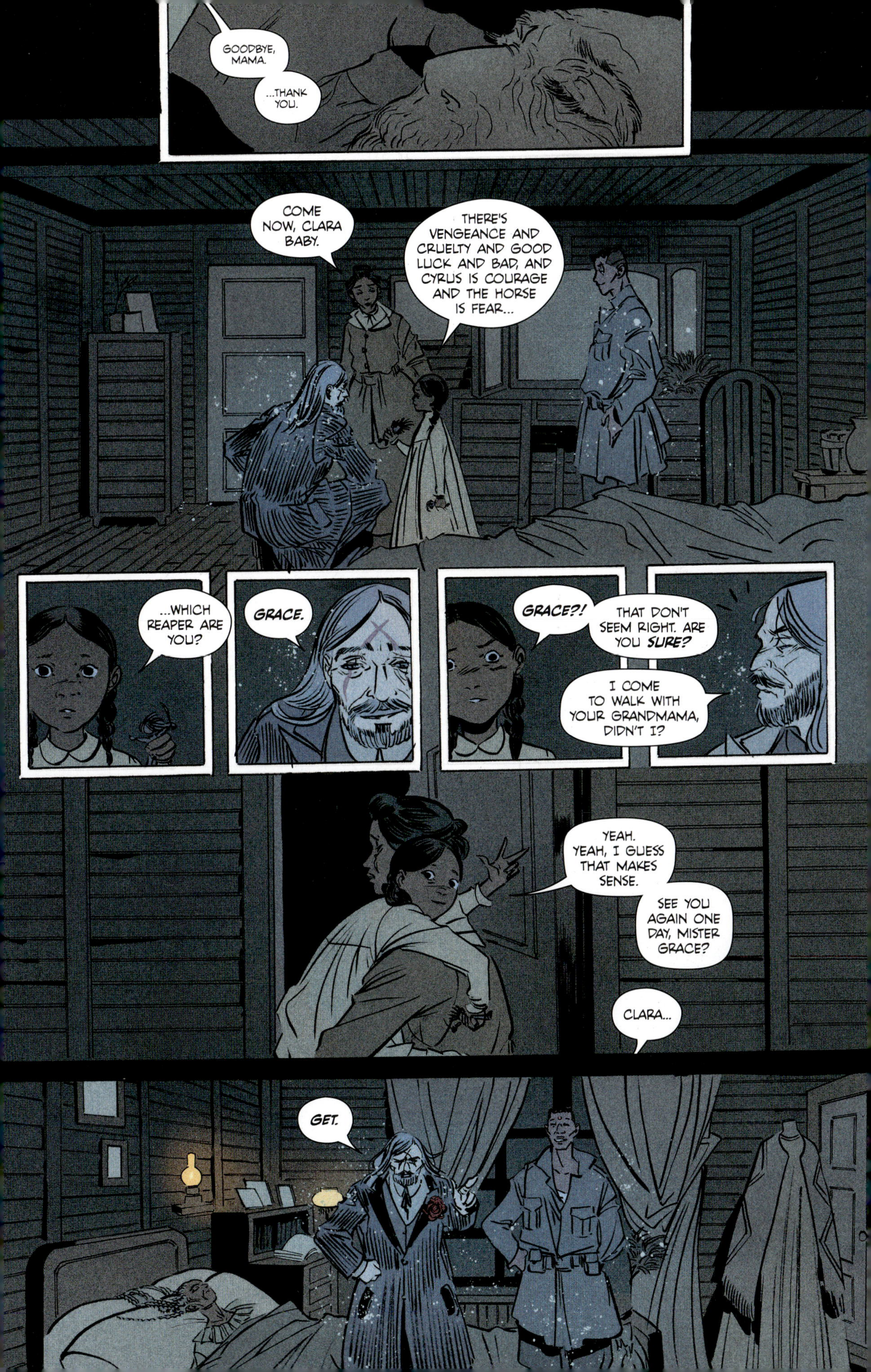
GOODBYE, MAMA.
...THANK YOU.
COME NOW, CLARA BABY.
THERE'S VENGEANCE AND CRUELTY AND GOOD LUCK AND BAD, AND CYRUS IS COURAGE AND THE HORSE IS FEAR...
...WHICH REAPER ARE YOU?
GRACE.
GRACE?!
THAT DON'T SEEM RIGHT. ARE YOU SURE?
I COME TO WALK WITH YOUR GRANDMAMA, DIDN'T I?
YEAH. YEAH, I GUESS THAT MAKES SENSE.
SEE YOU AGAIN ONE DAY, MISTER GRACE?
CLARA...
GET.

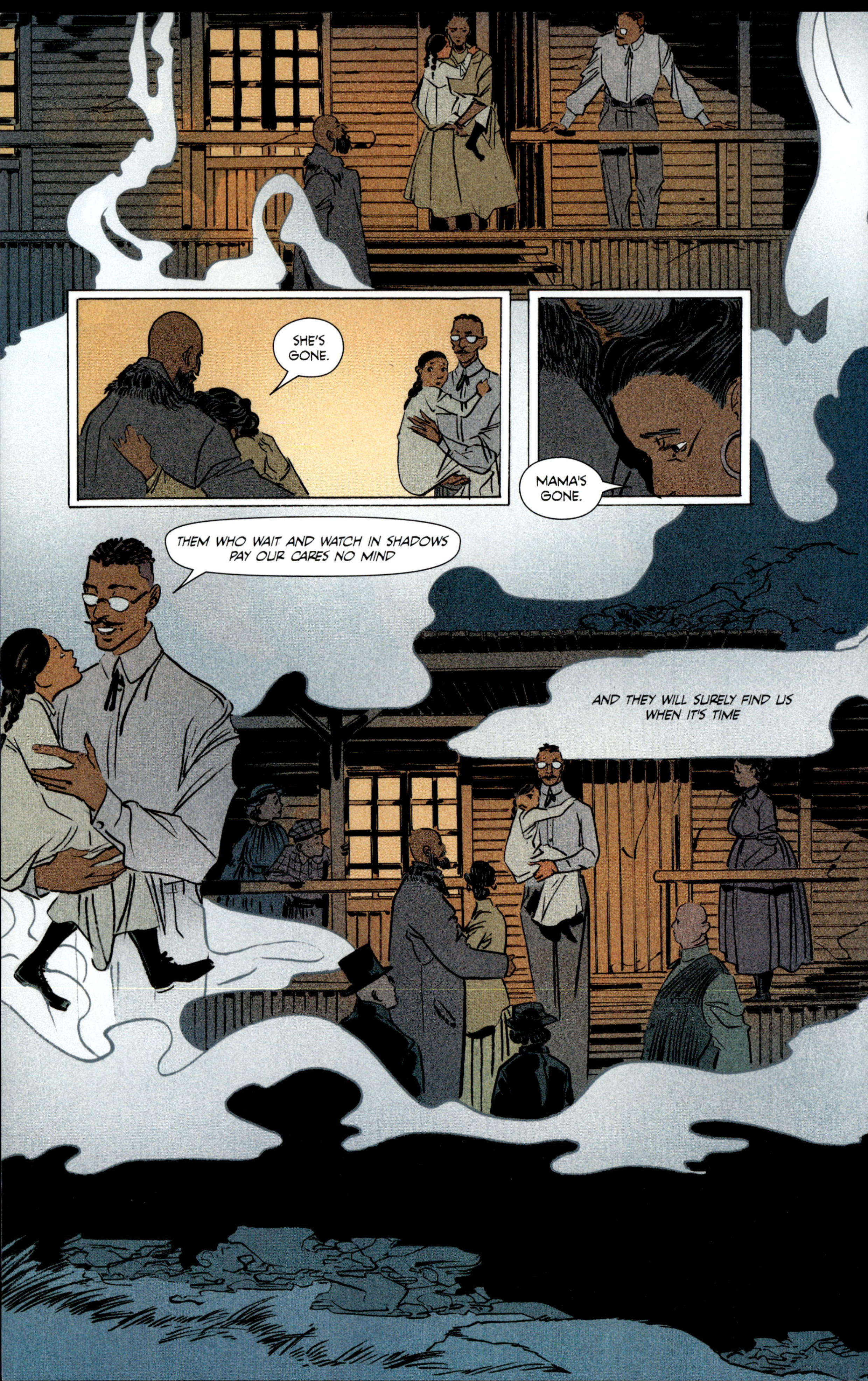
SHE'S GONE.
MAMA'S GONE.
THEM WHO WAIT AND WATCH IN SHADOWS PAY OUR CARES NO MIND
AND THEY WILL SURELY FIND US WHEN IT'S TIME

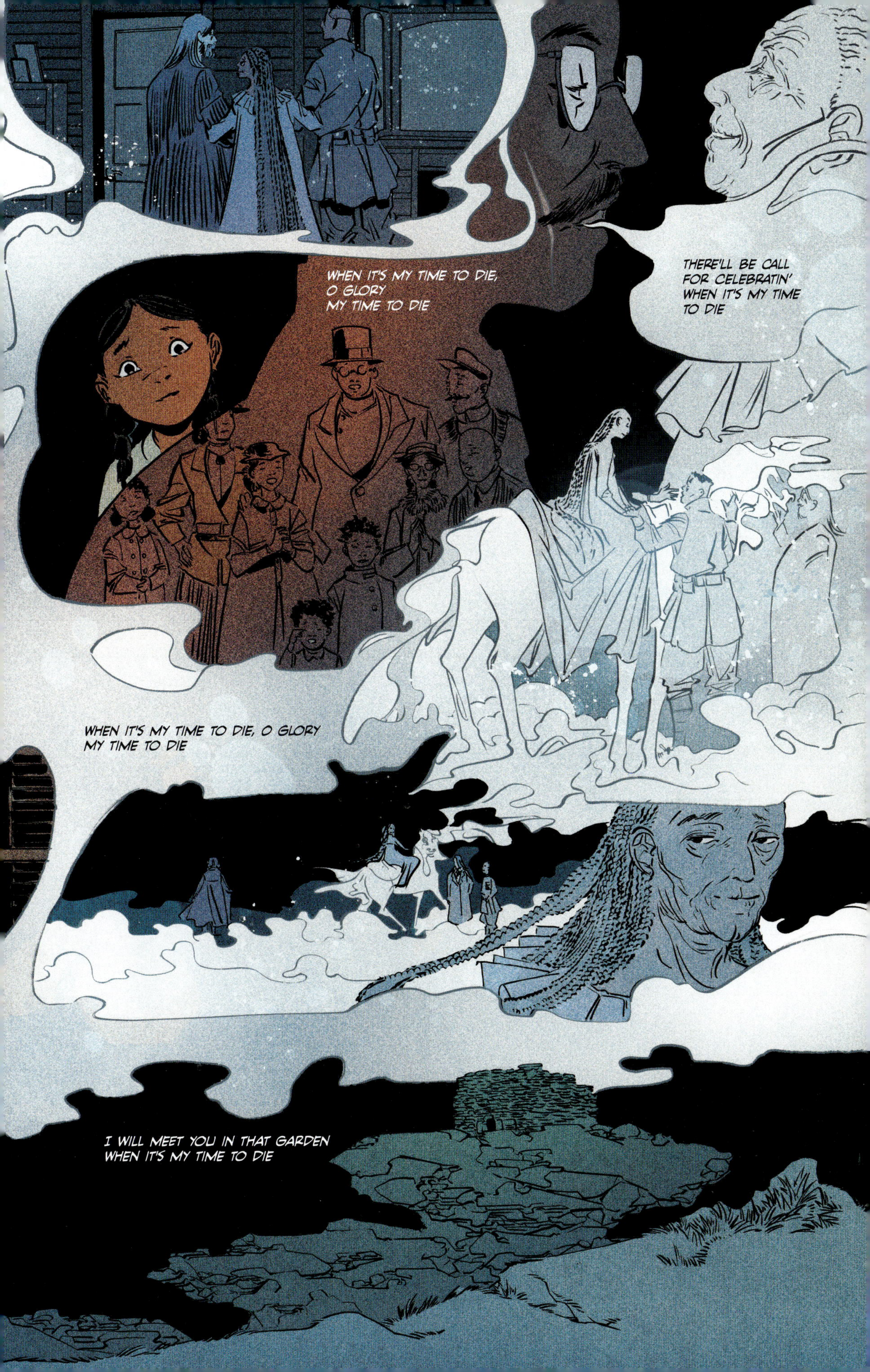
WHEN IT'S MY TIME TO DIE, O GLORY MY TIME TO DIE
THERE'LL BE CALL FOR CELEBRATIN' WHEN IT'S MY TIME TO DIE
WHEN IT'S MY TIME TO DIE, O GLORY MY TIME TO DIE
I WILL MEET YOU IN THAT GARDEN WHEN IT'S MY TIME TO DIE

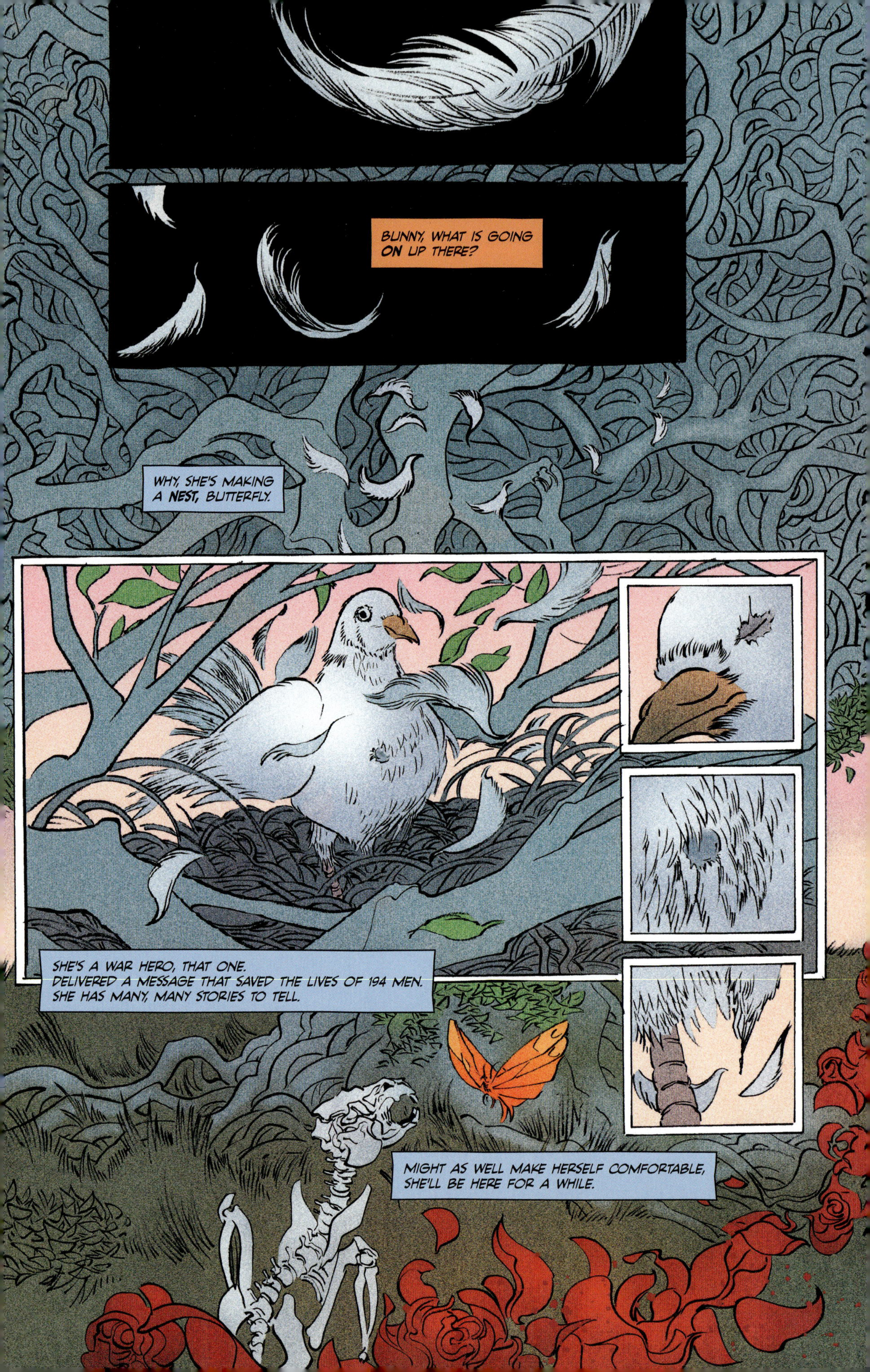
BUNNY, WHAT IS GOING ON UP THERE?
WHY, SHE'S MAKING A NEST, BUTTERFLY.
SHE'S A WAR HERO, THAT ONE. DELIVERED A MESSAGE THAT SAVED THE LIVES OF 194 MEN. SHE HAS MANY, MANY STORIES TO TELL.
MIGHT AS WELL MAKE HERSELF COMFORTABLE, SHE'LL BE HERE FOR A WHILE.

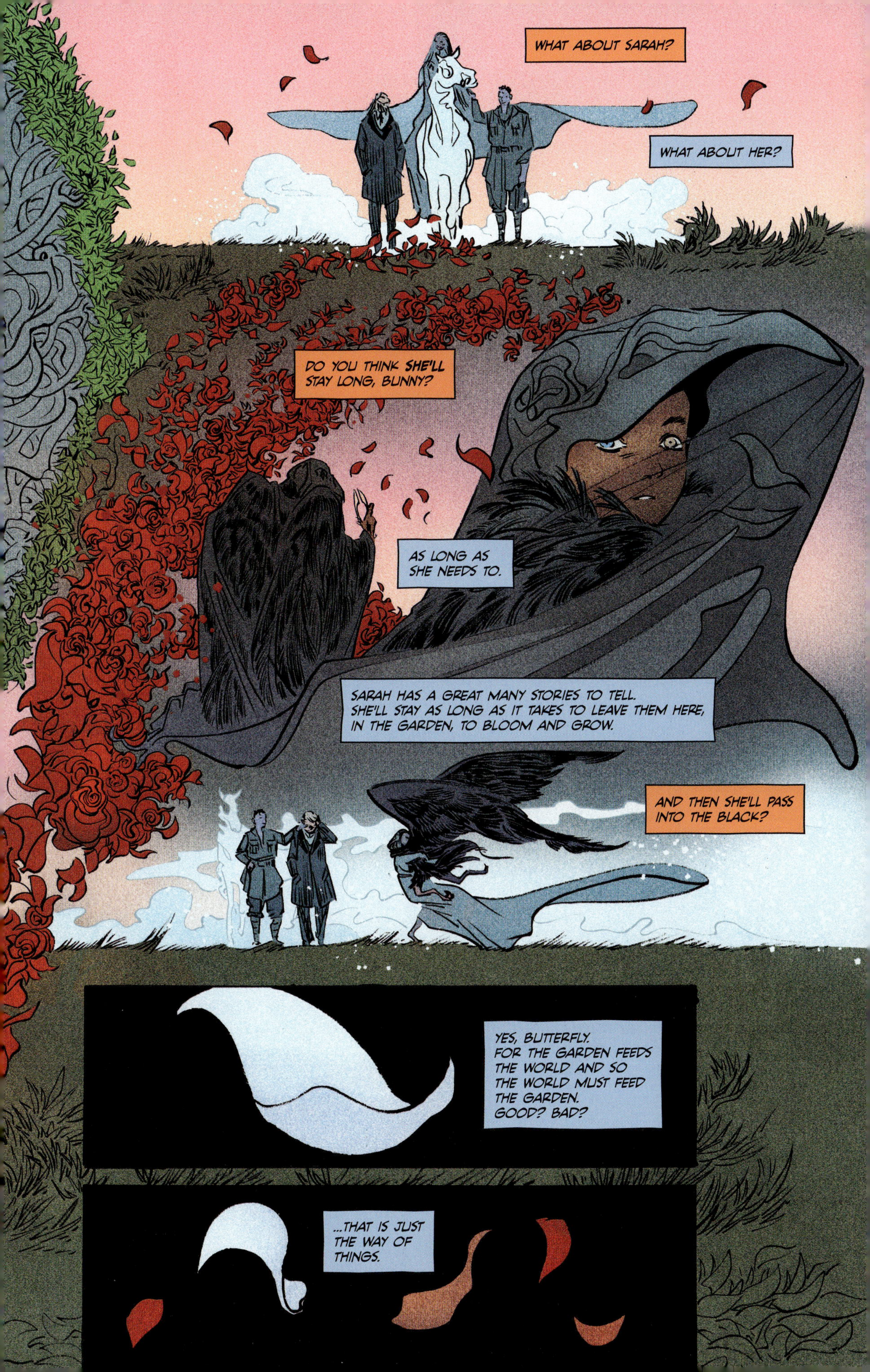
WHAT ABOUT SARAH?
WHAT ABOUT HER?
DO YOU THINK SHE'LL STAY LONG, BUNNY?
AS LONG AS SHE NEEDS TO.
SARAH HAS A GREAT MANY STORIES TO TELL. SHE'LL STAY AS LONG AS IT TAKES TO LEAVE THEM HERE, IN THE GARDEN, TO BLOOM AND GROW.
AND THEN SHE'LL PASS INTO THE BLACK?
YES, BUTTERFLY. FOR THE GARDEN FEEDS THE WORLD AND SO THE WORLD MUST FEED THE GARDEN. GOOD? BAD?
...THAT IS JUST THE WAY OF THINGS.

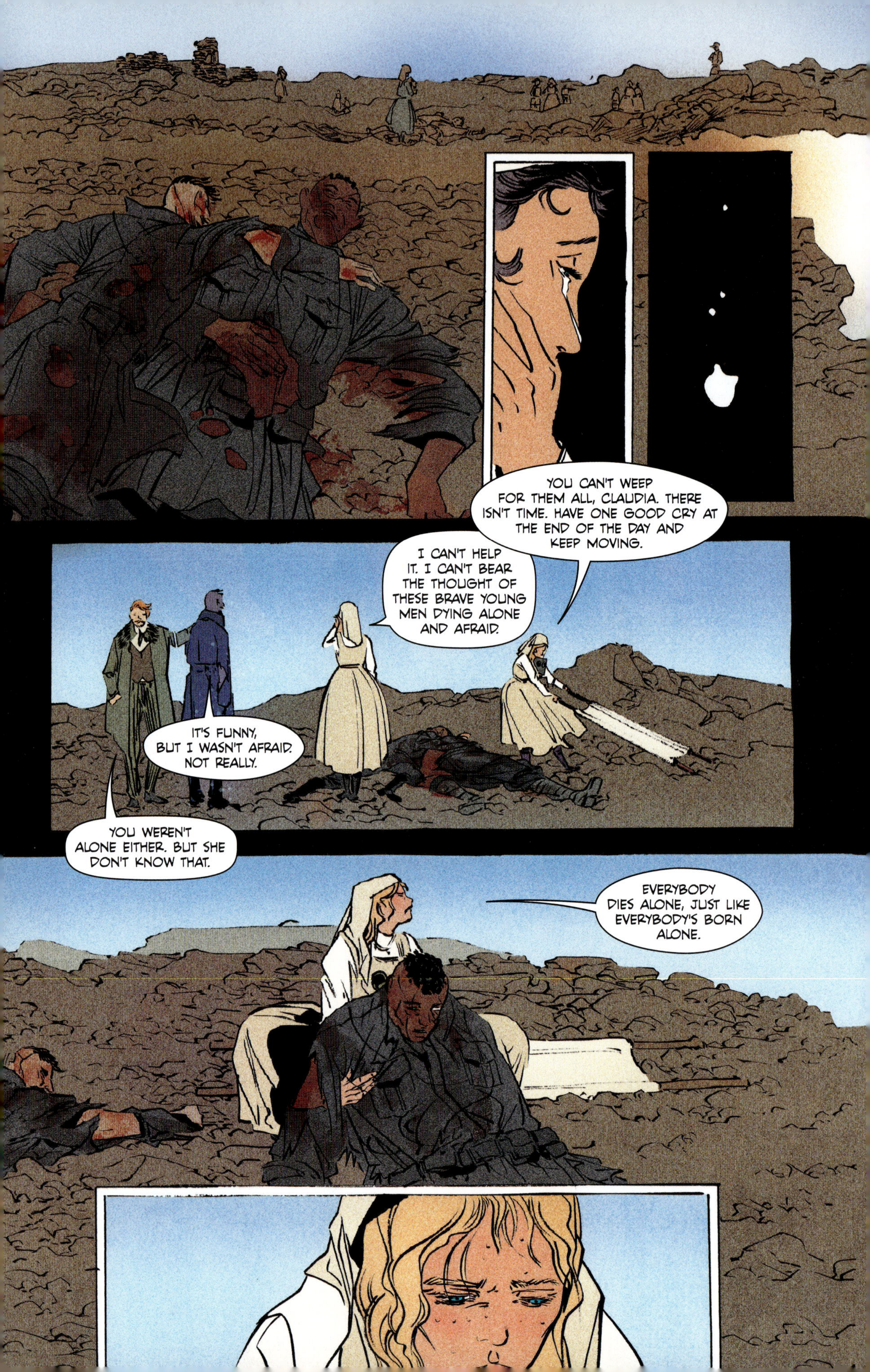
YOU CAN'T WEEP FOR THEM ALL, CLAUDIA. THERE ISN'T TIME. HAVE ONE GOOD CRY AT THE END OF THE DAY AND KEEP MOVING.
I CAN'T HELP IT. I CAN'T BEAR THE THOUGHT OF THESE BRAVE YOUNG MEN DYING ALONE AND AFRAID.
IT'S FUNNY, BUT I WASN'T AFRAID. NOT REALLY.
YOU WEREN'T ALONE EITHER. BUT SHE DON'T KNOW THAT.
EVERYBODY DIES ALONE, JUST LIKE EVERYBODY'S BORN ALONE.

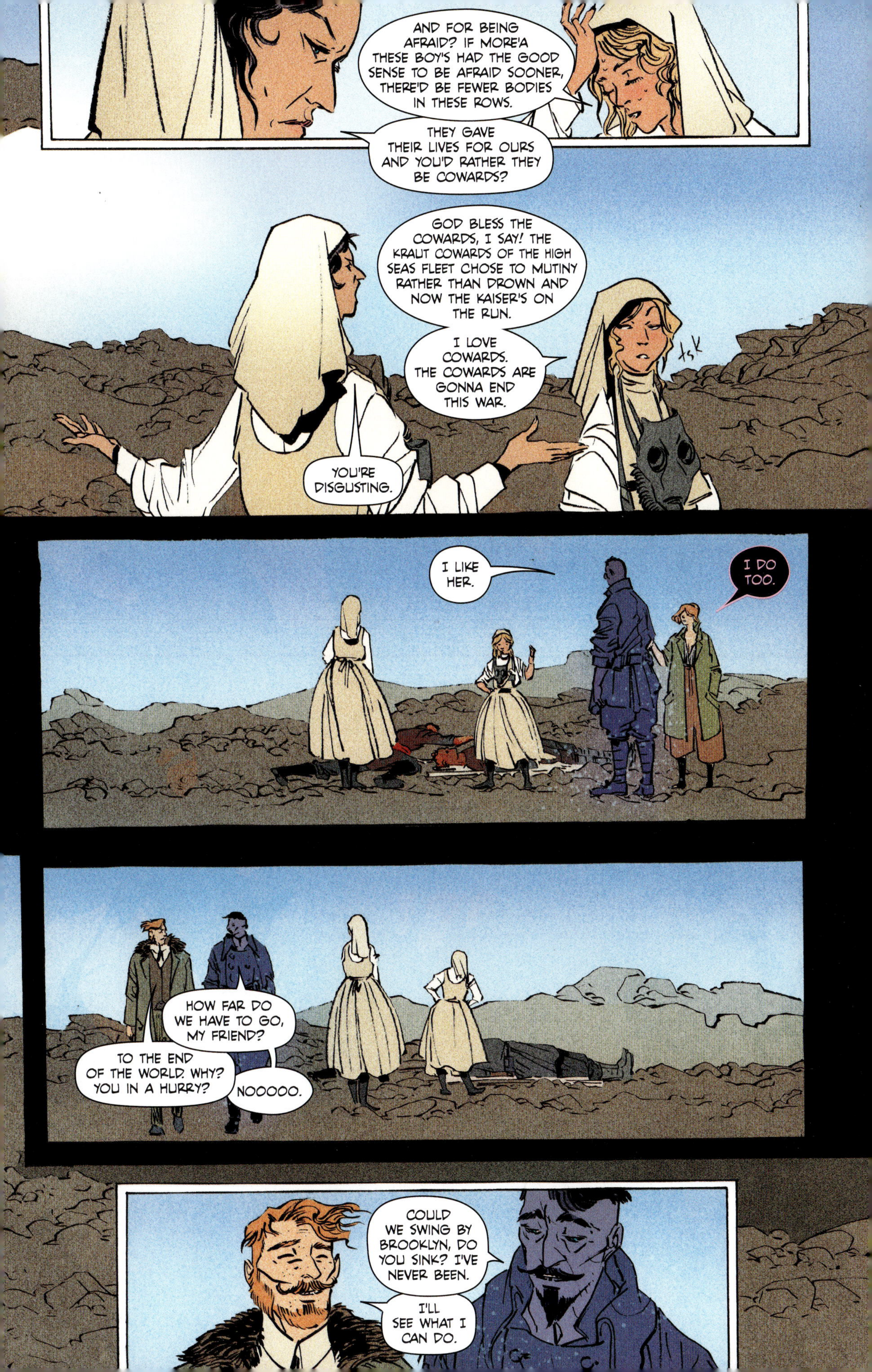
AND FOR BEING AFRAID? IF MORE'A THESE BOY'S HAD THE GOOD SENSE TO BE AFRAID SOONER, THERE'D BE FEWER BODIES IN THESE ROWS.
THEY GAVE THEIR LIVES FOR OURS AND YOU'D RATHER THEY BE COWARDS?
GOD BLESS THE COWARDS, I SAY! THE KRAUT COWARDS OF THE HIGH SEAS FLEET CHOSE TO MUTINY RATHER THAN DROWN AND NOW THE KAISER'S ON THE RUN.
I LOVE COWARDS. THE COWARDS ARE GONNA END THIS WAR.
tsk
YOU'RE DISGUSTING.
I LIKE HER.
I DO TOO.
HOW FAR DO WE HAVE TO GO, MY FRIEND?
TO THE END OF THE WORLD. WHY? YOU IN A HURRY?
NOOOOO.
COULD WE SWING BY BROOKLYN, DO YOU SINK? I'VE NEVER BEEN.
I'LL SEE WHAT I CAN DO.

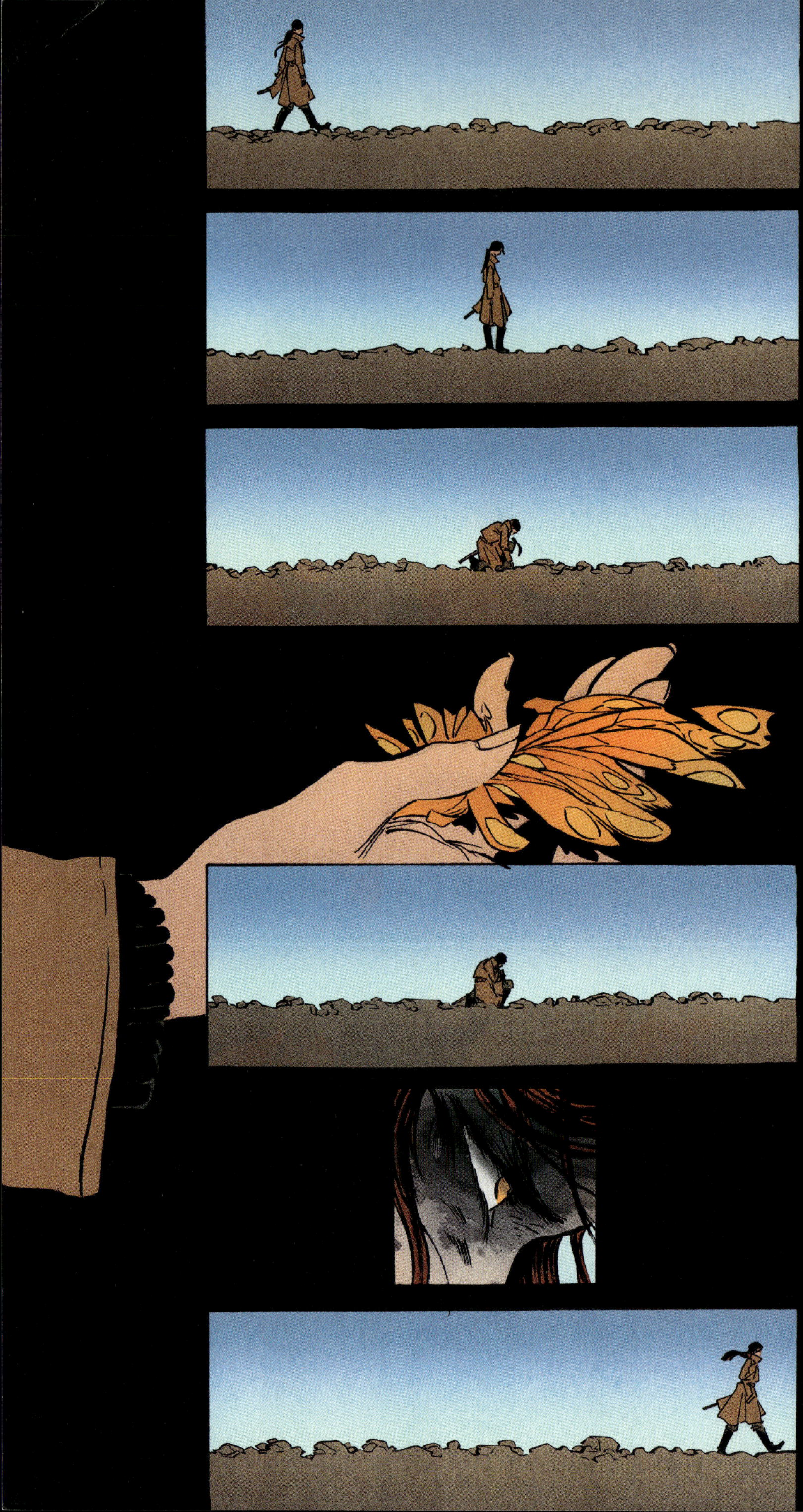

DEATHFACE GINNY WILL RETURN IN **PRETTY DEADLY VOLUME 3.**

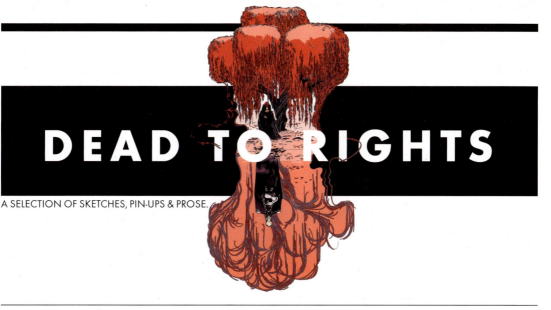

DEAD TO RIGHTS

A SELECTION OF SKETCHES, PIN-UPS & PROSE.

Falling Up

ORIGINALLY PRINTED IN PRETTY DEADLY #1.

1.
Papillion, NE. 1977. Ish.

My gymnastics coach – a kid not even half the age I am today, but an adult to my young eyes – urged me to let go. He'd catch me and carry me through the dismount, he said. I willed my hand to release, my fingers to uncurl, but they wouldn't. They couldn't. I could not.

Coach made a joke, something I remember thinking was cruel or intended to be cruel, but I was too divorced from the moment to be wounded by it. I knew when I left that day I would not return and my mind had moved on to wonder where I would spend Tuesday and Thursday evenings from there on out. (Spoilers: On the floor of my room reading comic books and listening to terrible records.)

I held Mom's hand and my chin unusually high as we made our way to the car that evening. Children long to know themselves and I had just learned something new about me. From then on if anyone asked what I was afraid of, I would have an answer.

I am afraid of falling.

2.
Hahn, Germany. 1981.

We were running for our lives, my friends and I, and my terror was such that the world around me turned red, red like the white rabbit's eyes; red as a default, red as a base.

We were running through a dream house – not an expensive condo, a dream house, a house in a dream, with all the attendant dead ends and irrational staircases. We were making our way up, toward the roof.

Not until we burst out into the crimson night did it dawn on me that we'd doomed ourselves, running up, up, up, to the rooftop, up to where the house would eventually end. The rest of the boxcar children kept going, not even slowing, right off the edge of the aging manor where they seemed to hang in the air for a moment..

And then they flew.

It was a nightmare, some three decades ago, but I recall in harrowing clarity the feeling of betrayal and inadequacy as I watched my compatriots take to the sky.

Does everyone know how to do this but me?

I felt the hot breath of our pursuer on my neck before I turned to face him and woke myself with a scream.

3.
Austin, TX. 1986.

I sat with another sixteen-year-old girl at the back of a college auditorium as a very serious man read a very serious poem about a sentient pile of dead bodies in the Holocaust. The pile – the "heap," I think he called it – spoke. The very serious man screamed the pile's dialogue. The very serious man used a diaphragmatic thrust to belt lines like "lick my puss-filled wounds!" so loud they shook the room.

There is nothing funny about the horror of the Holocaust. And yet.

We'd won a contest to get there, stayed up nearly all night preparing for... for whatever it was that we expected a collegiate poetry symposium to be. We were teenagers, under-rested and over-confident, and if the program of old lady's verses and art therapy slide shows set us up, the anthropomorphic screaming sick-covered heap knocked us down.

The harder we tried not to laugh the funnier it became. They ought to have asked us to leave. I can't imagine why they did not.

At the peak of our assholery, our own high school English teacher took the stage. That we were likely facing some sort of disciplinary action already only added to the comedic value.

"Before I begin, I'd like to read a piece by Guillaume Apollinaire," he said and his voice took on the quality of a warning.

The verse was simple.

> 'Come to the edge.'
> 'We can't. We're afraid.'
> 'Come to the edge.'
> 'We can't. We will fall!'
> 'Come to the edge.'
> And they came.
> And he pushed them.
> And they flew.

I recalled my red house dream and the parity stopped me cold.

4.
New York, NY. 2000.

The morning after my 30th birthday I leaned over the bathroom sink and watched streaks of red blood and blue toothpaste circle the drain.

I was two months clean and sober and I'd tried to climb out of my skin that year. I'd quit my job, cut my hair, dumped my boyfriend and moved into a shitty little two-bedroom apartment that I shared with five members of a rap/metal fusion band called TEAM SPYDER. I was trying to escape me, disguise me, fool me, but the faster I ran, the closer I followed.

The two of us – Old Me and New Me – spent the afternoon riding the Coney Island rollercoaster with Maggie, our guru. Maggie was strange and sexy like a French film. She wrote books and collected dead words and horrible men. We wanted to be her.

The Cyclone looked to be held together by gum. Old Me and New Me white-knuckled the safety bar and braced ourselves hard against every quick turn, afraid that gravity would smash us into Maggie and we'd crush her with our cumulative weight. Our thighs ached from the great effort it took to sit still.

Not six inches to our left, Maggie was on a different ride entirely. Ginger Rogers to the Cyclone's Fred Astaire, she deftly anticipated every turn, eyes closed, beaming. At the crest of the first drop she threw her hands over her head and screamed in celebration as we fought the inevitable, pulling up hard against the metal, as if we could muscle the car to take flight.

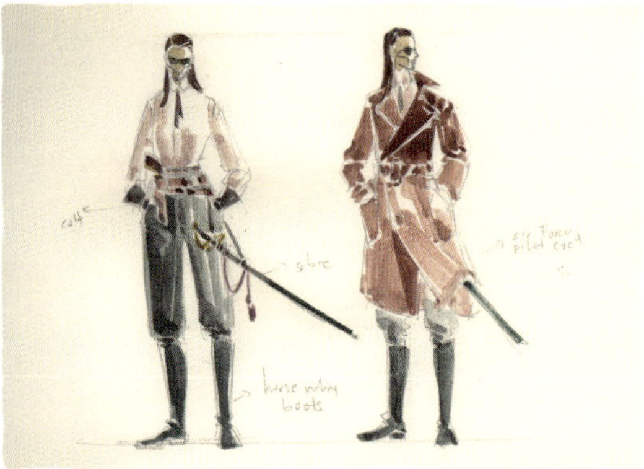
cuff
sabre
horse whip boots
pilot coat

5.
Kansas City, MO. 2005.

Ivan Brandon invited me to write for an Image anthology called 24SEVEN. Andy MacDonald would draw. I wasn't consciously aware of it then, but I've since learned I write not by picturing but by listening.

When I listened for that story, I only heard noise. Every angel, devil and writer-I-wanted-to-be, spoke at once in a deafening chorus. I tried to discern my voice through the cacophony, but eventually I gave up.

(It never gets better until I give up. I don't know why I don't give up sooner.)

When I came back, I wrote about the noise. I wrote about a Collector, a boy who took something – a literal thing, a souvenir – from every interaction. Eventually the Collector was so encumbered by the weight of what he carried that he was lost, hidden in his pile – his heap – of things.

I wrote myself into a corner – a rooftop, unsurprisingly. I wanted to say something and I'd said it, but I needed an ending.

The boy and I threw ourselves off the roof. Just before impact, the junk fell off the boy, revealing wings.

Old Me turned to New Me as the Collector fell skyward, "I didn't know he had those."

New Me answered, "Neither did he."

We called the story "Leap."

6.
New York, NY. 2009.

Emma Ríos and I sat face-to-face for the first time in a coffee shop around the corner from the Javits. There was an open notebook between us and I was trying to explain the story as I saw it in terms of a shape – something like a capital letter "D," lying on its back.

A straight line, left to right, and then an arc back to the starting point.

"An arrow shot East, then pulled back in a natural curve to the West. See?"

Emma looked at the page, at me, at the page again, at me again, and then, with no good reason to do so, made the decision to take the leap. Though it would be another couple of years before we would draw up contracts and work on PRETTY DEADLY in earnest, the core of it, the heart of it, exists in echoes of that moment.

7.
Portland, OR. 2011.

I'd landed my first ongoing comics gig, writing Carol Danvers as Captain Marvel for Marvel Comics. I was terrified of failing on the big stage.

In developing my take on the character, I decided Carol, a super-powered recovering alcoholic, got high as a deliberate Icarus, flying to the edge of space, passing out and relying on her body's ability to absorb friction as heat to jump-start her heart before she barreled into the earth.

In reviewing my 17 issues, I find my subconscious decidedly unsubtle.

8.
Portland, OR. 4 days ago.

Backmatter should have been done but I hadn't started this piece, the last piece. I had a million excuses, all legit, but all noise. So much noise.

I had to get something on the page, so I tricked myself, the way I've learned to, by deciding that every word I put down is poorly chosen, that I am giftless, and the best I can ever hope to do is continue to occasionally suck less, progressively, a little more each time, continuously failing up.

I gave up.

I started writing about Emma in the coffee shop just to get words on the page. I thought, "She decided to take the leap." I thought about leaping and falling, falling and flying. Blood and toothpaste. Maggie and the Cyclone.

I thought about the D-shape. The D-shape was dumb.

Maybe not dumb, but wrong. Like the Wild West Show and the dying grandmother and the circus owner, that D-shape was a piece of PRETTY DEADLY that we would discover didn't belong. We scraped those parts away, bits of granite that didn't contain the sculpture. A few of them, I suspect, will find their way into other things. Or in later arcs, perhaps.

I thought about how this book didn't start to come together until I gave up. Until I gave up trying to make it one thing and invited the monsters and rivers of blood and bunnies made out of bones to come on in.

I realized that Emma surrendered first. She decided years ago to take the ride with her hands over her head, screaming, and I see that glee reflected on her pages; her lines a tense flirtation between passion and control.

What Emma did in New York over coffee and my inane scribbling she would do again and again over the years in reassuring emails and silent support. She doesn't judge me for my reluctance to let go. She shakes her head and calls me "Sister Kraken" for my tendency to disappear into the dark places for days at a time. She's certain I'll be back with something for her, even when I am not.

I love this book. I don't talk about the products of my labor in those terms because I don't want to appear arrogant, I tell myself, or unseemly, but really I don't do it because I don't want to be embarrassed by it later. And while it's true that I prefer each issue over the last as the book teaches us how to make it (Issue 3 is my favorite right now, but I suspect that's only because we haven't yet finished Issue 4), I think here my affection is grounded in something other than my fickle assessment of its quality.

Looking back now, I wonder if Emma and PRETTY DEADLY aren't trying to teach me to fall.

– *Kelly Sue DeConnick*

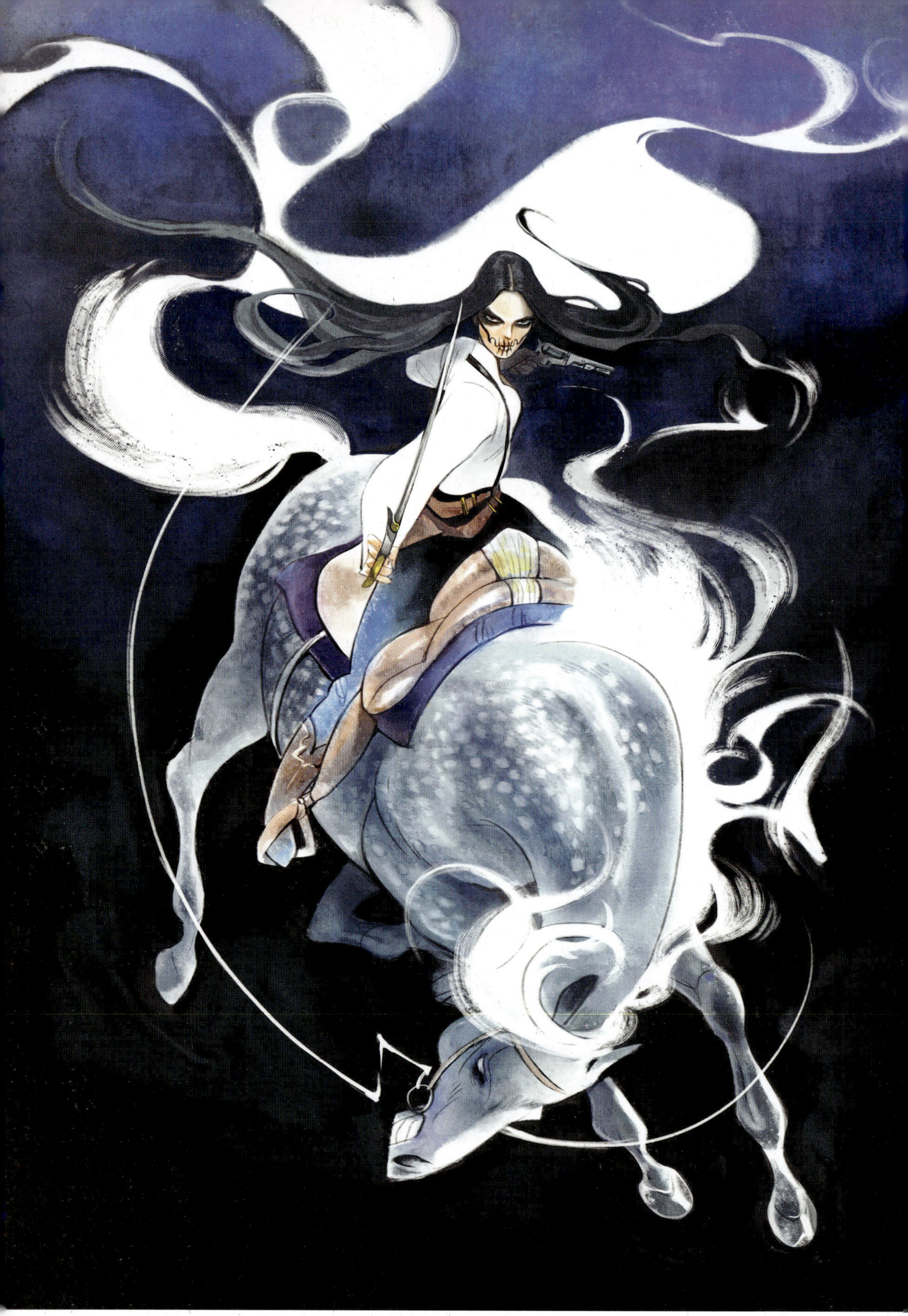

PIN-UP BY **HWEI LIM**
@MADAOBA
LALAGE.TUMBLR.COM

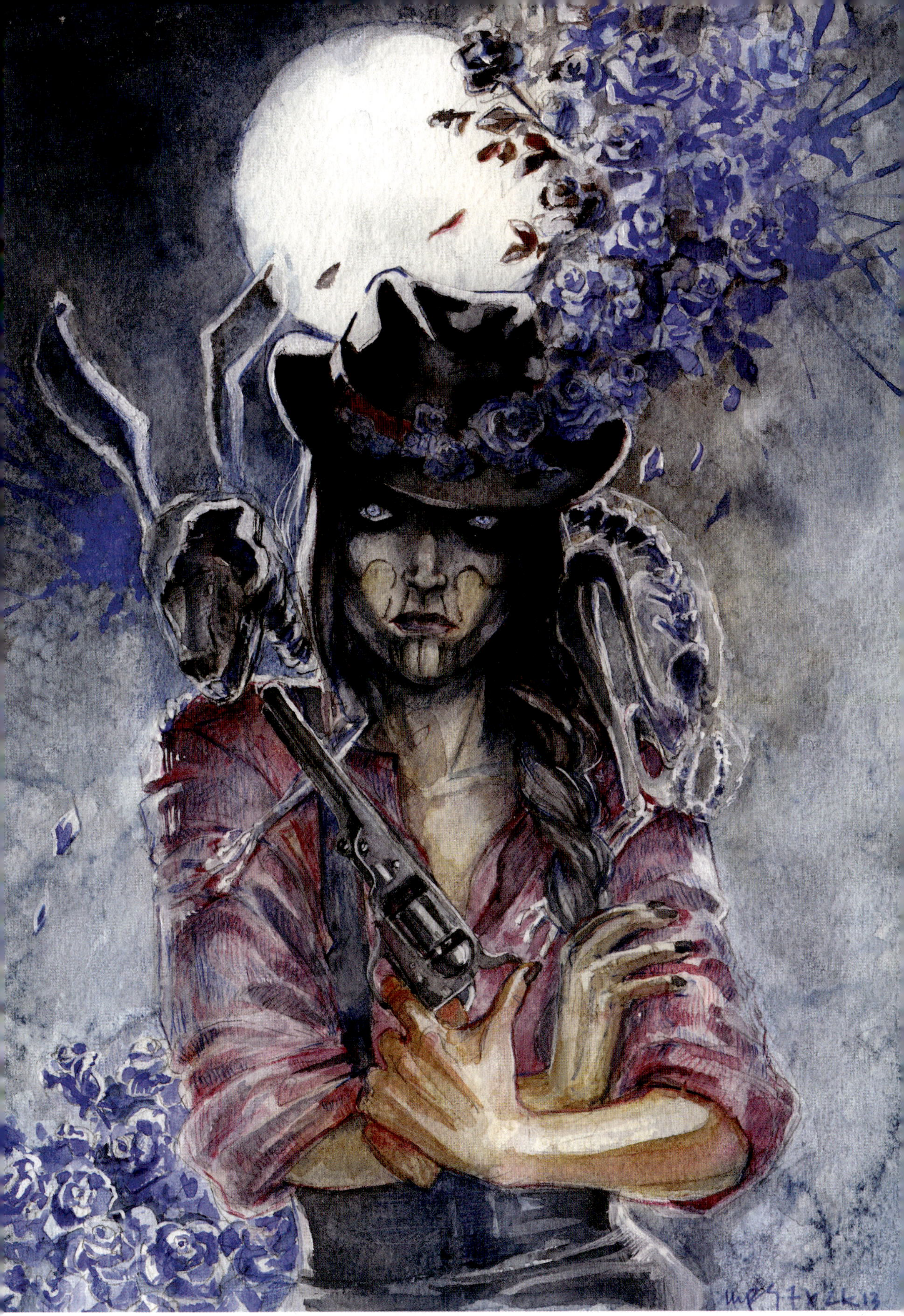

PIN-UP BY **KAŚKA GAZDOWNA**
@GAZDOWNA
GAZDOWNA.PL

The Disgrace of the Scoundrels Johnny Coyote and the Lady Molly Raven as Seduced by a Beguiling Moon

BY CHAD COLLIER WITH ILLUSTRATIONS BY SUMMER SUZUKI
ORIGINALLY PRINTED IN PRETTY DEADLY #1&2.

PART ONE

Moon wasn't always free.

Was a time when Moon's light was tethered to a dusty tract of earth, locked away behind barbed wire. Only a crafty few could evade the fence-riders' patrol, could pass unnoticed long enough to bathe under Moon's cooling glow.

Was a time when two such creatures found themselves on Moon's land, under a Joshua tree. Johnny, because he didn't much care for fences; and Molly, because trespassing was a secret treat, a burning thrill, not unlike the whiskey that passed between them. Molly trusted Johnny to be Johnny, and Johnny trusted Molly to... well. Times were rough, and allies were allies even if they didn't always sit together easy.

Johnny took a swig from the bottle and handed it to Molly. She took a mouthful.

"Seems a shame, sometimes, that it's locked away like this," he said.

Molly grinned, her smile a shark flashing in Moon's glow. "I dunno. I like not having to share, sometimes."

"You just like being where you ain't welcome."

Molly considered the possibility for a moment and then, "Can't it be both?" which was close as she could come to a concession.

He leaned back and sighed. "Ever wonder what it would be like, not to have to sneak in here for once? To stroll in, chest high, knowing you had a right..."

Molly laughed. "You wanna own the Moon, Johnny? You don't ask for much."

"Wouldn't have own it... could just borrow it a little while." Johnny had another drink.

Molly watched him lean back, watched the silvery light of Moon play against his face. "You serious?"

"Might be. Could be. If I could reach it, I'd slip it right in my pocket."

"Moon ain't something you can steal," Molly said, but the thought crept through her, carried on the alcohol, bleeding into her fingertips and toes until they tingled with possibility.

The crickets chirped. The bottle was passed, once, more than once. To anyone watching, it would seem like the conversation was done.

"We ain't got to steal the Moon," Molly said, puzzling it out.

"We don't, huh?"

"Nope."

The silence and the crickets skittered away, fleeing as if a mountain lion had passed their tree. Molly continued.

"Riders, and a fence, Johnny. Someone owns this land."

He turned to face her. "What you propose is a might bit more serious than trespassing, milady."

But she went on as though she hadn't heard the trepidation in his tone. "Where there's an owner, there's a deed. Deeds are law. We swipe the deed and..." Molly trailed off.

"And then we waltz into the courthouse and say, 'Hello! We just so happened to have found this deed!'" He finished her sentence for her, chuckling sweet and low.

She didn't laugh, though. Didn't even smile. "That deed holds the Moon. We don't need no courthouse, we just need the paper. The paper's enough."

He turned it over in his mind for the time it took to drain the bottle, and she allowed it, knowing that if she pushed, he'd balk.

"I don't suppose you know where a fella might keep such a deed," said Johnny, as he idly twisted the empty bottle into the earth.

Molly smiled her shark smile again and her eyes shone black in the moonlight.

PART TWO

The old house creaked and groaned. Molly and Johnny picked their way carefully down the hillside and over the broken fence.

"I expected a bank," Johnny whispered.

"It's more'a deposit box," she replied. "Now hush."

Molly pulled open the front door, glanced in quick and waved Johnny through.

There were cobwebs in every corner, dust on every surface. Someone had lived here once. Then they hadn't.

"Looks okay for now," Molly said. "What we want's upstairs."

Johnny followed. "You'd think old abandoned place like this would be looted three ways from Sunday."

"Ain't no looter gonna touch this place."

They came to a bedroom door at the top of the stairs. Molly went right in.

A single lantern lit the room. In the bed lay an impossibly old man. Johnny was sure he was dead, mummified even, and was about to say as much when the body took a soft, gasping breath. There was a pause and then the breath rattled back out.

"That ain't right," Johnny hissed.

"Damn straight." Molly turned and looked to the far wall. "There it is."

"It" was a massive iron gun safe. Johnny wondered briefly how anyone'd even managed to get it up here, let alone how the old house held it up.

Molly turned to the bed, brushed the old man's cheek with her fingers and pulled at his shirt, revealing a loop of twine, a large brass key at the end.

Johnny blanched. His eyes bore into Molly. "Whose safe is this?"

Molly held his stare and remained silent.

Johnny cussed again between his teeth as Molly leaned over, grabbed the key, and jerked the cord free.

The old man's eyes went wide and turned towards her in shock. Then he smiled as his last breath rattled free. The lantern's flame flickered.

Molly went to the safe, turned the key, and swung the massive iron door wide. When she found what she was looking for she stopped and held it out. The paper trembled in her hand. The print wavered from black to silver and back again, sparking opalescent off the lantern's flame.

"We should go," Molly said, heading out of the room. Johnny followed, dazed. She made for the front door.

Johnny almost ran into her, his objection lost to the wind as he looked over her shoulder. There, at the foot of the steps, stood Death himself.

Death stepped to Molly Raven and plucked the deed from her fingers. She started to speak and Death waved his hand.

She turned to Johnny, her eyes wide, and he watched in horror as they turned to obsidian glass. She reached for him, falling away at the same time, folding into herself. Her last word stuck in her throat. With a sound not unlike the old man's last breath and a puff of loose feathers, the space that had held Molly Raven became a large black bird.

Johnny turned to Death, who was already walking away. Molly swooped down on Death and snatched the deed back out of his hand. She flew up to the top of the dead tree in front of the dead house and tore the deed to shreds, furiously eating bits as she went.

Johnny laughed despite himself and as Moon's light slowly washed across the land, Johnny's world went black.

And that is how Raven freed the Moon.

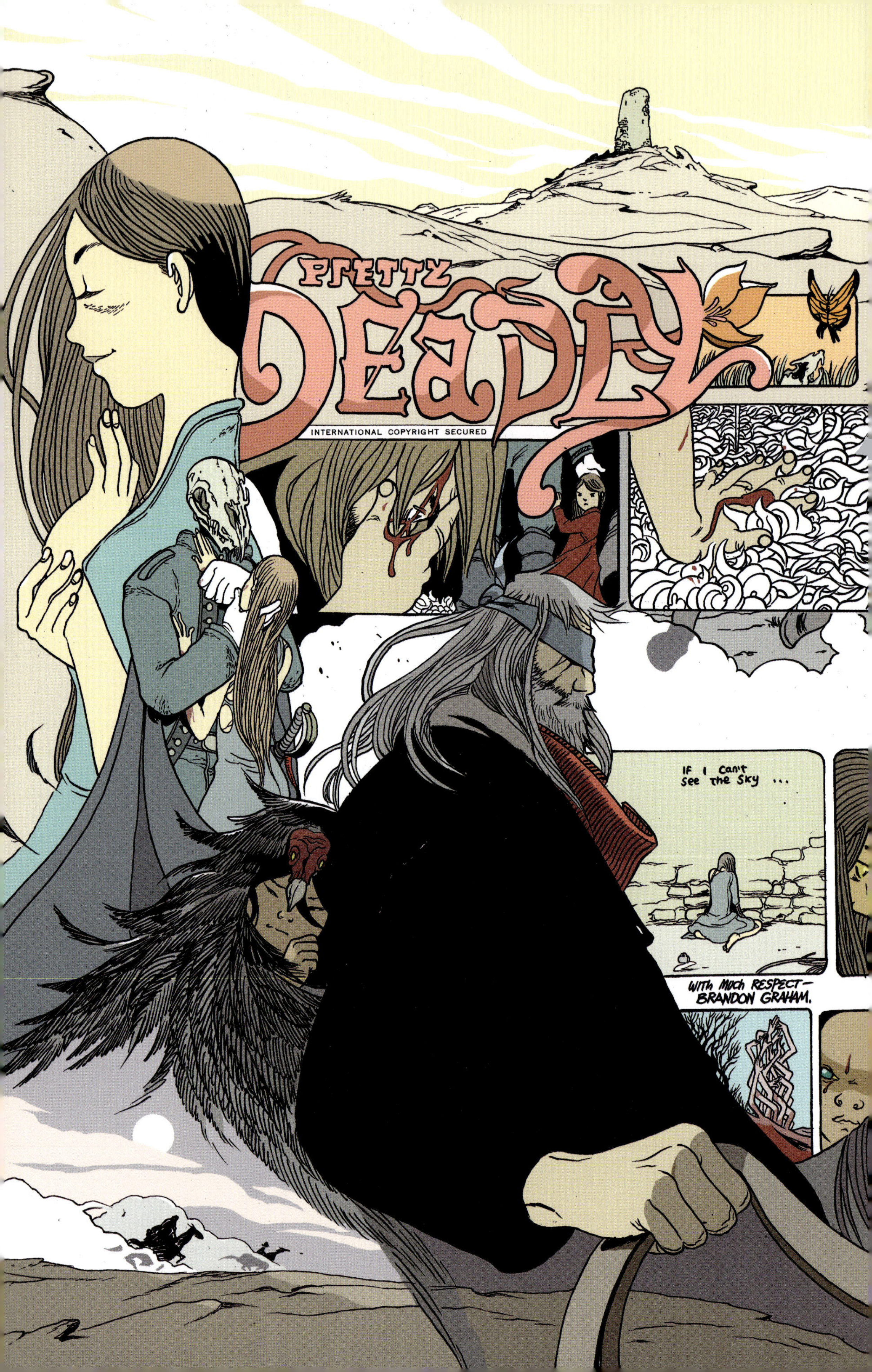
PRETTY DEADLY
INTERNATIONAL COPYRIGHT SECURED
IF I CAN'T SEE THE SKY ...
WITH MUCH RESPECT— BRANDON GRAHAM.

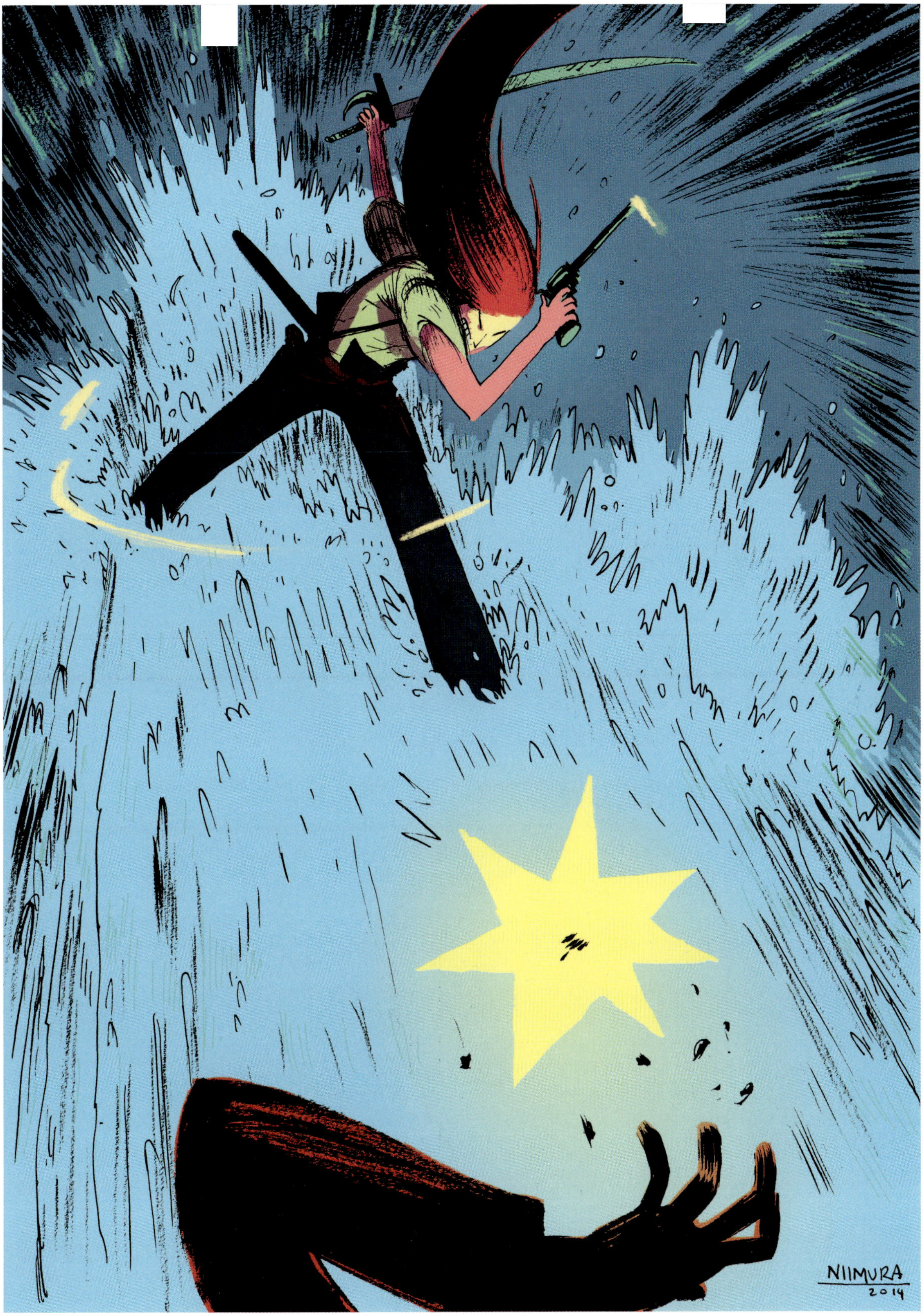
NIIMURA
2014

LEFT:PIN-UP BY
BRANDON GRAHAM
@ROYALBOILER
ROYALBOILER.WORDPRESS.COM

THIS PAGE:PIN-UP BY
KEN NIIMURA
@KEN_NIIMURA
NIIMURAWEB.COM

SHOTS TAKEN - KELLY SUE AND EMMA TALK PROCESS

ORIGINALLY PRINTED IN PRETTY DEADLY #7.

1. KSD: Let's talk about the World Tree. That was a you-thing for sure — I've told the story a few times about how the script says, "I dunno, maybe a tree" and then this MAGNIFICENT beast of tree came to be and now I can't imagine the world without it. We had talked about this place, this World Garden where Death and the Soul of the World reside, as being shaped like a donut. It exists surrounded by the REAL world on all sides but has a portal to "the black." I feel like there's something of that mirrored in the conception of the tree, but I can't put my finger on it exactly. Am I projecting? Tell me about how you came to this spectacular tree.

ER: I remember talking at some point about our ghostly world being somehow an inverted reflection, or a symmetry: A valley would translate into a mountain, an ocean into a desert... When I think about trees there is an enigmatic similarity on how the roots and the branches grow, and I started imagining this concept as related, where maybe the roots on one world could be branches in the other and so on, like Life and Death recycling and retro-feeding each other. That's how it all started, I think.

Besides, I like drawing trees, and leaves, with those thin lines that almost feel like sketching. All those flying particles all around to depict romantic or epic winds, so useful to create the atmosphere in this book in particular.

In general, the inking feels so loose it's relaxing, so maybe I was just looking for an excuse, heh.

2. KSD: The hand-drawn sound effects. Here you've used them to guide the reader to the next panel — this is a difficult spread to navigate at first glance. But I love them every time you do them. How do you translate sound to image?

ER: I think a lot about manga and about how well they do this in Japanese comics. Our alphabet can't integrate that well, shape speaking, but still, you can play a bit with it with more "pop" results. PRETTY DEADLY, though, is a book in which I can't help not seeing sound effects much. It's as if everything flows better in silence, more dramatically, just like those beautiful duels in old samurai films. I'm heavily influenced by that stuff. I think we both are always trying to be minimalistic enough to not let onomatopoeias — or sounds — interfere with the aesthetics or the mood of the book because of this feeling. That's why when we need them I really try to do a heavy integration with the art, that sometimes

even feels just too subtle to understand. For this I try to follow the steps of other incredible artists like Frank Quitely. It's not easy, and I always struggle a bit, but I'm rather happy with the results so far.

What I did in this page in particular feels a bit like cheating to direct the eye of the reader, it being such a weird layout, but I have no regrets.

3. KSD: We talked about the donut-shape of the World Garden

meaning that Sissy could "see" the world in any direction. Easy for me to say, harder to actually conceptualize in a way that could be drawn. What I think I'm seeing here is Sissy pulling a piece of sky out, opening a window to the "real" world. Am I reading that correctly? And if I am, can you talk about that progression?

ER: Yeah, for this I tried to open holes in the sky. In my head the sky could melt into drops of water or retract like mixing incompatible liquids, as if the Garden

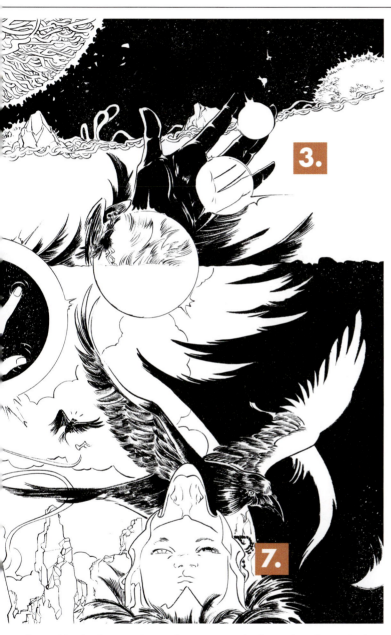

3.
7.

and everything that happens in our other world were all about changing states. Vegetation, ground, light, weather and sky transforming continuously as if time flowed unnaturally.

Here in particular what I tried to do was use the shining star you mentioned in the script, the one that was getting close. I turned it into one of these holes by Sissy's touch, so she could somehow reach another sky and invite this other reality to come in the shape of another circle, the one with Molly.

It's nuts but also really inspiring to me to figure out solutions for these kinds of lyrical landscapes. So challenging it makes me sound like a crazy person.

4. **KSD:** The donut! And also the slice of the sky? Goddamn, Emma. You floor me. I don't know that that's a question. Just wow.

5. **ER:** *Haha, the idea of a toroidal space is fascinating, but also really difficult to depict. I feel I cheated again here, a bit, and really want to try harder on this. But I think we both are moving in the right direction and I'm really glad you like it.*

6. **KSD:** Tell me about the inversion here?

ER: *It's basically the symmetry game, Sissy invades the reality in negative space, as some kind of multiverse exchange. Haha why does all of this have to sound so pretentious? Holy shit. I'm kinda blushing while writing this stuff, I swear.*

7. **KSD:** And then we follow the sound of her whistle through the vista. Are those spaces based on any particular geography?

ER: *Yeah, Far West red mountains in my head. The kind of landscape I would enjoy flying over if I were Molly.*

KSD: What about the technical stuff? You ink with a brush, yeah? Tell me about your tools, and in particular about how you achieve those feathers – so real I can feel them.

ER: *My favorite pen is the Pentel Pocket Brush. It took me a bit to get used to it but now it feels so versatile, and fast, I can use it almost like sketching with pencils. Besides this one, I use some Stadler liners to work on architecture and backgrounds here and there.*

I work with graphite pencils first, then I scan the pages and turn the lines not blue in Photoshop. Then I print those and apply the inks to scan them again and have the finals. I do the covers with digital colors in Photoshop, too, but I always feel a bit insecure and slow doing those, in comparison.

Learning how to ink was a real struggle to me, I swear. I ruined so many pages and I was told many times that I was turning my beautiful pencils into chunky shit and incomprehensible layers. I felt so insecure and it was such a long way to realize that I needed to relax and forget about accuracy while doing the inks. Now that I feel super comfortable, and can even see the brush almost like another extension of my body, I can laugh about it, but it was hard to get here. If someone is feeling angsty about this, please, do not despair, practice makes everything possible.

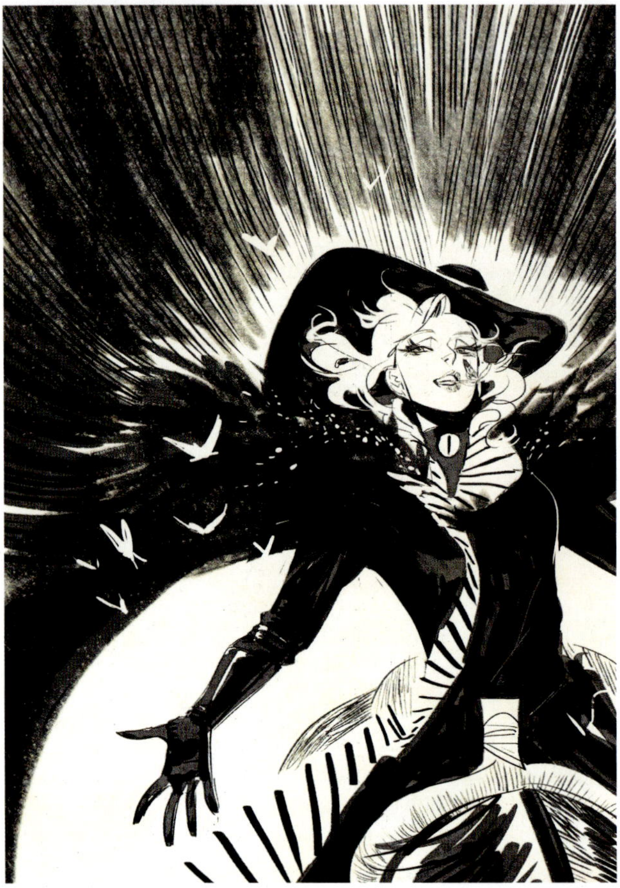

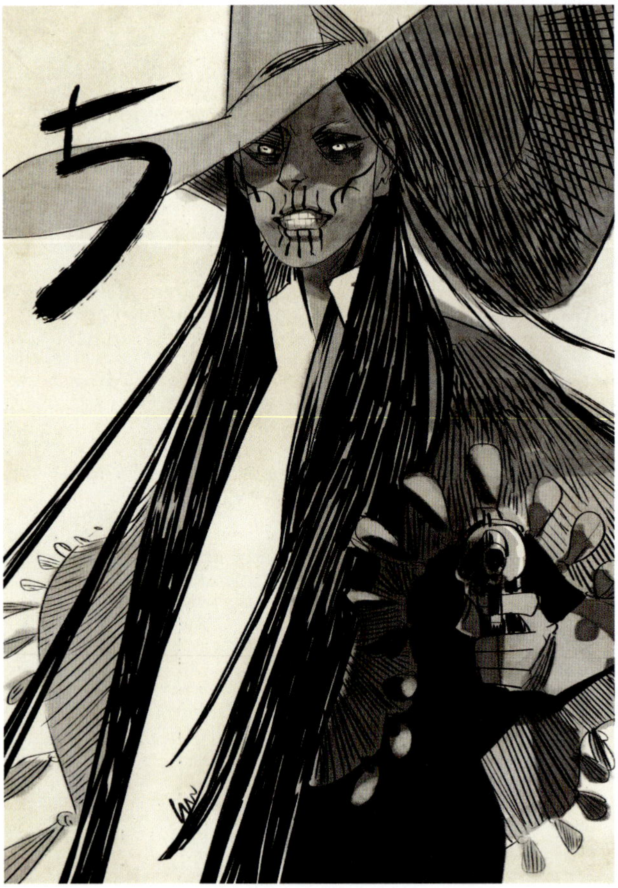
5

RIGHT:PIN-UP BY
XULIA VICENTE
@TAKITAKOS
XULIAVICENTE.TUMBLR.COM

THIS PAGE:PIN-UPS BY
HWEI LIM
@MADAOBA
LALAGE.TUMBLR.COM

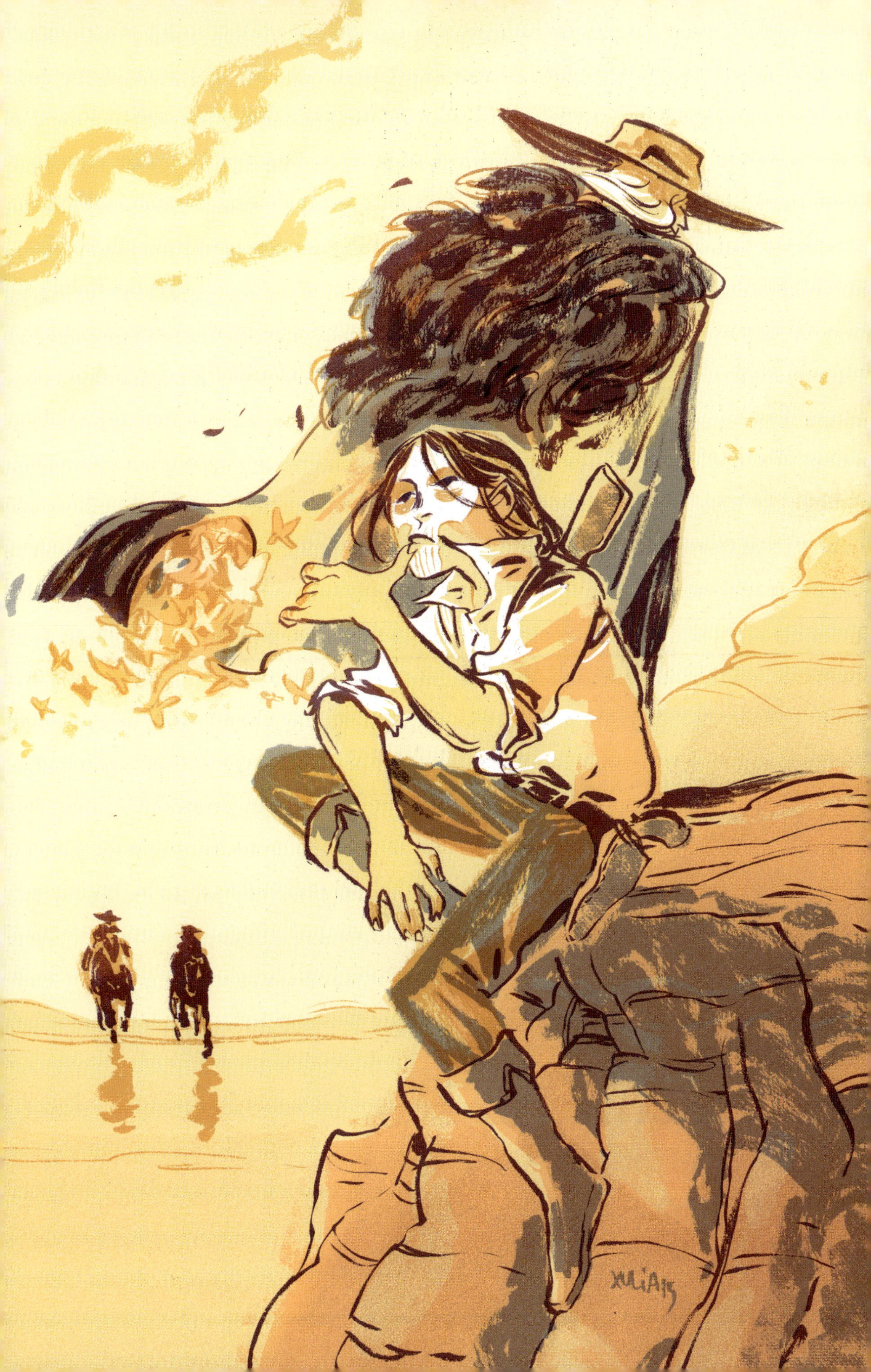

SHOTS TAKEN - KELLY SUE AND EMMA TALK PROCESS
ORIGINALLY PRINTED IN PRETTY DEADLY #8.

INITIAL DRAFT OF PAGE 13 FROM ISSUE #8 (AS SENT TO EMMA WITH NO PANEL DIVISIONS):

[This is the page where we're going to try and explain why nobody has mentioned the weird ladies standing in the middle of the battlefield with no gas masks on. THINK GOOD THOUGHTS!]

Down at the southern end of the trench, far away from Melvin and Theo, Cyrus stands ready to man a machine gun, while Alice takes her place in the trench beside him, prepared to take on any comers who manage to get past the machine gun barrage and Cyrus's fellow soldiers.

(The gas should be thinned out here too.)

Okay, I have two ideas for how we communicate that the other soldiers don't see Alice: pick your preference? Or if you've got a third idea, as always, I'm totally listening.

1) When Cyrus talks to Alice, you frame tight on the two of them, but when we see from the perspective of the other soldiers we're back and wide enough that it's clear she's not cut out of the shot, rather she's just. Not. There.

Or

2) Do one of those things you do where you frame one element of a larger shot. Alice exists inside the smaller frame, but her body does not continue outside into the larger frame while Cyrus's does. This, again, would need to be shot from the POV of the other soldiers.

I think either option will WORK, it's a question of what's the most elegant. I'm inclined toward the former. What are your thoughts?

HERE ARE THE BEATS AND DIALOGUE:

Cyrus's eyes are wide as he looks out past us at the enemy soldiers closing in. Alice is right over him/next to him, whispering into his hear.

CYRUS
There must be hundreds.

BIG ALICE
Hold your fire, Cyrus.

Now from the POV of the Sergeant, who is walking the line and is a few yards away from Cyrus. *Alice is not visible.* Cyrus is.

SERGEANT
Hold your fire, Cowboy.

Still right up next to Cyrus, but now looking at the Sergeant as she speaks. Frame Big Alice and Sergeant. No one is looking AT her.

BIG ALICE
Don't unleash until they're close.

Cyrus returns to the frame.

BIG ALICE
Then, when you run out of bullets, lay down. Play dead.

CYRUS
Why me?

CYRUS
Why is my life worth saving more than Carter? Or Melvin? Or Sarge?

She smiles. The point:

BIG ALICE
It's not. You don't earn good fortune BEFORE you get it, fool. You earn it AFTER.

BIG ALICE
Fire on my count. 3... 2... 1...

Again, Alice isn't visible.

SERGEANT
FIRE...!

Cyrus, wide-eyed, fires the machine gun at the oncoming soldiers.

SFX
RATTA TATTA TATTA

HERE ARE SOME OF THE OTHER IDEAS FOR SOLVING THE PROBLEM, AS DISCUSSED BETWEEN EMMA AND KELLY SUE IN EMAIL:

KSD: How do you feel about the other soldiers seeing them as kind of shadowed soldiers? Only Cyrus sees them as themselves? Then if [x] dies, when he dies for a moment he sees them as they are?

ER: *Like in silhouette? Hmm... I think turning them into soldiers, with this little space to explain the things, would be more confusing, maybe? Think letting them stand in the middle. I could make soldiers go through them, as in phasing, like Kitty Pryde. But when I see the scene written I think I'll be able to figure out something, I think in these pages I sent you, it is noticeable that the soldiers don't see them, or that something weird happens. Jordie can always play with coloring the lines on them, in a different color than black, to make them different from the soldiers.*

KSD: All right, let me see if I can make that work in script?

ER: *Another doubt, if we do them look like somebody else in real life, what would have happened with Foxy if, for example, in the scene with Sarah in the first issue, somebody else aside from Clara or Verine would have entered in the room? As the scene is drawn it feels like he is disappearing.*

Jordie did a great job there changing the palette on him, to cold colors, alone.

KSD: No, no, I'm saying let me try it the way you suggest — with a soldier running through them.

There are going to be people who will have trouble with the idea that a figure that isn't solid can wield a knife or throw a punch, but I think if we just operate with the idea that they're solid or not as they choose, it's fine.

ER: *Ah! Okay.*

Here is another idea that just came to my mind, we could decompose in frames, mirroring the hits drawing them and making them disappear, leaving the soldiers being hit alone like in this cool scene in Ghost In The Shell. Could be rather creepy.
https://www.youtube.com/watch?v=w1BhezbxCPc

FINALLY, THE LETTERING SCRIPT FOR PAGE 13 (MODIFIED UPON RECEIPT OF INKED PAGES):

PAGE 13
[This is the page where we're going to try and explain why nobody has mentioned the weird ladies standing in the middle of the battlefield with no gas masks on. THINK GOOD THOUGHTS!]

Down at the southern end of the trench, far away from Melvin and Theo, Cyrus stands ready to man a machine gun, while Alice takes her place in the trench beside him, prepared to take on any comers who manage to get past the machine gun barrage and Cyrus's fellow soldiers. (The gas should be thinned out here too.)

Okay, I have two ideas for how we communicate that the other soldiers don't see Alice: pick your preference? Or if you've got a third idea, as always, I'm totally listening.

1) When Cyrus talks to Alice, you frame tight on the two of them, but when we see from the perspective of the other soldiers we're back and wide enough that it's clear she's not cut out of the shot, rather she's just. Not. There.

Or 2) Do one of those things you do where you frame one element of a larger shot. Alice exists inside the smaller frame, but her body does not continue outside into the larger frame while Cyrus's does. This, again, would need to be shot from the POV of the other soldiers.

I think either option will WORK, it's a question of what's the most elegant. I'm inclined toward the former. What are your thoughts?

CLAYTON: BALLOON PLACEMENT ON THE LATTER HALF OF THIS PAGE IS GONNA BE ROUGH. I HAD A GO IN THE ATTACHED SCANS, BUT DEFER TO YOUR WISDOM.

PANEL 1
Down at the southern end of the trench, far away from Melvin and Theo, Cyrus stands ready to man a machine gun, while Alice takes her place in the trench beside him, prepared to take on any comers who manage to get past the machine gun barrage and Cyrus's fellow soldiers. (The gas should be thinned out here too.)

CYRUS
There must be hundreds.

PANEL 2
Cyrus's eyes are wide as he looks out past us at the enemy soldiers closing in. Alice is right over him/next to him, whispering into his ear.

BIG ALICE
Hold your fire, Cyrus.

PANEL 3
Now from the POV of the Sergeant, who is walking the line and is a few yards away from Cyrus. *Alice is not visible.* Cyrus is.

SERGEANT (TAIL TO 4)
Hold your fire, Cowboy.

PANEL 4

BIG ALICE (TAIL TO 5)
Don't unleash until they're close.

BIG ALICE (TAIL TO 5)
Then, when you run out of bullets, lay down. Play dead.

PANEL 5

CYRUS
Why me?

CYRUS
Why is my life worth saving more than Carter? Or Melvin? Or Sarge?

BIG ALICE
It's not. You don't earn good fortune BEFORE you get it, fool. You earn it AFTER.

BIG ALICE
Fire on my count. 3... 2... 1...

PANEL 6

SERGEANT
FIRE...!

PANEL 7
Cyrus, wide-eyed, fires the machine gun at the oncoming soldiers.

BIG ALICE
FIRE...!

SFX
RATTA TATTA TATTA

FOLLOWING PAGES:

LEFT:PIN-UP BY
FAREL DALRYMPLE
FARELDALRYMPLE.COM

RIGHT:PIN-UP BY
VALENTINE DE LANDRO
VALENTINEDELANDRO.TUMBLR.COM

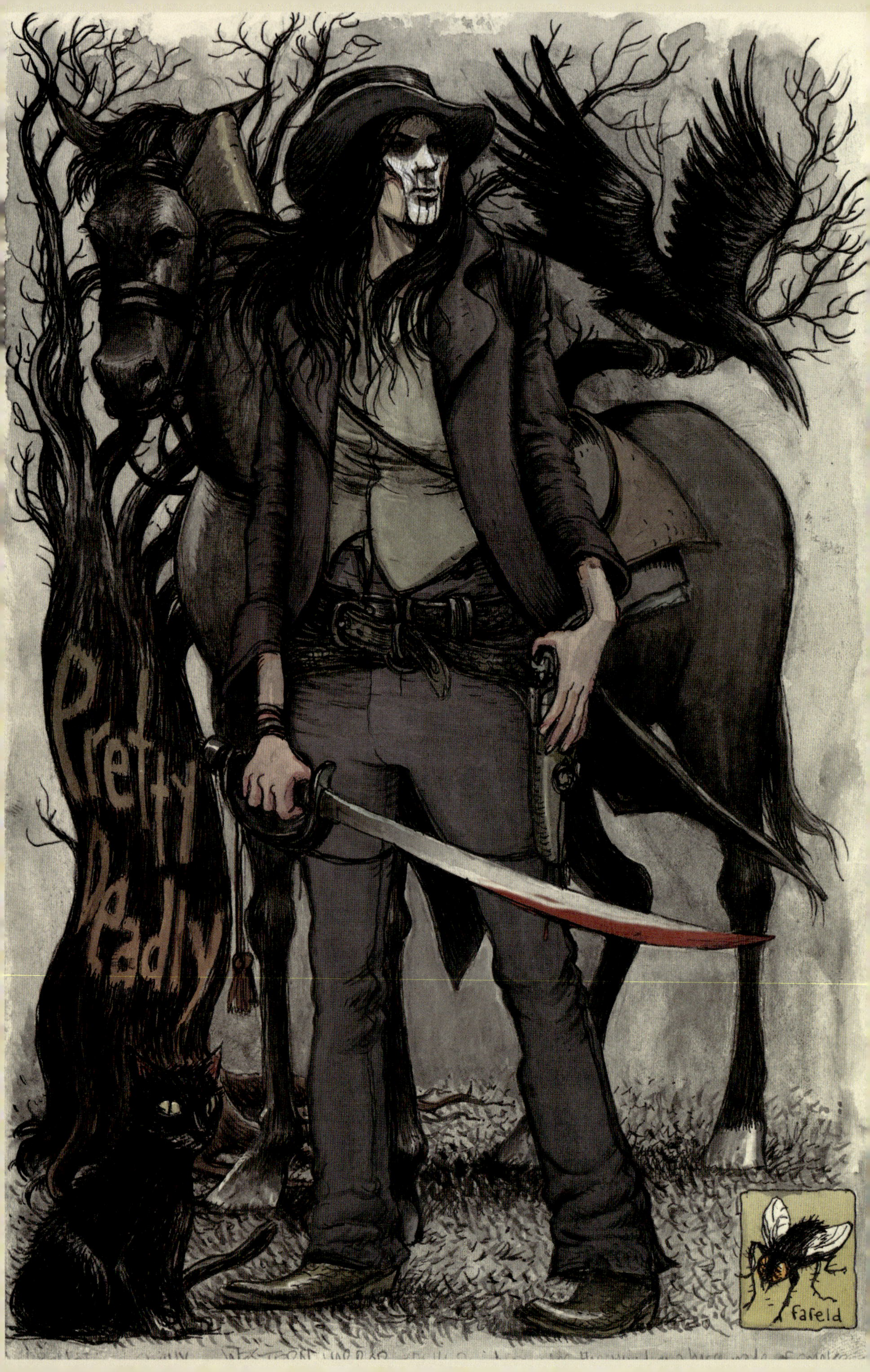
Pretty Deadly
fafeld

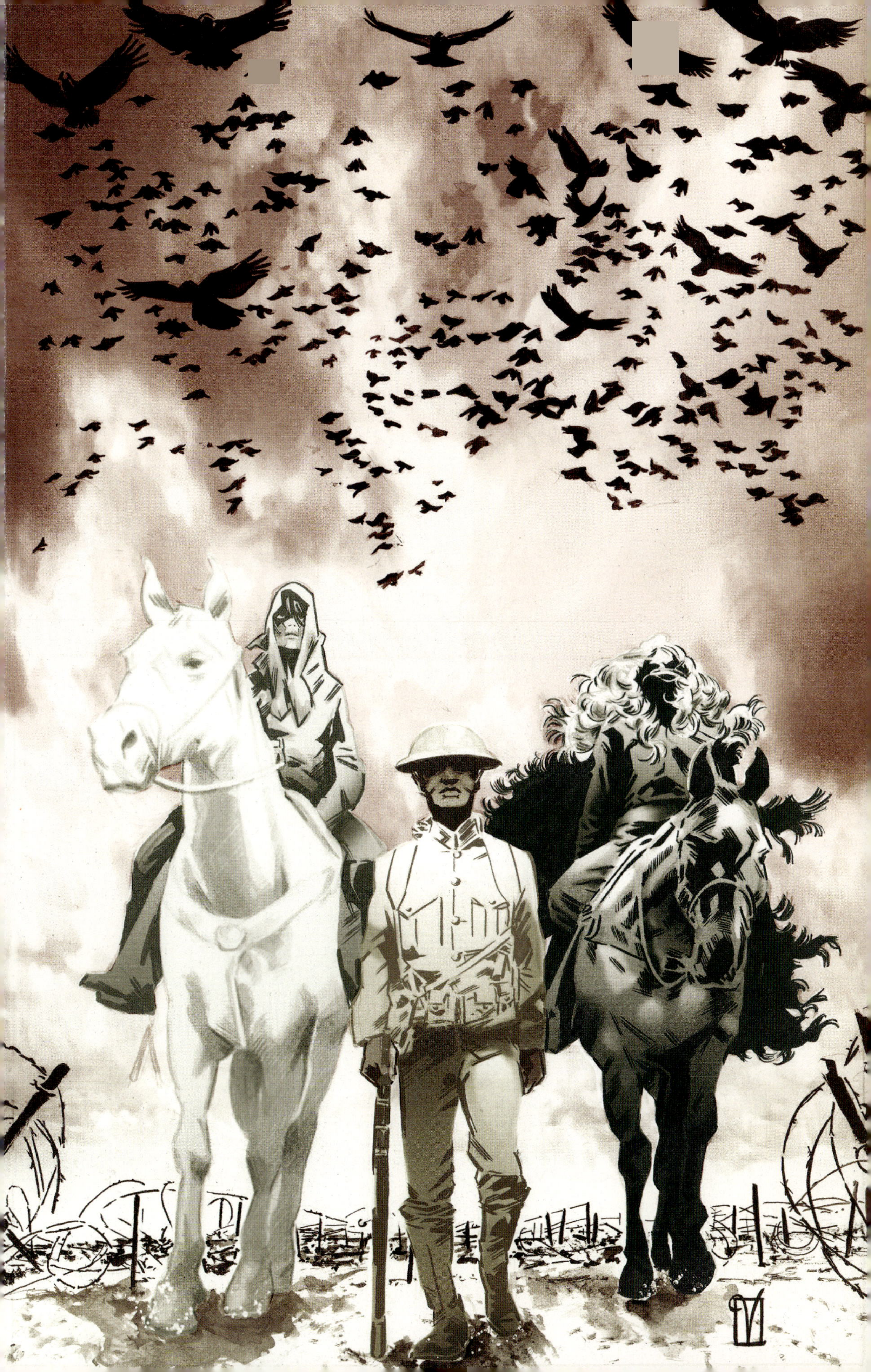

KELLY SUE DECONNICK is best known for surprise hits like Carol Danvers' rebranding as Captain Marvel and the Eisner-nominated mythological western, PRETTY DEADLY; the latter was co-created with artist Emma Ríos. DeConnick's most recent venture, the sci-fi kidney-punch called BITCH PLANET, co-created with Valentine De Landro, launched to rave reviews. DeConnick lives in Portland, Oregon, with her husband, Matt Fraction, and their two children. Under their company Milkfed Criminal Masterminds, Inc., DeConnick and Fraction are currently developing television for NBC/Universal.

EMMA RÍOS is a cartoonist based in Spain. She shifted her focus to a mix of both architecture and small press until working on comics full-time in 2007. Having worked for Boom! Studios and Marvel, she returned to creator-owned production in 2013 thanks to Image Comics. She currently co-edits the ISLAND magazine with Brandon Graham, and co-creates PRETTY DEADLY with Kelly Sue DeConnick and MIRROR with Hwei Lim.

JORDIE BELLAIRE is an Eisner award-winning colorist who has worked on many titles with many publishers. Her credits include, PRETTY DEADLY, NOWHERE MEN, MOON KNIGHT, INJECTION, AUTUMNLANDS, THEY'RE NOT LIKE US, X-FILES, VISION and others. She lives in Ireland with her famous cat, Buffy.

CLAYTON COWLES graduated from the Joe Kubert School of Cartoon and Graphic Art in 2009, and has been lettering for Image and Marvel comics ever since; working on such titles as INVINCIBLE IRON MAN, DAREDEVIL, SPIDER-GWEN, BITCH PLANET, PRETTY DEADLY, THE WICKED + THE DIVINE, and far more than can be counted in one sitting. His Twitter handle is @claytoncowles, and he lives in upstate New York with his cat.